George

Within Changi's Walls

A record of civilian internment
in World War II

Edited and with an Introduction by
Emma G. Peet

Marshall Cavendish Editions

© 2011 Marshall Cavendish International (Asia) Private Limited

Published by Marshall Cavendish Editions
An imprint of Marshall Cavendish International
1 New Industrial Road, Singapore 536196

All rights reserved

No part of this publication may be reproduced, stored in a retrieval system or transmitted, in any form or by any means, electronic, mechanical, photocopying, recording or otherwise, without the prior permission of the copyright owner. Request for permission should be addressed to the Publisher, Marshall Cavendish International (Asia) Private Limited, 1 New Industrial Road, Singapore 536196. Tel: (65) 6213 9300, Fax: (65) 6285 4871. E-mail: genref@sg.marshallcavendish.com

The publisher makes no representation or warranties with respect to the contents of this book, and specifically disclaims any implied warranties or merchantability or fitness for any particular purpose, and shall in no events be liable for any loss of profit or any other commercial damage, including but not limited to special, incidental, consequential, or other damages.

Other Marshall Cavendish Offices:
Marshall Cavendish International. PO Box 65829, London EC1P 1NY, UK • Marshall Cavendish Corporation. 99 White Plains Road, Tarrytown NY 10591-9001, USA • Marshall Cavendish International (Thailand) Co Ltd. 253 Asoke, 12th Flr, Sukhumvit 21 Road, Klongtoey Nua, Wattana, Bangkok 10110, Thailand • Marshall Cavendish (Malaysia) Sdn Bhd. Times Subang, Lot 46, Subang Hi-Tech Industrial Park, Batu Tiga, 40000 Shah Alam, Selangor Darul Ehsan, Malaysia

Marshall Cavendish is a trademark of Times Publishing Limited

National Library Board, Singapore Cataloguing-in-Publication Data
    Peet, George L.
        Within Changi's Walls : A record of civilian internment in World War II / George L. Peet ; edited and with an introduction by Emma G. Peet. – Singapore : Marshall Cavendish Editions, c2011.
        p. cm.
        ISBN : 978-981-4328-85-2 (pbk.)
    1. Peet, George L. – Diaries. 2. Changi POW Camp (Changi, Singapore) 3. Concentration camp inmates – Singapore – Diaries. 4. Prisoners of war – Great Britain – Diaries. 5. Prisoners of war – Singapore – Diaries. 6. World War, 1939-1945 – Prisoners and prisons, Japanese. 7. World War, 1939-1945 – Personal narratives, British. I. Peet, Emma G., 1968- II. Title.
D805.5
940.53175957092 -- dc22   OCN704887349

Cover photograph shows the author on his way to work at *The Straits Times*, c. 1938. Other images: SXC.hu (Andrew Eldridge, Shlomit Wolf, B.S.K., Kriss Szkurlatowski)

Cover design by Lock Hong Liang
Printed in Singapore by Times Printers Pte Ltd

CONTENTS

Introduction by Emma G. Peet v

Last letters home before internment 1

BOOK I: CHANGI GAOL 7
    The Fall · 7
    Karikal · 14
    The Gaol · 16
    Settling Down · 24
    The Day's Work · 31
    The Community · 42
    Life in the Sun · 56
    Rice, Rice, Rice · 67
    Changi University · 91
    The Early Days · 97
    Within the Walls · 110
    Three in a Cell · 116
    Our Health · 125
    East and West · 132
    Ugliness · 141
    Human Nature in Changi · 152
    Under the Stars · 156
    The Women · 158
    The Last Six Months · 159
    Sime Road Camp · 162

BOOK II: SIME ROAD JOURNAL 169

First letter home on release from internment 245

*Letter from the author to his
children in Australia, 1941*

INTRODUCTION

My grandfather, George Lamb Peet, was born in Secunderabad, India, on May 27, 1902. He was born the son and grandson of poorly paid Methodist ministers and grew up in England following the ministers' circuits. At school's end, the only affordable profession that attracted him was journalism, and George's first placement was as junior reporter on the *Essex County Standard* in Colchester during the Great War.

In 1923 George decided to apply for a job as a junior reporter at *The Straits Times* in Singapore; he was successful in his application and was soon leaving Colchester and heading off to the unknowns of Asia. The salary was $300 a month as junior reporter; he covered such subjects as the crime beat, the courts and the municipal council of Singapore. "It was like stepping into another world," he wrote, "marked by social lines rigidly drawn down the years by colonial convention." Being the son of a Methodist minister, Grandpa was more conscious than most colonials of the injustice of discrimination and Singapore was certainly a far cry from his bedsit in Colchester—this is a theme that you become aware of while reading his diaries.

Whilst living in Singapore, George met Lora Buel, an American teacher working at the Methodist Girls' School. On May 23, 1930, they married in Kuala Lumpur, in the Wesley Church on Petaling Hill. They bore three children: George B., Lorinne and Ronald.

George worked in Kuala Lumpur in the early 1930s before being recalled in 1934 to the Straits Times head office in Singapore to serve as the Assistant Editor; after a time he rose to Acting Editor.

On September 3, 1939, George was seconded to the role of Director of Information in the Straits Settlements government, and thus became privy to highly classified information. In 1940, acting on confidential advice, George sent his wife and children to the sanctuary of the U.S.A.; this proved to be a life-saving decision. George himself remained in Singapore. After nine months Lora, wanting to be closer to her husband in Singapore, moved the little family to Bolingbroke

Parade in Manly, New South Wales, Australia. George was to be reunited with his family there whilst on four months' leave in 1941, before again returning to his post in Singapore. This was to be their last reunion until the war ended in 1945. George wasn't able to flee Singapore before the fall as "every fit man under 60 must stay and play his part in the defence of Singapore," the last remaining Europeans being evacuated only when it was realised that Singapore was to shatter and burn.

From my family's recollections, in February 1942 George boarded the *Giang Bee*, an old island freighter and one of the last to leave Singapore, with his second-in-command from the Department of Information as well as some newspaper colleagues. George in later years said that whilst on the ship he had a "premonition" the boat would be sunk and that he smelt "the stench of death" on the boat's decks. At the risk of leaving his only route of escape behind him, he hailed a passing sampan and climbed aboard to return to the shellfire and the hell that Singapore had become, in the face of the invading forces.

Grandpa's colleagues were on the other side of the boat and didn't see him alight from the ship. Devastatingly, the *Giang Bee* was bombed and sunk by the Japanese, with much loss of life, including many of George's former colleagues. One of the few survivors happened to be George's 2IC, and as George was one of the first men hunted by the Japanese, his companion was quickly captured and tortured by the Kempeitai — the Japanese secret police — to ascertain Grandpa's whereabouts. Fortuitously he could not divulge the story of George's survival as he had not seen him get off the boat, and it was assumed George had drowned and perished.

Once back on land, Grandpa headed to the Cathay building and took shelter in the basement. When the surrender of Singapore was imminent, he made his way back to his home at Mount Rosie, where he found an Australian machine-gun regiment taking refuge. There, after the British surrender, he was given an Australian private's uniform, and then marched in with the other Australian soldiers under the assumed surname of "Dunphy," the name of his cousins in Australia. George grew a moustache and beard as disguise, and spent three months in an Australian Imperial Force (A.I.F.) camp. He must soon have realised that his English gent's accent would sooner or later give his identity away, and somehow managed to get himself placed in the civilian camp at Changi Prison. He is still on the WWII Changi Prison Register as "George Dunphy," not Peet, and with the occupation of rubber planter.

Lora had no news of her husband's survival for all of 18 months after the sinking of the *Giang Bee*, until a radio message from the Red Cross got through to the Dunphys in Australia. His relatives handed on the message to Lora as both she and the children were mentioned by name in the message, and that is when Lora realised he had survived.

George's identity was discovered by the Japanese halfway through his internment, even with his moustache and beard; it is thought the camp's Japanese librarian recognised him. During a Japanese military police enquiry where, according to Grandpa, fifteen out of 45 internees died at the hands of the Japanese, he miraculously escaped torture, perhaps because any information he could have provided at that point was out of date and hence useless.

This is where George's story begins. His records and journal were written while in the Sime Road Prison camp after the stint at Changi and these are his recollections, opinions and observations as written at that time during the war. George takes a very fair view of his treatment during his internment, which is partly due to the measure of the man but also because he experienced internment as a civilian, not as a prisoner of war. From George's observations the civilian internees seem to have run the camp themselves and had little contact with the Japanese. Mary Thomas was a civilian internee in both the Changi and Sime Road camps as well, and supports his views in her excellent account of camp life, *In the Shadow of the Rising Sun*, where she feels that compared with the horrors of the European camps, the Changi and Sime Road camps had probably the best conditions, despite the lack of food, overcrowding and lack of resources.

In August 1945 the war ended. Just days after the declaration of peace, George got together with a couple of colleagues from his former life in newspapers — Henry Miller and Eric Jennings (who had also survived the internment) and a couple of Indian typesetters. On September 7, 1945, using a hand press, they got the first post-war edition of *The Straits Times* on the streets of Singapore. That provided a massive and much-needed psychological boost to a nation of people that had been invaded, overpowered, shelled and burned so devastatingly.

Six weeks after the first edition of *The Straits Times* was produced, the Royal Australian Air Force flew George to Sydney to reunite with Lora, George B., Lorinne and Ronald. He subsequently returned to Singapore to take up the position of the first post-war Editor of the newspaper.

The opinions expressed in these diaries are Grandpa's alone; I have transcribed his writing faithfully from his manuscripts, my only additions being Malay translations and crucial background information (in footnotes). In reading George's account it is important to remember that he had no access to a dependable news source so some "facts" may not be completely accurate.

I began transcribing Grandpa's diaries in order to give a copy to my father and extended family so we could all share in his experience. Like many internees he rarely spoke of his internment, and owing to the poor condition of the diaries, they couldn't be shared around the family.

I would like to give my thanks to George's three children: my father, George B.; my Uncle Ron, for entrusting me with the transcription of the diaries; and a special thanks to my Aunty Lorinne, for allowing me access to the diaries as well as entrusting me with the transcription. I would also like to say a huge Thank You to my mum, Gillian, who spent countless hours editing my drafts of Grandpa's work and researching literary and musical references for me. Without her help my "Grandpa George Project" would have been much more of a labour than a labour of love.

Emma G. Peet

LAST LETTERS HOME BEFORE INTERNMENT

11 Mount Rosie Road,
Singapore
January 30, 1942

My Dearest Lora,

Three letters from you yesterday! What a blessing to be still getting letters like that. I wonder how much longer.

I wrote to Aunt Elsie after reading your news about her heart attack.

It must be dreadful for you now, listening to the news alone in the living room, with the children asleep. I don't suppose you knew until a few days ago how serious the situation was, and I couldn't tell you in letters even if I had wanted to.

By the time this letter reaches you the seizure of Singapore Island will have begun. I am not qualified to express an opinion on whether we can hold out, but, looking at it from a civilian point of view, I am not optimistic. It all depends, I suppose, on how quickly help comes—and on various other factors not worth discussing in a letter.

Next day I am continuing this in the office. Last night we had the usual air-raid alarms and it was impossible to do anything except snatch some sleep between visits to the dugout. In the end, though, I got quite a good night's sleep.

I am greatly enjoying Le Doux's company. We try to find time for a stroll in the evenings. Unfortunately we both very much dislike the other man in the house and I am pondering ways and means to solve the problem. One cannot put up at a time like this with petty selfishness, grumbling at the cook, and so on. Actually poor old Cookie is doing pretty well, considering everything. (Later: the misfit is leaving!)

Hobart and Tyler Thompson have had a narrow escape. They escaped, with a shaking, by sheltering in a drain. Almost all the mission people have gone.

The causeway was destroyed today and the seizure of the island has begun.

February 1 Sunday afternoon in the office. If you only knew the difficulties under which this letter has been written thus far! Yesterday I got only a few lines written. Today I had hoped for a quiet day but have not been able to return to this letter until now (five o'clock) at night; no sooner do I settle down to write to you than the siren goes. And there have been so many distractions that it has been difficult to concentrate. One long procession of worries, problems, anxieties, departmental and personal (other people's problems), has passed through my office in the last two or three days, and I have been almost at the end of my tether, trying to cope with them all and do my job as well. However, the situation has simplified now that most of my female staff have evacuated or are about to do so.

But why my writing about such things when I know what you must have been going through in the last few days! I know how you must have felt last night when you heard the news of our withdrawal into the island, and I wish so much that I could have been with you to comfort you. I was in the little house with my family in spirit and was conscious of you all with peculiar reality and vividness.

There are very grim weeks ahead, and the strain on you will be almost beyond bearing at times. But I know you will bear it and carry the responsibility of the home and children for both of us. I am very proud of your courage and strength and practical common sense and that quality called spirit — all those things which I mean when I tease you about your pioneer American inheritance. Thank God you have it now. It will stand you in good stead in the days to come. I am perfectly content, knowing that Georgie, Lorinne and Ronnie are in your hands, and I know that you will shield them as far as you can against the horrors amid which we are living and keep their little lives sunny and unclouded.

My dear, I cannot be sure that I shall get through this. Nobody can. I have no illusions about the situation. The coming siege will be a very dangerous time to civilians as well as soldiers, and if the Japanese take the place it will mean a long period in an internment camp for Europeans, if the Japanese act as they did in Manila and Hong Kong.

If I don't get through, you'll know that you, and through you the children, have given me the greatest happiness I have known in life. And if I do get through — well, what happy times there will be when this is all over! After what I have seen in the last two months poverty has no terrors for me, or failure in life in a material sense. Close contact with war makes one realise the things that really matter in life, and I look back on many aspects of pre-war Singapore — its class barriers, its wages policy, its company directors, its press, its lack of any hope or progress of the masses or even for the clerical class — with detestation. So I feel I have burnt my boats, materially and spiritually, and can face whatever the future may bring. The only thing I still care about, apart from my family and my friends, is my Malayan library! And I have a plan whereby that may remain intact whatever may befall.

This is looking on the dark side, I know. We shall put up a hard fight for Singapore and help may come in time. But in writing to you, my wife, I will write as I really feel in my innermost heart, not as I have to write for propaganda purposes. I have by no means given up hope — for I do not know what the Allied command in Java may be able to do — but neither am I deluding myself about the realities of the situation as I see them here. (I know very little about our military strength — the army seem fairly confident about holding out if the civilian population can stand it — and I am thinking mainly in terms of the civil population and the conditions which may arise for them.) Well, we shall see.

I *know* you'll stand the strain of the coming days, and, it may be, of a long period of uncertainty and separation, and when worry gets you down, draw consolation and faith in life from the children, as I do here. Kiss them all for me, and all my love to you.

George
P.S. Some stamps for Georgie's book.
Keep them for the next wet day!

11 Mount Rosie Road,
Singapore
February 9, 1942

My Dear,

No letter from you this week. I fear it was lost in that Qantas tragedy. After the announcement that the air service had been suspended I sent you a cable, as I thought you might be without letters for a while, but since then the service has been resumed. That's something to be thankful for.

Celeste has arrived safely in India. Margaret Waite has gone, I need hardly say, not back to Australia. All my female staff have also evacuated except two Chinese typists and a Malay girl typist. Hobart is still here.

Most of the people in our building have departed. Quite right, as they were employed by the Home government, not the local one, but rather depressing just the same.

Le Doux, as I expected, is exerting an admirable influence on our household staff, particularly Cookie, and I look forward to his company in the evenings. The "laki" who used to annoy you so, would now do so more than ever, for he has, I suspect, deserted from the R.G.F. and is now strutting about in finery, living on ayah, and not doing a stroke of work. Le Doux and I are considering action of some sort.

Two days ago Cookie piled all his family and goods onto a lorry and sent them somewhere else, the reason being that soldiers have suddenly descended upon our suburb.

We get sufficient food but life is getting more difficult. I shall probably live partly in the office. Where do you think I was the other day when their sirens sounded? In Quenzer's chair! Can you imagine a more horrid situation! We postponed the operation and went downstairs hastily.

A letter from my mother arrived today. I am sending it on to you. I am so glad to see that she is serene and contented at last. The food parcels we sent from Sydney arrived.

I was glad to hear that you are sending Lorinne and Ronnie to the Brighton Girl's School. How I should like to see them setting off! You will not be quite so tied to the house now, although I'm afraid you won't feel in the mood to go into Sydney while the present situation continues. I'm rather more optimistic than when I last wrote, but the Allies will have to look lively if they are to stop the Japanese encircling Singapore via the Netherlands East Indies and then starving us out. We had our first shelling today. Everyone may have to live more or less beside a trench to dive into, as the troops do. I suppose we can, but I don't see how any office work is going to be done. I wouldn't be sorry if it came to that!

Don't worry too much. Remember that I am only one of the many thousands here. When the children go to school you must do some painting. It'll all end some day. Good night, my dear.

George
P.S. A few stamps enclosed.

BOOK I
CHANGI GAOL

[1]
The Fall

When Singapore surrendered to the Japanese on the evening of Sunday, February 15, there were about 3000 British civilians left in the city. Nearly all the white women and children in Malaya had been sent away while the invaders were advancing down the peninsula, but the Straits Settlements government issued an order that every fit man under 60 must stay and play his part in the defence of Singapore. Consequently, no one was able to get a permit to leave except on production of a medical certificate or with special permission from the government. Actually some hundreds did get away without permits, getting on board the refugee ships on the pretext of carrying luggage or simply walking up the gangway unchallenged. When the ships were being got away from Tanjong Pagar under the ever-present threat of raids, confusion, crowding and haste were such that it was impossible to carry out a strict examination, particularly during the first week.

Whether the men who did leave without permission were justified in doing so was the subject of bitter debate, but more of that later. At a rough estimate, about five-sixths of the male British civilians resident in Malaya remained behind in Singapore and fell into the hands of the Japanese. The younger men of the peacetime white community were almost all in the volunteer forces of the colony and the Malay States and were consequently mobilised with their regular forces. They numbered about 1000. In addition there were about 2500 British residents, mostly middle-aged and elderly, from all parts of the country, in Singapore at the time of the surrender, and a small number of white women.

It was said afterwards that the Japanese military authorities were surprised and annoyed to find so many white civilians left in Singapore when they entered the city, having anticipated that there would have been wholesale flight, which would have saved them the trouble and responsibility of looking after such a large body of internees.

On the last day of the siege all these people were living in temporary quarters in the centre of the city, in their offices in many cases or in hotels and flats, having been driven in from their homes in the suburbs, which were by then under shellfire and very close to the actual fighting at some points. That last Sunday, like the day before it, was a day of hell for Singapore. Air raids were continuous, and the city lay helpless before the enemy bombers, which skimmed the roofs of Chinatown, searching for the few anti-aircraft guns which still gallantly carried on.

The Royal Air Force — what was left of its few and inferior Malayan squadrons — had gone to new bases in Sumatra and Java, and not a single British aircraft was to be seen in the sky. The navy had left some days before, except for a skeleton staff left behind, and even that had nothing to do, for by that time no shipping was left in the port. The army still maintained an unbroken perimeter of defence five or six miles from the centre of the city, but the enemy were on the Mount Faber range in the West, penetrating into the Holland Road and Thomson Road suburbs on the inland side, and at Siglap on the East Coast. Meanwhile, the ground floors and cellars of all the comparatively safe buildings in the city were packed with British, Australian and Indian deserters — only a small portion of the 60,000 troops under General Percival's command on the island, but still eloquent of the demoralisation that had set in. Shells were falling steadily among the crowded and terrified masses of Chinatown, and the crack snipers' rifles were heard in the very heart of the city. Ten operating theatres were working simultaneously and unceasingly at the General Hospital, and even then it was impossible to cope with the flood of civilian and military casuals, while at many points in the city the dead lay unburied in the humid heat and the sewers were leaking into the water mains in the streets ripped open by bombs and shells.

Great fires were burning at many places and every informed person knew that the outlook was hopeless although even at that stage there were still a surprising number of people who did not know the real position and did not believe even at that stage that Singapore would fall. Had not the *Sunday Times* come out that very morning with reassuring headlines? Had they not been told that if only Singapore would hold out a little longer, the sky over the tortured city would be "black with American planes"? Were not the most sensational and convincing rumours circulating about the Americans landing in Penang — rumours which we now know to have all been deliberately invented and put about to keep up morale!

Such were the conditions prevailing in Singapore on the last day of the siege. In the afternoon of that Sunday people began to whisper that negotiations were going on, and in fact the Colonial Secretary, the late Mr Hugh Fraser, had gone out that morning to negotiate the surrender but had been sent back by the Japanese with a declaration that they would accept no signature other than that of the British commander-in-chief himself. Consequently that afternoon Lieutenant-General Percival motored out to Bukit Timah, accompanied by two officers, one bearing a white flag and the other the Union Jack, and signed the document setting out the terms of capitulation dictated by the Japanese commander-in-chief, General Yamashita. It is said that when the British commander attempted to bargain he was cut short by General Yamashita with a curt remark, "We give you your lives, but that is all."

That evening, soon after dark, the shutters of a big window in the Cathay building, the tallest building in the city, were thrown open and the interior was seen to be open and blazing with light, brilliant and conspicuous, high above the rigidly blacked-out city. That window opened out of the headquarters of the Malay Command (which had been moved from Fort Canning) and was a sign and signal to the population that Singapore had surrendered and the hell of bombing and shelling was over at last. Then, the church bells began ringing, and, for the first time since the days of peace, a long line of motorcars moved out along Stamford Road and Orchard Road with their headlights full on, carrying people out to their suburban homes to retrieve their belongings.

The sensation of relief, after the horrors of the last few days, was immense. That night people had a meal in quiet and relative comfort, and wondered what the next day would bring forth.

The following morning the Japanese army moved in, picked troops, under strict discipline, and took over the city in an orderly manner, while long columns of white and Indian troops, without their weapons now, moved out to temporary prisoner-of-war camps. A communiqué, distributed as a handbill, was issued by Sir Shenton Thomas — a tragic finale to a distinguished colonial career. It was signed by him not as Governor of the Straits Settlements and High Commissioner for the Malay States, but bore only the plain and significant signature, "Sir Shenton Thomas."

The white civilians were required to register at the Municipal Building but were otherwise left alone that day, except that some of them were peremptorily turned out of their temporary quarters. The next morning, however, word was passed around that they were all to assemble on the Padang, bringing with them only "one suitcase and clothing sufficient for nine days."

Accordingly, courses of several thousand Europeans gathered on the green expanse of the Padang, and waited for four hours, under the supervision of Japanese army officers, while they were being sorted out and then addressed by Major Kato. Men employed in the Municipal service and in certain government departments were ordered to stay behind and carry on essential services of water, sanitation, electricity, post and telegraphs and so on, and the remainder — the large majority — were ordered out to Katong and were told that they would have to walk there and carry their own baggage. The assemblage was watched from the balconies of the Municipal building by a number of Japanese military officers, but there was no ill-treatment.

There followed one of the most dramatic episodes in the history of Asia. Europeans, the former rulers of Malaya, government officials, merchants, miners, planters, straggled through the streets of Singapore before the eyes of the Asiatic population of the city. The behaviour of the crowds, which lined the route, was noteworthy. There was no cheering or taunting or laughter, no hostile demonstration, such as might have been expected at that time and in those circumstances, having regard to the frightful disillusionment and disgust which had been left in the minds of the Asiatic population by the British military debacle and the exposure of the falseness of the propaganda as to the strength of Malaya's defences. What actually happened, on this occasion, however, was that the Asiatic population showed neither hostility nor sympathy as they watched this humiliating parade of their former rulers and bosses pass by. That sea of Chinese, Indian and Malay faces were completely impassive. It was if they were stunned, dazed, numb, and unable to react as they would have done to such an extraordinary sight in normal times.

At the time of writing these words, in the Sime Road internment camp nearly three years after the surrender, one almost requires a definite effort of memory to realise just how extraordinary that spectacle was at the time. Since then we have had all sorts of new experiences and done all sorts of things which we would never have dreamt of doing in our former peacetime existence — for example, hauling firewood carts along the public roads like the slaves of ancient Egypt, or digging and woodcutting naked to the waist in full view of the traffic passing along Bukit Timah Road — and in consequence we have lost a great deal of our former pomposity. But, on that day, February 15, 1942, we had just been thrown rudely and abruptly from our status as the ruling class of Malaya.

In the eyes of the populace we were not simply "internees," as they came to regard us later, but government officials, professional men, heads of mercantile firms, managers of rubber estates, managers of tin mines — in general, a parade of those who had held all the most prominent, authoritative and best-paid positions in pre-war Malaya. Social and political reversal and upheaval sudden and amazing beyond belief, a humiliation of the white man such as had never been known in the history of the Far East. Yet the leading impression left in the minds of the British civilians who took part in the march was the strange and utterly expressionless character of the sea of faces past which they filed. The truth was that the Asiatic population, like ourselves, had been so stunned by the ordeal of the last few days and the shock of the fall of Singapore that they were unable to think or feel normally. In our own cases that state of mental and emotional numbness lasted for weeks after the surrender.

Later, when we came to talk it over, intense bitterness was expressed by some internees, particularly the older men, at having been forced to walk to the first internment camp in that way. They interpreted it as an act of intentional and vindictive humiliation, an expression of anti-white hatred in our conquerors, a propaganda tableau for the benefit of the Asiatic population. But it is doubtful whether it was really as purposive, calculated or significant an affair as that. Those complainants whose racial pride and colour feeling were so deeply hurt by the march to Karikal probably read far too much into it. It is sufficient to assume that the Japanese army authorities, with a hundred and one problems on their hands, saw no reason why they should provide lorries to convey us to the internment camp when their own troops were moving into the town on foot and the prisoners of war were foot-slogging to their camps, and, above all, they were extremely angry at the destruction of all the petrol stocks in Singapore by the British authorities before the surrender.

As a matter of fact, a large majority of the internees were perfectly fit and quite capable of walking the six miles to Siglap, even though most of them were unaccustomed to walking during the hottest part of the day. On the other hand, there was a large number of old and elderly men, several hundred of them, to whom that walk was a very severe physical strain, and for whom transport certainly should have been provided. Indeed, that apparently was the original intention, for the elderly men were told while they were on the Padang that they would be sent out in the lorries, but after waiting several hours a Japanese officer stated that no lorries were available and they would have to walk. Two lorries were provided for baggage, but most people had to carry their own.

Actually the march to Siglap was much more exhausting for all concerned than it need have been because the direct route along Grove Road was barred and the procession had to take a long and devious route, via Serangoon Road and Geylang Road, necessitating a walk of some hours in the blazing sun. On arriving at Siglap long and straggling columns of white prisoners were directed into a large seaside property known as Karikal and the Joo Chiat police station, and there the internment began. (Temporary camps: Karikal, Joo Chiat station, the convent school and two compound houses for the women.)

A number of civilians who were living in the Raffles Hotel escaped internment for two more days, the order to assemble on the Padang having failed to reach them. Japanese officers moved in to the hotel but left the white residents undisturbed, and it was not until the Thursday after the surrender that Major Kato, the officer in charge of the internees, came to the hotel and was astonished to find a large number of white civilians still living there. Highly indignant, he ordered them forthwith to go to the internment camps and to go there on foot. That march, which followed the same devious route, was particularly trying because the party included a number of women and children. One woman carried her baby the whole way. Another dragged her possessions in a receptacle that had formed part of air-raid precautions equipment, while leading a young child with the other hand. The behaviour of the Japanese soldiers detailed as guards both on the Tuesday and Thursday was not unsympathetic, and there was no violence or brutality, while one or two guards went out of their way to be helpful, fetching drinking water for exhausted internees and even carrying their baggage for them. One man, an employee of the telephone company in Singapore, died from heart failure a few hours after arriving at Karikal, but there were no other fatalities at that time, even without food, water, bedding or sanitation of any kind at first.

[2]
Karikal

The three weeks spent in temporary camps at Siglap may be quickly passed over. Hunger, thirst and acute discomfort of every kind characterised the first few days. The Japanese provided no rations at the beginning but they gave us lorries and permits to go into town and allowed us to forage for ourselves, so that we were soon well stocked with tinned food. Having many members of the Singapore mercantile community in our ranks, our foragers knew just where to go in their expeditions into town — expeditions by no means devoid of the possibilities of unpleasantness, for the new regime had not yet settled down, and European civilians moving about the town or trying to pass through the barbed wire barriers which shut off all the main streets were quite likely to run into trouble, even though they were furnished with official permits. Extraordinarily good work was done by our foragers in those early days, and we reaped the benefit of their efforts for a long time afterwards, but our palate was still used to peacetime menus in those days, and one actually heard people complaining that they were "sick of the everlasting sardines." They had little thought then that the time would come when the thought of a couple of Californian sardines with their rice would seem as remote and as delicious as the most expensive meal they had ever had at the Raffles grill room.

The sanitation at Karikal, as might be expected with many hundreds of people crowded into a compound intended for only three or four families, was appalling, and the general unpleasantness was worsened by the fact that the place had been left in a filthy condition by the troops who had occupied it before the surrender. The sudden change over to a diet totally lacking in fruit and green vegetables, coupled with the psychological effect of open trench latrines, resulted in universal demand for laxatives in those days. Another of the trials at Karikal was being dive-bombed all night long by swarms of mosquitoes, and as most people in the camp had never passed a single night in Malaya without a mosquito net, and now had to do without that amenity, they passed sleepless nights.

In the Joo Chiat police station conditions were worse, if anything, as they had not the pleasure of sea-bathing and they fared worse in rations than in Karikal.

Some revealing glimpses of this body of Europeans, suddenly uprooted from their homes and jobs, having lost everything they possessed, trying to adjust themselves to this upheaval are to be had in the campus newspaper which was started in Karikal with commendable enterprise and promptitude within three days of our arriving there. A few extracts may interest readers now living a normal life of freedom in comfortable homes.

"Arrived at Karikal on the p.m. of February 17th to find a dirty mess of things as left by Indian soldiers, half-empty tins lying all around, camp-beds, blankets, bits of clothing, etc., etc., in indescribable filth. We are given no bedding, no food, simply pushed into the place to fend for ourselves as best we could, no sanitary arrangements of any sort, very little water, only one tap in each house.

"February 19th. Amazing progress at cleaning up the place and burying and burning the filth. Some start at sanitary arrangements, absolutely no privacy for any of nature's functions. Had begun to eat a little the previous night from the stores of food that our five scroungers were gallantly bringing us. The spectacle of the Singapore merchant princes, Malayan rubber and tin magnates, and the "Heaven-born" themselves, scrubbing floors, cleaning out drains, picking up rubbish, and bathing in their birthday suits, is something that has a most piquant flavour for even the most kechil among us!"

But this was merely the preliminary phase of the internment. It was inevitable, with so large a body of internees to deal with, and with the confusion inevitably attendant upon the occupation of a large city by an invading army, that heavy discomforts and trials should have been experienced by the British civilians at this phase of their internment, and it was no use and foolish to grouse unduly about it. For that matter, the Japanese civilians whom our own police had taken from their homes at half an hour's notice on the night of the Japanese landing at Kota Bahru had not had too good a time in the immigration depot at Port Swettenham and elsewhere, and our arrangement had been cut and dried a long time beforehand, whereas the Japanese, having no notion of the number of British civilians they would find in Singapore, had to improvise arrangements on the spur of the moment.

Accordingly they sent us to Siglap temporarily. After three weeks there we were told that we were to be transferred to Changi Gaol, and again, we would have to walk there and carry our own hand luggage. Soon again a long procession of Europeans was seen on the roads of Singapore. It was a six-mile walk to the East Coast Road and Changi Road, and if it had not been for the weight of the suitcases, kitbags, bedding and other things with which people were weighed down, it would have been not an unpleasant hike by the sea to Bedoh and through the countryside along the Changi Road. However, lorries followed the procession and picked up some of the older men when they were too exhausted to walk farther. A particularly distressing feature was that Sir Shenton Thomas was made to walk too. He finished the journey in a lorry, but we all felt that this was an unnecessary indignity. A few days later the women and children followed us, and were also made to do the journey on foot, a tragic spectacle in view of the privileged, relatively luxurious and socially exclusive status enjoyed by the white women in Malaya before the Japanese conquest.

[3]

The Gaol

Changi Gaol, which was to be our home for the next two years, was the long-sentence prison of the Straits Settlements, having been built to replace the old prison in Singapore. As gaols go, Changi Gaol was no doubt as up-to-date and attractive as any prison in the world, for it had been opened only six years before and was supposed to incorporate all the most modern ideas of prison design. However I fear that we failed to appreciate its attractions and were surprised to find how like the old conception of the gaol, a place deliberately made as grim, forbidding, ugly and comfortless as possible, Changi Gaol proved to be. We were inclined to think that all the improvements in design benefited the warders rather than the inmates of the cells, and some of us were even led to speculate, for the first time in our lives, on the wisdom or curative effect of confining human beings for 5, 10, 15, 20 years in that vast cage of concrete and iron. I for one often thought while in Changi of an ultramodern prison in Soviet Russia, described in one of Maurice Hindus's books, in which criminals are actually cured of their antisocial tendencies instead of merely being punished and then let loose to take a further revenge on society. At any rate, it is certain that no one who lived as an internee in Changi Gaol will ever again be able to read of a criminal being sentenced to ten years' penal servitude with the same indifference and utter lack of imagination that he used to feel before this experience. And he knows, as very few citizens who approve of and defend our penal system, just what a sentence means.

At the same time, one must admit that to the reader of these recollections the fact that we were interned in Changi Gaol may sound worse than it really was. The word "gaol" can have such unpleasant associations that the choice of that particular building for an internment camp may seem to anyone living in normal peacetime an act of intentional cruelty on the part of our conquerors and an experience of peculiar indignity and humiliation for us. Indeed that trying type of internee who spent half his leisure time brooding on our grievances, real or imaginary, was continuingly comforting his mean little soul with the thought that special revenge would be expected after the war for our having been put in gaol, instead of a block of military barracks or a camp of wooden hutments, or in hotels or in our own houses in the suburbs of Singapore, for there were actually people among us who argued, quite passionately, those were not unreasonable expectations.

When one reminded them that our own government had put the Japanese male internees from Malaya into the very gaol in which we were interned, and that the Japanese internees in India and Australia were not accorded the luxuries of hotels and suburban residences, they still refused to admit that sauce for the Nipponese goose was sauce for the British gander.

The truth was that from our own point of view as well as that of captors, Changi Gaol was by far the most suitable building in which they could have confined us and that we were fortunate to have been put there. It was at that time the only building on Singapore Island in which the larger body of civilian prisoners, including women and children, could have been housed under even barely tolerable conditions. Changi Gaol had emerged from the assault on Singapore completely undamaged, having been left alone by the Japanese bombers and artillery under the mistaken assumption that the Japanese internees were still there. In consequence there was not even a shrapnel scar in all the vast complex of buildings, and the essential services of water, sanitation, lighting and cooking were intact. Consequently we were saved the acute discomfort suffered by the British and Australians' prisoners of war in the neighbouring camps at Changi during the first two or three months. While they were bathing from anti-malarial drains and rationed to very small amounts of water, we had daily shower-baths, plenty of water for drinking and cooking, and excellent facilities for washing clothes in a spacious and well-equipped laundry. While the prisoners of war were having difficulty in cooking their meals, owing to the fact that some 40,000 prisoners were at first crowded into barracks intended for a much smaller number, we took over a large kitchen equipped with the most up-to-date steam-cooking equipment, all complete and in working order and requiring only alteration from oil to wood fuel to be brought into use immediately. While the prisoner-of-war camps were totally without lighting (even one heard in their hospital), they looked enviously at Changi Gaol lit up like a great liner until ten o'clock at night. While the prisoners of war were hastily constructing trench latrines, a huge three-storey barrack full from top to bottom with dysentery patients had no sanitation except "jambans" (the entire sewage system of the Changi cantonments having been wrecked during the fighting), the civilians in Changi Gaol had a latrine in working order in every one of the 700 cells, and a number of other water-flush lavatories elsewhere; true, the sanitary facilities in that part of the Gaol occupied by the male internees was most inadequate, since the cell latrines were not used for defecation, but it was adequate in the women's camp and in the hospital. Again, while the prisoners of war were living in barracks damaged by shells and bombs, with great holes in the roofs and walls in some blocks, getting soaked every time a rain squall swept across the open through the verandas of the upper storeys, the civilians in Changi Gaol were housed in perfectly dry waterproof and undamaged buildings. Thus we see the hardships which we might have had to endure had we been put elsewhere during those early months after the fall of Singapore, when the aftermath of war had still to be cleared up. Considering our numbers, the fact that we had with us 400 women and children who had no desire to be put elsewhere away from their menfolk, and a high proportion of infirm and elderly men, it was clear that we were fortunate to be put in Changi Gaol. Gaol or no gaol, it was the best place for us at that time.

Since the reader of these recollections is not, we hope, familiar with the interior of Changi Gaol, it now becomes necessary to give a sketch of this vast cage of concrete and steel in which over some 3000 European captives lived during the Second World War. Outwardly, standing up starkly amid the rubber and coconuts of the Changi countryside, the Gaol looks rather like a modern adaptation of a mediaeval fortress with its high encircling wall and outer walls curved outwards at the top and surmounted at intervals by projecting watchtowers, its great blocks of cells and its high tower. A steel portcullis, electrically operated, is fitted into the main entrance archway, and in the latter part of our captivity there, this was lowered every night. Inside the walls of the Gaol is a veritable maze of yards, corridors, workshops and cells.

After passing through the main gate one enters a large hall beneath the tower, with small rooms on either side; here, in our time, the Japanese had their guardroom and offices, together with our own camp officials. The rooms in the tower above were used as cells for internees undergoing trouble. It was known to the internees as the "main gate" and anyone who was summoned to the "main gate" at once felt a most unpleasant premonition of trouble which might vary from a mere reprimand to something much worse. Those who went through the internment will remember that frequently heard item of gossip, "So-and-so is in the tower," and the ominous sound of it in those days.

Two internees, who were regarded as being in a special category, spent a year in solitary confinement in the tower — and emerged from that ordeal surprisingly well and cheerful. One reads in a book on prison life that solitary confinement is a terrible punishment and causes men to go more or less insane after a few weeks of it. No doubt that is so in normal circumstances, but these things are relative, and those two Europeans who spent a year alone in the tower of Changi Gaol had just come from infinitely worse conditions in prison camps in Palembang and in the Outram Road prison in Singapore, so it seemed a relative luxury to find themselves in a clean, well-lit room, with decent washing and sanitary facilities, and given comparatively good food and books to read. After all that they had been through, the solitary confinement was, for some time, a period of rest and recuperation, which will give some idea of the physical and mental strain which some people experienced in the early days after the conquest.

From the entrance hall below the tower one emerges into a courtyard. On the right hand is the hospital, on the left a large storeroom used for rice and so on, and straight ahead is the entrance into the main part of the prison. After passing through the bottleneck formed by this entrance one comes to the kitchen and beyond it the laundry, while to the right and left corridors lead to two great three-storey buildings in which the convicts live. Each of these buildings is divided into two self-contained blocks, each with its own exercise yard, its own workshop and dining room on the ground floor and its three floors of cells above. Beyond this complex of buildings but still within the walls are two empty spaces intended for future expansion. The whole prison is surrounded by double walls, the inner one about 25 feet high and the outer one nearly twice that height, with a road between, the total area thus surrounded being eleven acres. The corners of the huge rectangle formed by the outer wall, and halfway along each side, are the curious watchtowers, looking rather like the bridge of a ship, mentioned above.

In normal times these watchtowers are provided with a powerful searchlight at either end, and warders were always on duty in them, but in our time the Japanese did not post guards in them. Everywhere inside the Gaol one is confronted with high walls and steel bars. Every corridor, every window, has its iron grille, while massive steel doors cut off the interconnecting blocks and floors. The utmost ingenuity has been applied to the problems of making the Gaol escape-proof, and the unfortunate beings caged in it were regarded as dangerous animals rather than human beings.

By living within those walls as an internee and reflecting on the life led by a long-term convict, who unlike ourselves, never saw the outside world from the day he passed through the main gate until the day of his discharge, one could not help recalling the account of the treatment of convicts given by Major McNair in his book, *Prisoners Their Own Warders*, in the days when Singapore was still used by the East India Company as a penal station for criminals sentenced to transportation from India. Those Indian convicts, up to the middle of the 19th century, worked all over Singapore, making roads and bridges and all kinds of public works. St Andrew's Cathedral and the older part of Government House were built by them. Major McNair says that attempts at escape were infrequent, and that the convicts were much healthier in body and mind than those in other prisons known to him in which they were confined strictly within the walls. Indeed, one can easily see that that must have been a much more natural, interesting, and at the same time useful life than that led by a convict in Changi Gaol, with all its so-called improvements, in our enlightened 20th century. Be that as it may, Changi Gaol certainly seemed to us internees as escape-proof as the result of the ingenuity of man any prison could be, for even if the convict succeeded in getting out of his own block, with its barriers of walls and bars on every side, he still had to climb the inner boundary wall cross the girdle road which was regularly patrolled, and then scale the outer wall and run the gauntlet of the searchlights. However, all this did not depress us, for we had no desire to escape and made no attempts to do so. No sensational escape stories will be contributed to the literature of the Second World War by the internment camp in Changi Gaol.

The real objection to the use of Changi Gaol as an internment camp was not that it was a Gaol or that incarceration there inflicted any special stigma or humiliation; the real trouble was that it was utterly inadequate for the number of captives crowded into it.

The Gaol had been designed for 700 convicts, and we numbered just under 3000 at the beginning of the internment and 3400 by the time we left Changi for the Sime Road camp two years later. Actually that figure of 700 as a maximum capacity of Changi Gaol under normal conditions is somewhat misleading, since it refers only to cell accommodation, whereas during the internment that accommodation was supplemented by the use of workshops as dormitories. Nevertheless, the overcrowding was bad enough in all conscience, as would appear from further details of our life at Changi that will be given later in this book. This was another aspect of the captivity on which the grievance-ridden type of internee brooded long and bitterly, and, it must be admitted, with ample justification.

But let us look at it from the Japanese point of view. They had 60,000 prisoners of war on their hands, besides ourselves, after the fall of Singapore. They had also a large garrison of their own army, as well as naval and air units, to accommodate on Singapore Island. Obviously the number of large buildings available for an internment camp was limited, with many other needs to be met. It has been argued that we might have been put into the spacious grounds and buildings of the mental hospital, known under the Japanese regime as Miyako, but that was required as a hospital for the civil population, the General Hospital in Singapore having been taken over as the Japanese army hospital. Again, the Japanese might have put the British women and children among the very much pleasanter surroundings of St John's Island, as our own government had done with the Japanese women and children. But against that it must be pointed out that our women and children wanted to be with their menfolk and would have strongly objected to being put in a separate camp 20 miles away. Moreover we were prisoners of an army on active service, not of civilian authorities with a civilian peacetime outlook. (The internment camp from first to last was under the direct control of the Japanese High Command in Singapore.)

The Japanese, at the time when the internment began, had just finished a campaign in Malaya during which their troops had endured living under active service conditions in Malaya for two months, sleeping in the open in all kinds of weather, and were still engaged in fighting their way through the swamps and jungles of Burma. Presumably they thought it no great hardship for the British civilians to live in the dry and weatherproof buildings of Changi Gaol, even if they did have to sleep on the concrete floor and in a space three feet wide. The Japanese are themselves a Spartan people, and their view of the conditions in the Changi internment camp was probably quite different from our own. They would have thought that those conditions were reasonably good, judged by their own standards of comfort and having regard to the circumstances of the time. In any case they could not be expected to take into account the relatively luxurious standard of living of the European in peacetime Malaya and his consequent reactions to a cell in Changi Gaol. I say this not by way of apology or special pleading for our captors, but to show that their tolerance of what appeared to us to be disgraceful overcrowding and discomfort in the internment camp in Changi Gaol may not have been attributable to deliberate callousness or cruelty but merely to a different racial point of view, together with consideration of expediency.

It must be remembered that the Japanese military authorities at the time had every reason to treat us with the greatest strictness and caution. We formed the larger part of what had been the governing class of Malaya before the Japanese conquest; we had occupied positions of great authority and influence. One can easily see that from the Japanese point of view it was imperative to isolate us from the Asiatic populace as promptly and completely as possible. The best way of doing that was to put the whole body of us behind the walls of Changi Gaol, whereas there would have been an obvious disadvantage from the Japanese point of view in splitting us up into two or three separate camps, which is what would have been necessary if any serious attempt was to be made to relieve the overcrowding at Changi. So considerations of political and administrative expediency must have influenced the Japanese. At the same time, one must admit that positive hostility towards us as British civilians probably entered into the matter too, for the Japanese at that time were not only animated by intense feeling against the British and Americans but had an additional and purely local reason for resentment against us. The Japanese army had expected to release their own people, but when they entered Singapore they found that the Japanese internees had already been sent to India. They were naturally angered over that, and we British civilians who had stayed behind had to bear the brunt of their disappointment. Be that as it may, the above remarks probably represent a fair statement of the Japanese point of view with regard to the use of Changi Gaol as an internment camp.

[4]
Settling Down

And so our new life at Changi began. The long procession of weary humanity straggling along the Changi Road streamed into the Gaol and filled the tiers of cells and the workshops and dining rooms on the ground floor to the very limit of their capacity. Into each cell, normally occupied by one convict, went three internees and their baggage. On the ground floor the official allowance of floor space to each man was seven feet long by three feet wide (actually less in some places), and into that space the internee, who only a month before had been living in a spacious and comfortably furnished house of his own, had to cram his suitcase, his camp-bed or mattress (if he had one), his eating utensils and other oddments, and himself.

Those great, densely packed dormitories on the ground floor indeed presented an extraordinary sight and invariably gave an unpleasant shock to new internees seeing them the first time. The degree of crowding in them may be judged from the fact that an area of floor space the size of a tennis court held 109 men. But the cells above were just as bad. These cells were of uniform size and design throughout the prison (except a few specially built for European convicts). These were ten feet long by six feet wide and twelve feet high. In the centre was a solid concrete slab, 18 inches high, which was in normal times the convict's bed. This was known to the internees as the "sarcophagus." The only window was a small aperture at the top of the wall, well above the reach of a man, so that the occupant of the cell was never able to look out at the outside world. There was a water-flushed latrine of the Asiatic squat type in the cell, and this was used by internees not only as a urinal but as a sink for ablutions and washing eating utensils, fresh clean water being kept in the cell in a bucket or kerosene tin for these purposes. The cell had a strong, heavy steel door, with peepholes in the upper and lower parts of it, but the cells were never locked during the internment, internees being free to come and go as they pleased. Just under the ceiling was an electric light which served two adjoining cells, but the bulb was of such low candle-power that it was almost impossible to read after dark.

Here was an instance of indifference to the welfare of convicts which impressed us strongly. It was a practice in peacetime to lock up the unfortunate convict in his cell at four o'clock every afternoon, and to keep him there until dawn the next day. (On Sundays he spent practically the whole day locked up in his cell.) Yet with these long afternoons and evenings and nights in the cell, our humane prisons department could not even provide an electric light strong enough for reading. No wonder that it was thought necessary to include in the Gaol an iron-barred structure exactly like a cage in a zoo, in which convicts who became mentally disordered were put for observation.

During the internment each cell was occupied by three men, one sleeping on the sarcophagus and the other two on a narrow strip of floor space on either side of him. In the former dining rooms downstairs men slept on the concrete tables and underneath them.

The women and children were better off, whilst being strictly separated from the men. That part of the prison that was used for European and Eurasian convicts in normal times was allotted to them, and they had plenty of space, judged by Changi standards. In no case had they to live more than two to a cell, which was no worse than sharing a cabin on a ship, and some of them even had the supreme luxury of a cell to themselves. Moreover, having an entire block to house only 400 persons, including children (the number later increased to 500), they were able to use the big rooms on the ground floor for recreation and meals. The amount of space available to them in the yards in their part of the Gaol was proportionally very much larger than the yard space in the men's area. The women could have least get away from each other, whereas we could not.

The Gaol at the time we entered it was completely bare of furniture, except the fixed concrete benches and tables in the dining rooms (which we were unable to use as dining rooms) and the heavy fittings in the kitchen and laundry; so these 3000 European suddenly found themselves required to live without such familiar necessities as chairs, tables and beds. Consequently a complaint known as "concrete rheumatism" became common in those early days. Some people had camp-beds at the beginning, but a large majority had to sleep on the concrete for some months, many of them with nothing more than a piece of sacking or a blanket between them and the concrete (there were no wooden floors anywhere in the Gaol). When they sat outside in the yards outside, internees had again to rest their protesting posteriors on the bare concrete, during the early days. Here the Japanese undeniably showed a lack of consideration, for if they had only given us a little time to prepare for internment, and some indication of the conditions we should have to meet, it would have been easy for us to have provided ourselves with bedding from our own houses.

These hardships — hardships in the most literal sense — which we had to endure in those early days at Changi, were, however, ameliorated with remarkable rapidity. A certain number of camp-beds were bought in town with our own funds, though not nearly enough, and other people managed to provide themselves with bedding of some sort, even if it was only a couple of motorcar cushions or a home-made mattress made with rice sacks stuffed with coconut fibre. Moreover, it became possible to make charpoys (bedsteads). There was a fully equipped carpenter's shop in the Gaol when we moved in, and we were allowed to buy tools in town, so that in time every block had its own carpenter's shop, in addition to the central one. From the shops you might, if you were lucky, get a charpoy or camp-bed in the course of time. If you knew the right people you got it quickly; if you did not, you had to wait a very long time, and even then you might be unlucky. This was only one of the many instances of unfairness, favouritism and racketeering which were so common in our life in Changi, in spite of determined efforts by our own camp authorities to check them, and which are apparently ineradicable in a community living under these conditions. Thus one found men over 60 still sleeping on the floor two years after the internment began, while young, fit men were sleeping on beds obtained from the camp workshops, for many months. In any case the output of beds was slow and limited, and as many as 800 men were still sleeping on the floor in the second year of the internment, according to an official letter sent to the Japanese authorities, while many continued to do so until the Japanese authorities themselves tackled the question after the transfer to the Sime Road camp in 1944.

Substitutes for chairs were provided more quickly. If the reader of these recollections could have visited Changi Gaol in the days when there was an internment camp, he would have been surprised and amused to see that almost everyone he met in the corridors was carrying a small wooden stool. These stools, made out of grocer's provision boxes and so on, were turned out by the carpenter's shop in hundreds, so that soon it was no longer necessary to sit on the concrete, although these stools at best were hard and uncomfortable. One of the longings one felt throughout the captivity was to sit in an ordinary chair again and rest one's elbow on an ordinary desk or table, instead of sitting in a cramped, uncomfortable position on a hard wooden stool one foot high, trying to write on one's knees. Until one actually lives under these conditions one does not realise how much the back is supported and rested by the chairs, settees, armchairs and long chairs of the rattan type used in normal life; and in fact many of us were troubled with a continual backache until our bodies became adjusted to the new conditions in Changi, although we relieved this as much as possible by sitting with our backs against the concrete walls of the prison yards. Later in the internment some people were able to replace the stools with a more comfortable and handier folding type made with canvas seats, while a few internees even possessed themselves of folding chairs with backrests. But the majority never sat on anything more comfortable than a small wooden stool during the three or more years of the internment.

To take the place of tables and cupboards (for which there would have been no room in the men's camp even if they had been available), we fitted up boxes and makeshift shelves on the walls above our sleeping places. The concrete would not take nails, so we had first to bore a hole in the wall, then plug the hole with a piece of wood, and drive the nails into the wooden plug. In this way, and by means of wire supports fastened to the bars of windows and so on, the walls of the big dormitories on the ground floor quickly became covered with makeshift cupboards and shelves, while the unlucky tenants who were allocated spaces away from the walls had to keep their worldly goods on the floor. The cells were fitted up in the same way. There were a certain number of tools in private hands, and some internees showed notable skill and ingenuity in fitting out their cells, while others had perforce to be content with a bare minimum.

The main problem at first, however, was one of organisation. With a Gaol suddenly filled with a European population as large as that of a small town, and with everybody living under cramped, arduous and utterly novel conditions, the confusion, which existed at the beginning, can easily be imagined. But if there was one asset which we possessed in superabundance, it was the capacity for organisation. There were many in our ranks who had held important executive positions in ordinary life, in civil service, in government departments, in mercantile firms, on rubber estates, mines and so on. Therefore the manifold complexities of our new communal life in captivity were tackled with impressive promptitude and ability. The presence among us of almost the entire European staff formerly stationed in the prison was a great help, as they were familiar with the working of the kitchen, laundry and so on, and we also had the services of experienced cooks and other personnel of the catering department of the liner *Empress of Asia*, who were accustomed to cooking and serving food on a large scale.

The first days at Changi were indeed hungry and wretched, but the process of settling down went ahead fast, and within two months we were a highly organised and smoothly running community, a veritable little township within those walls. From the first the Japanese left the internal organisation and management of the camp entirely to ourselves, and they also expected us to do all our own work, although they never employed us on outside work unconnected with the camp, as they did the prisoners of war. We adopted the former prison system and organised the camp in four separate blocks, three for the men and one for the women. Each block had its own elected head, known as the Block Commandant, and the general body of internees also elected a supreme head known as the Camp Commandant, who was the recognised intermediary for dealing with Japanese officials in charge of the camp. Later the Japanese objected to the term "commandant" in these titles and instructed us to use "representative" instead. The Camp Commandant thus became the "Men's Representative," and a very responsible and arduous position it was.

The first occupant of it was General Macrae, who had come to Singapore in charge of the Indian Red Cross and for some reason was interned with us instead of joining the prisoners of war. The fact that he was a regular soldier of high rank, although retired, undoubtedly made it easier for us to deal with the Japanese and the difficult times immediately after the surrender, for our captors, perhaps naturally, always seemed more friendly towards soldiers than civilians, so far as the prison camps were concerned. The successors of General Macrae were Mr Johns, formerly a surgeon at the General Hospital, Singapore; the late Mr Adrian Clarke, formerly legal adviser in the F.M.S.; Mr N.A. Worley, formerly a Malayan civil servant and judge; Dr Glyn Evans, of the Malayan Medical Service; and Mr C.E.(?) Collinge, manager of the well-known mercantile firm of McAlister and Co. Other positions of high responsibility in the camp were those of camp quartermaster and fatigue officer, and there were secretarial and office staffs as well. In addition to these officials, every dormitory on the ground floor and every floor of the cells had its own elected representatives and its own quartermaster, fatigue officer and shopkeeper (of whom, more anon). We also had our own Financial Committee to manage camp funds, Judicial Tribunal, and camp police force to maintain discipline and enforce rules made by the Japanese authorities and by our own officials.

For the professional and technical needs of the community we had an abundance of qualified personnel, the best that Malaya had possessed in peacetime, in fact, so that there was no difficulty in staffing the camp hospital, the dental surgery and other clinics, the block dispensaries, the public health and sanitary services, the vegetable gardens, the school for the children, the electrical and water services, the carpenter's, the tinsmith's and blacksmith's shops, and all the other activities of a completely self-contained community. Whatever need arose, we always seem to be able to find someone with the necessary expert knowledge. For example, the time came when we had to make charcoal; this had been a purely Chinese industry in peacetime Malaya, Europeans having nothing to do with it; yet when the call was made, internees with the necessary knowledge came forward, and in no time we were producing large quantities of charcoal from stumps of rubber trees. This was but one instance of many that could be given.

Here may be mentioned that a number of British civilians were not interned until much later but were retained in Singapore, to carry on the municipal and other essential public services. Thus there were over 100 members of the peacetime European community living in Singapore for some months after the Japanese occupation began, and as well as a nucleus of posts and telegraph staff in Kuala Lumpur and an odd P.W.D. engineer or two elsewhere in the country. These people lived in a state of semi-imprisonment, being treated reasonably well and allowed a measure of relative freedom, but they always had the uncomfortable feeling that they were under strict surveillance.

They were certainly fed much better, and were more comfortably housed than we were in Changi Gaol. They also had the great advantage of being able to prepare for internment and were thus well-provided with beds and bedding, clothing and food reserves when they were eventually sent into the internment camp. Two of the last British residents of Malaya to arrive in the camp were the medical officer and the superintendent of the leper settlement at Sungei Buloh, Selangor, who had lived a solitary life in that rural spot for two years before they were interned. A few elderly men who had retired and settled down in Malaya were also left alone for a long time, but eventually they were all rounded up and bought to Changi with their wives and families.

There was a group of Dutchmen who had been working in the bauxite mine on Bintang island and who came in late, and two separate parties of Norwegian seamen, one of whom had survived one of the most remarkable voyages in the history of the sea, 91 days from the time that their ship was bombed and abandoned off Java until they arrived at Port Blair in the Andamans, only to find the Japanese already in possession. The entire Chinese crew died during that odyssey, but Scandinavian toughness and seafaring tradition carried the Norwegians through. The other group of Norwegians had been captured by a German raider in the south Atlantic, taken to Japan, and there put on board the crack German liner, *Scharnhorst*. This ship left for Europe, intending to try to run the British blockade but got no farther than the Straits of Sunda, where she was torpedoed.[†]

[5]
The Day's Work

Let us now take a look at Changi Gaol as it was on a typical day during the internment; this will be the best way of finding out the extraordinarily varied activities being carried out. We will begin our tour of the camp in the front courtyard, at 9.30 a.m., when the day's work is about to begin. The yard is crowded with internees waiting to go on fatigues, and we are struck at once by their clothing, which would have been in

† [There are records of a battle in the Straits of Sunda in 1942 where enemy vessels were sunk but it did not involve the *Scharnhorst*. The author did not have access to reliable news sources, so he was reporting events secondhand. — Ed.]

the highest degree unconventional, if not improper, in the days when those same internees were members of the peacetime British community of Malaya. They are all bare to the waist, wearing only a pair of shorts or lap-laps. Nearly all are bare-headed, the topee of former days being conspicuous by its absence, and many are going barefoot as well. But more of Changi fashions in dress later: it was one of the most interesting aspects of the internment. The internees we see mustered in the yard are mostly those who are going on fatigues outside the Gaol, and we thus make the pleasant discovery that internment in Changi Gaol does not mean perpetual confinement behind those walls; on the contrary, quite a large proportion of internees go outside every morning and afternoon. Some men go outside regularly every day; others, perhaps twice a week.

Let us stand in the archway under the tower and watch the fatigue parties go out. Sikh guards armed with rifles, or, in some cases, only with lathis (sticks), accompany them, and they are subjected to a superficial search before they go out. (This practice was not instituted until halfway through the second year.) First comes a party of brawny fellows carrying axes and saws. These are woodcutters, who are going to fell trees in a nearby rubber estate to cut into logs for the kitchen furnace, all the fuel required for the camp being provided by ourselves in this way. Next comes a spectacle which we shall certainly find startling, if not shocking, if our standards and ideal conventions are still those of pre-conquest Malaya. What we see is a line of carts to each of which a party of men is, as it were, harnessed. Two men walk inside the shafts, holding them up, while the others are holding onto the long ropes with which the cart is pulled along. These are parties detailed of the fatigue known as "outside firewood." They will follow the woodcutters, load the carts and drag them back, the distance being about three miles there and back. Do not jump to hasty conclusions about those carts: the work is not nearly so bad as it looks, and I shall have more to say about that particular fatigue later, some of the pleasantest memories of the internment camp are associated with it.

Next there files through the gate a long line of men, the largest we have yet seen. These are the workers in the vegetable gardens outside the Gaol. For a long time we only had the vegetable garden inside the walls, but during the second year we were allowed to open up new ground outside, and soon there were extensive areas under cultivation around three sides of the prison. These gardeners worked inside a boundary wire fence, guarded by a few Sikhs.

The morning procession through the gate is still going on. Now comes a single cart, drawn as before by a gang of internees. They are going to load the cart with coconuts in a nearby kampong, where the camp has a contract with the Chinese dealer. This privilege was withdrawn by the Japanese after the Double Tenth, after which we got no more coconuts.[†]

Yet another cart comes into view. This is drawn by a gang which goes out every day to cut lalang, which is used by the gardeners for making compost.

Next pass before us two elderly and dignified gentlemen, equipped with a sickle and a pair of shears respectively. These are light-fatigue workers and they are going to trim the grass in front of the Sikhs' quarters. Shades of Kipling….

Finally we see several lorries pass out of the Gaol, each with a Japanese beside the internee-driver. The camp has six lorries, serviced entirely by volunteer mechanics drawn from our own ranks. The first two lorries that we see this morning are going into town to bring back rice and other commodities.

This is the most sought-after fatigue of all, because it affords an enjoyable drive, a view of the town, a chance to buy tobacco and other comforts, and a meal in a Chinese eating shop in town. (This was another privilege that was withdrawn after the Double Tenth.)

Another lorry passes out carrying internees equipped with carpenters' tools. They are going to wreck an abandoned bungalow near the coast to supply the camp with urgently needed timber.

[†] [The Double Tenth was the burning of warehouses and the cutting of telephone lines on October 10, 1943, by saboteurs, who Lieutenant-Colonel Haruzo Sumida of the Japanese Kempeitai believed were organised by the internees within Changi Gaol; after an investigation it was proven not to be the internees (Australian War Memorial website). — Ed.]

Last comes a lorry loaded with large metal bins, a pump and a length of hose. This party is going to the beach at Tanah Merah to bring back seawater, which will be condensed down to brine to supplement our supply of salt.

So much for the outside fatigues. Let us now take a walk through the Gaol and see what is going on. Before we go further, there are a number of activities here in the front courtyard that are worth noting. To begin with, we notice a gang of internees armed with brooms and squeegees heading for the archway under the tower. They're going to clean out the guardroom, including the adjoining lavatory, which penance is no doubt good for their souls. On our left we hear a loud whirring from the rice mill, where rice, soya beans and other cereals are ground to flour to add variety to our extremely limited cuisine.

At the entrance to the rice store, which is also the entrance to the women's camp, we see a curious ritual taking place. Two women internees come forward carrying between them a rubbish bin. They put the bin down. Precisely at that moment, and before the ladies have turned round to withdraw to their own arcanum, two men internees come forward and pick up the bin. Smiles are exchanged, but the ceremony is conducted in solemn and eloquent silence. Then another pair of ladies appears with another rubbish bin, and again a pair of men comes forward, and so on until the supply of rubbish bins is exhausted. This particular fatigue has a quaint and rather pathetic purport, although you would never know it unless you were told. This is nothing less than a meeting of husbands and wives, mothers and sons, sisters and brothers, and even, most tragic of all in such circumstances, a young man and his fiancée. So strict is the separation between the men's and women's camps that the Japanese do not even allow husbands and wives to meet, so that they and other close relatives have been separated for many months, with only a wall between them. But even a momentary meeting is better than none, so the husbands, sons and brothers are specially put on this daily fatigue of emptying the women's rubbish bins, thus enabling them at least to see each other. Special pains are taken to put husbands and wives, parents and children, sisters and brothers on this fatigue simultaneously, thus enabling them at least to see each other for a few seconds, even though they may not speak.

But let us pass on. In front of this we see another odd spectacle: the role of youths seated on stools and vigorously scraping coconuts backwards and forwards on a type of saw-toothed metal scraper mounted on a board, which is kept in position by sitting on it. These are some of that distinctive element in the camp known as the "Asia Boys," of whom we shall hear more later, as they are engaged in grating coconut to be used in the rice-flour buns which are served to us at tea. On our right the camp carpenters are busy, and in another corner the motor mechanics who service the lorries and cars. And amid all this din and bustle two harassed-looking gentlemen are typing at a small table. These are the joint editors of the campus newspaper, a typed bi-weekly sheet called the *Changi Guardian*, and we see them in the agonies of trying to gestate copy amid distractions such as the busiest newspaper office has ever known.

That exhausts the interest of the front courtyard, and we may now pass through the bottleneck passage leading into the interior of the Gaol, camp police office on left, quartermaster's store nearby. First we come to the kitchen, where the not inconsiderable feat of providing three meals a day to 3000 people is the daily routine. The kitchen in normal times was serving fewer than 700 persons; thanks to the highly efficient steam-cooking equipment it is possible to prepare the great quantities of food required for a camp of this size. The cooking is of a simple nature, however, the staple articles of the camp diet being only rice and soup. There is also a bakery, where a sort of bread is made with rice flour or any other sort of flour that may be available. Considering that in normal times the cooking in European households in Malaya was done almost entirely by Chinese cooks, even the women of the white community rarely doing anything themselves in the kitchen, to say nothing of the men, it is astonishing to see this busy scene in the kitchen at Changi Gaol, with its all-European staff busily engaged in peeling and cutting up vegetables, filling the steaming boilers and slinging heavy wooden tubs about as if they had been doing it all their lives. Actually a good many of them are not amateurs, for the *Empress of Asia* personnel naturally gravitated to the kitchen, this being the sort of work they had been doing at sea. Most internees were thankful to be able to leave the kitchen to the "Asia Boys" and other merchant seamen, preferring to work in the open air or to spend their time in reading and study rather than work in that steamy atmosphere.

There are, however, quite a number of members of the former white community of Malaya working in the kitchen and bakery, as well as the merchant seamen. The hours of work here are longer than those required of any other manual workers in the camp, except the woodcutters, and they are also inconvenient, for the task of cooking the camp's breakfast porridge begins at 5.30 in the morning. On the other hand, work in the kitchen offers very real advantages, opportunities for private cooking, and, one might add, stealing, for we have among us completely amoral types who would have thought nothing of stealing from the scanty food reserves of our community. But, apart from actual dishonesty, or "racketeering," if you prefer the term used at Changi, the kitchen offered the supreme inducement of double rations, so that the kitchen workers never went hungry while the rest of the internees were pulling in their belts. But with all its faults the kitchen does a very good job of work, considering the number of people to be fed, which by the way, includes the women's camp as well as the men's, and abuses of this sort are apparently ineradicable in any kitchen, as we found to our cost during the internment.

Resuming our tour, we pass through the kitchen into the boiler room, where internees are at work feeding into the furnaces the three tons of firewood a day which they consume. This is one of the most unpleasant jobs in the camp, requiring practically a twelve-hour shift, but volunteers have come forward to take it on as a permanent fatigue — in other words, a regular daily job.

Next up is the laundry, one of the greatest assets or amenities of Changi Gaol as an internment camp. Here 2000 men wash their clothes, and most of them bathe here as well. The laundry is spacious and furnished with large water tanks, tables and an automatic dryer, while hot water is available close by. During rush hours the place is packed but even so it represents an amenity far superior to anything available to our prisoner-of-war neighbours in the Changi barracks. Our visit being made in the morning, the laundry is almost empty. There is a gang of internees scrubbing the floor and tables, while another group is washing sheets and other linen from the camp hospital. We find that in addition to its proper function the laundry accommodates several other camp activities. On our right as we enter is the boot-maker's shop, where half a dozen amateur boot-makers working with scanty materials repair as best they can the heavy wear and tear in the camp footwear. On the left is the camp library, stocked mainly with 5000 books donated by the Japanese authorities. This invaluable institution is housed in a room so small that one cannot understand how thousands of internees ever manage to circulate through it; but they do. Here we notice also bookbinding in progress. The books are in continuous use, and if it were not for a number of internees who have volunteered to do the bookbinding, in addition to their ordinary fatigues, the well-thumbed volumes would have fallen to pieces long ago.

Also in the laundry is a dental surgery, where three dentists well-known in peacetime Singapore give free dental treatment. They can only take on temporary or urgent work with the equipment available, but they perform an invaluable service.

In another corner of the laundry we come upon an artist at work. His prosaic practical function is that of camp signboard painter, for he is surrounded by notices reading, "Make way for ration parties," "Do not take to the lavatory," and so on; but these are mere bread-and-butter jobs, and we have only to look around to see that this ugly little concrete room is a real artist's studio in which serious work is being done. How artistic inspiration or aesthetic experience is possible in an environment of such consummate ugliness one cannot imagine, but evidently it is; and enviable indeed is he who can achieve that degree of detachment from the sordid realities of life in Changi Gaol.

The most incongruous sight of all in the laundry is a devotee of music seated at a piano, attempting to practise a Chopin sonata amid the splashing of water, the hubbub of conversation, the whirring of the electric drying machine, the banging of hammers in the boot-maker's shop, the flushing of a nearby lavatory, the coming and going from the dental surgery, and the bustle in the adjacent library. Of all memories of Changi Gaol, that lone pianist carrying on on his wooden dais amid all that din and confusion is one of the quaintest and at the same time most pathetic. One can imagine no purer bliss than that which that pianist will experience when he sits down again to a good instrument in his own house in a perfectly silent and empty room.

Now let us leave the laundry and get some fresh air. We pass through a narrow door and find ourselves in what looks like a big market garden. What a relief it is to drink in the fresh air and sunlight and rest the eyes on green plants after that interminable maze of concrete walls and barred windows from which we have just emerged. Here we are in the inside vegetable garden, a space of just under two acres outside the main complex of prison buildings but still inside the walls. The gardeners turn out regularly every day, as distinct from those internees who only do the compulsory minimum of two fatigues a week. Many of the men working here are planters, their former outdoor life having inclined towards this kind of work, but there are plenty of men from sedentary peacetime occupations as well.

Experts of the former Department of Agriculture supervise the work in the gardens. This area at which we are now looking is extraordinarily productive, yielding results as good as those of Chinese market gardens despite the poorness of the sandy soil. As already mentioned, this was for a long time the only vegetable garden that the camp possessed, and without it the internees would have been entirely without green vegetables and therefore without vitamin C, iron and other minerals essential for health. The need was met by intensive cultivation of the creeping spinach known as Ceylon spinach and later the erect, large spinach known as bayam, and also by cropping the sweet potato bed for leaf rather than root. This was probably the first time in the history of Malaya that sweet potato leaves had been used for human consumption, the leaves of this vegetable having been used only for feeding pigs in normal times, and it was certainly the first time that this had been eaten by Europeans.

At the time of our tour of the Changi internment camp the outside gardens have come into being (we saw the outside gardeners going out to work earlier in the morning), so the supply of green vegetables is better than it was, but even now it is only sufficient for the vegetable soup served at midday and an extra spoonful of savoury spinach served at the evening meal. Looking at the green expanse of the inside garden, and remembering that those beds are being constantly and heavily cropped, you may ask how the manure problem has been solved, having regard to the fact that the camp has no pigsties, the Chinese market gardener's main source of manure. The answer, in the Changi internment camp, was simple: urine. Unpleasant as the use of this human waste product is on aesthetic grounds, it would never be possible for the internees to keep up the production of vegetables without it, for they have no other means of replenishing the earth except a little lalang compost, the garden refuse which is carefully dug back into the soil, and a very occasional lorry load of sludge which they are allowed to fetch from the sewerage works in town. The use of urine for this purpose is not open to the same objections that have led public health authorities in Malaya to ban the Chinese gardener's traditional practice of using human excrement as manure, and the chemistry of the soil converts the nitrogen, phosphates and other substances in urine into forms assimilable by plants. By this means yields of vegetables amounting to nearly 40 tons per acre per year were obtained by the amateur European gardeners in the Changi internment camp.

There are one or two other interesting activities in the inside garden that we may glance at before we move on. In one part we see a gang of grimy internees busy around a deep, smoking pit. They are making charcoal—the fuel which is used for various purposes in the camp—by burning the stumps of rubber trees. In normal times charcoal-burning in Malaya was a purely Chinese industry, and the European residents had nothing to do with it. Yet when it became no longer possible for the Changi internment camp to buy charcoal in town a call went forth for internees able to meet this need, volunteers with the necessary knowledge at once came forward, and in no time the camp was producing its own charcoal, just one of the many instances which could be given of how it was possible to find specialised knowledge and experts on almost any subject in this extraordinarily varied population of the Changi internment camp.

Near the charcoal pit, in the girdle road between the inner and outer walls, we find a professor of Raffles College and several other internees operating a Heath-Robinson sort of apparatus in which the seawater, already mentioned, is condensed; and also in the girdle road are a group of internees engaged in making brooms out of coconut husk.

We are now ready to leave the vegetable garden, and as we pass out we note beside the doorway yet another instance of the ingenuity of the internees in improvisation: an improvised blacksmith shop with a home-made forge and bellows, made by the internees, surrounded by walls built of wattle, clay and rubble, a type of construction which still survives in some parts of rural England but is normally never used in Malaya.

Now we are at the doorway in the concrete wall and find ourselves in the gloomy atmosphere of the Gaol again. It is worthwhile pausing at this spot to look through the iron grille in front of us and note the peculiar activities going on in the small yard behind the boiler room. Here a gang of internees armed with thick cudgels are vigorously pounding a pile of empty tins. The camp kitchen uses large numbers of tins of sardines and so on, and the Japanese have given an order that the empty tins are to be flattened, for convenience in packing, and handed over to them, presumably for scrap metal for war purposes. Also in this yard we see another gang industriously straightening bent nails. The carpenters are so short of nails that a special fatigue is put on to the job of making use of all the nails which they get out of old woodwork. Yet another gang is working in this yard, burning the rubbish in the incinerator.

Passing this yard, we step for a moment through another doorway in the wall and again find ourselves in the open air. Here we are in an open space as large as the vegetable garden, known as the Main Yard and used for exercise and recreation. But our present purpose is only to glance at the camp tinsmiths, a gang of internees (managers and dredge masters of tin mines not many months ago), engaged in making bore-hole latrines — cylindrical holes in the ground 18 inches in diameter and about 30 feet deep. This type of latrine lasts a long time, prevents fly breeding and is by far the best defence against hookworm, dysentery and typhoid where modern sanitation is not available.

Leaving the yard, we pass along the long, dark corridor shut in on the outer side by an iron grille, with a high wall behind it, such are the delightful vistas afforded by Changi Gaol at every turn. In the passage we meet a former member of the "Heaven-born" and well-known planter conscientiously sweeping the concrete floor and exchanging badinage with acquaintances passing by. All passages in the Gaol are swept twice daily.

The last stop in our itinerary is the camp hospital. This is one part of the Gaol in which the general grimness and starkness of the architect's design has been relaxed, and where the convict was allowed temporary enjoyment of a slightly more cheerful atmosphere, the hospital group of buildings forming a separate little block of their own and being surrounded by comparatively pleasant, small, grassy courtyards. But even here every window has its bars and every grassy space its high grey wall. During the internment the hospital was always full, and many a Malayan career came to a sad end in the prison mortuary nearby. We find two wards full of medical and surgical cases, a separate ward for dysentery cases and another ward for old men and others who are not actually ill but need special attention and help in looking after their personal needs. Generally speaking, only minor operations are possible; some of the gravest cases requiring major operations cannot be treated at all, a terrible predicament for some of those who stayed behind. There are free consultations with the best surgeons and other specialists of peacetime Malaya, but instruments and other facilities are very limited and in no way compatible with those available in a normal hospital.

But in spite of great handicaps, the surgeons (members of the surgical staff of the General Hospital, Singapore) are at work in the stuffy little operating theatre every day, operating on cases of hernias (a very common trouble in the camp), appendicitis, haemorrhoids, and so on.

The hospital physicians are carrying on with the very limited supply of drugs and under discouraging conditions. A laboratory, eye clinic, massage clinic and dispensary are also attached to the hospital. In general, the hospital is staffed by members of the former government medical service in Malaya, while the private practitioners in the camp, of whom there are many, have assumed responsibility of the separate block dispensaries. The most remarkable feature of the camp hospital is that it has a purely amateur nursing staff who have volunteered for this work, but none of them had any experience of nursing in normal life. Inevitably they included at first the type of Changi pest who was always trying to get into a food racket, and who volunteered for work in the hospital merely in the hope of being able to steal the patient's food, but this type was gradually weeded out, and eventually the hospital had a really splendid body of orderlies, who won the admiration and gratitude of everyone who passed through their hands. The work, which called for a six-hour shift every day or night, at a time when the majority of internees were doing only two fatigues a week, attracted some of the best types in a very mixed conglomeration of human nature.

[6]
The Community

Before going on to describe the way we lived in Changi Gaol, and what captivity was like in its various phases and aspects, it is necessary to give a sketch of the population of the Gaol during this period, so that the reader will know what sort of people we were, for without this knowledge he will not be able to appreciate the very wide range of specialised skill and knowledge that was available to us in tackling our problems, nor understand our individual and mass reactions, nor realise the full significance of this extraordinary and utterly unprecedented episode in the history of Malaya.

Nationally, we were almost a homogeneous population, for all but a small minority were British and nearly all of us had been residents of Malaya before the war. There was quite a large Australian group numbering several hundred, mostly mining men, and a sprinkling of internees from the other dominions and the United States. The largest foreign group was the Dutch. The peacetime Dutch community of Singapore were not caught there when the city fell, having had the foresight to evacuate to Java shortly after the invasion of Malaya began; but we had two officials of the Dutch East Indies civil service and a police officer who had remained at their posts in the Rhio Archipelago; also a Dutch planter who with admirable courage had deliberately stayed on his estate on a lonely island in order to stand by his Javanese labour force, and a group of Dutch mining men who had been taken after the conquest of Java to work in the big tin mine on Billiton Island. The Dutch community in the camp eventually numbered about 40. They were peculiarly unlucky in being interned in Singapore instead of in their former possessions, for, judging from what we heard in letters, the internment camps in Java were much more comfortable and very much better supplied with food than ours was.

The next largest of the foreign elements in the camp was the Norwegian. We had about 20 Norwegian seamen amongst us, and we were struck by the contrast between them and some of our own merchant seamen from the slum districts of Liverpool. The Norwegians were quiet, well-mannered, well-behaved, notably intelligent, and quite without a class complex. It was the difference between the boy from a farm or fishing village and the product of an ugly and stunting industrial environment.

For a time we had with us some members the French community of Singapore, when the Japanese interned that part of the community which had allegedly identified itself with the "Free French Movement," while leaving the "Vichy Faction" free. After a few months however, the Japanese shipped the whole French community off to Saigon, and then our French internees went too.

We also had a few Greek seamen, one of whom was an all-in wrestler of gorilla-like physique but fortunately lamb-like disposition. He presented an extraordinary contrast with the other Greeks, who were known as the seven dwarfs, by the reason of their comic resemblance to the dwarfs in the film fairy tale well-known at that time. These little Greek seamen were one of the most pathetic sights in the camp, for they knew no English and were thus unable to take advantage of the library and other recreational facilities, with the result that they were figures of hopeless and dreadful boredom. Imagine sitting in Changi Gaol for two years with nothing to do except whittling a stick, and dreaming the while of the peace and beauty of the isles of Greece. However, they stuck it out somehow and one likes to think of them as sunning themselves in front of a wine shop on the quayside of some quaint little village port in their native land, and thanking God they are not in Changi.

This does not exhaust the list of nationalities represented in Changi Gaol. We also had one or two Russians, who were not enemy aliens from the Japanese point of view, a solitary Swede who was released after a while, a seaman from one of the South American republics aligned with the Allies, and, oddest of all a Cook Islander. What unkind freak of fate had been that had carried this simple, childlike Polynesian to spend the war in prison on Singapore Island instead of his native palm groves, I never discovered.

About a 100 members of the Eurasian community of Malaya were interned with us. The principle on which the Japanese acted in their case appeared to be that all Eurasians of the first generation were to be interned, but in practice they seem to have acted quite arbitrarily, for there were cases in which one brother was put in Changi Gaol while others of the same family were left free, and some of the Eurasian internees were of the second or third generation. A few of them had been educated at public schools and universities in England, and it was natural that the Japanese should have classified them with the British European community, but the majority of Eurasian internees seemed to us to be perfectly harmless people from any point of view and we could not see why the Japanese had bothered to intern them. Among the Eurasian element in the camp there was a handful of young hobbledehoys obviously from bad homes, who made themselves a general nuisance by their noisy and irresponsible behaviour, but the Eurasians as a whole were a harmonious and cooperative part of our community. They were mixed up with the camp population generally, so that one found Eurasians living in the same cells or side-by-side in the workshops with internees from the British Isles and other overseas countries, with the result that they got to know each other well, and the rigid colour bar that had formed so unpleasant and indigestible a characteristic of European society in Malaya before the conquest was blurred or obliterated in many cases.

At the same time, it must be admitted that the pre-war prejudice did rear its head more than once, the worst case occurring after the move to the Sime Road camp, when there was a redistribution of living quarters and all the Europeans from a certain floor of one of the Changi blocks suddenly found that they had been segregated and put into the worst hut in that particular area. However, it was quickly put right by the higher authorities of the camp.

We also had several Dutch Eurasians with us and were struck by their independent and confident bearing and standard of education — the fruit of the fair-minded and helpful treatment which this community has always received in the Dutch East Indies.

Now we come to the most distinctive, unassimilable and peculiar group in the camp. One day, after we had been in Changi Gaol about a year, a rumour went through the camp that a large number of Jews had arrived to join us. We repaired forthwith to the front courtyard to check this remarkable report, and found that it was so. There they were, about 100 Jews from Singapore, chattering, arguing and gesticulating amid their belongings. Nearly all of them were Asiatic Jews, born in Malaya, India, the Near East or the Middle East. Why they should have been interned, we could not imagine, for they could not be regarded as pro-British and half the community had been left outside. The sudden swoop of the internment net had been especially distressing for them, because they had had to leave their wives and children outside. A few of them were well-known business and professional men with a European background, and these mixed easily and naturally with the main body of the internees, but 90% of them had been petty traders or shopkeepers in the Asiatic quarters of Singapore and were quite unknown to the European internees.

The homogeneous nature of this group was accentuated by the fact they were not distributed through the camp but lived together as a separate unit, at first in the gloomy recreation recesses of the rice store and afterwards in the attap-roofed hut in the Main Yard. Special arrangements were made for them in the kitchen to enable them to observe their ritual rules regarding food as far as possible, but it so happened at that time the only meat we were getting was pork, which was used to flavour the midday soup two or three days a week, so on those days the Jews had to be content with an all-vegetarian menu. They took their share of camp fatigues, and showed a good spirit when they came in by contributing a very substantial sum of $35,000 to the camp funds, but from first to last, with the exceptions already mentioned, they were a community apart, living in a little world of their own, cut off from the main body of the camp population by barriers of language, race, colour, demeanour and traditions. As a group they were peculiarly noisy and excitable, by contrast with the stolid and reserved British internees, and the fact that they were perpetually jabbering in Malay and various strange languages accentuated the oddity. They quickly familiarised themselves with the intricacies of the black market in Changi Gaol, and soon dominated that aspect of our communal life. One was always hearing the term "the Jews" in camp, particularly in reference to the black-market supplies and prices. If you wanted to buy smokes or foodstuffs at fantastic prices you could always do so in "Aldgate," as the Jewish quarter of the camp was called. They were also prompt in starting the moneylending business, and any internee of reasonable standing could borrow from them, the loan to be repaid after the war with appropriate interest. In several ways their presence did undeniably benefit the camp, for their black-market activities were welcome to those internees who had money to spend and increased the amount of food and tobacco available in the camp, even if it was not equally distributed, and in the absence of a proper camp canteen, that was a useful or at least defensible activity.

Again, the Jews were abundantly supplied with funds, and their lending and trading activities made it possible for other internees to replenish the camp funds, which proved particularly timely during the lean times at Sime Road. On the other hand, the fact that the Jews had this apparently unlimited supply of money led to ill-feeling in the camp, for they were always to outbid anyone else for anything they wanted. For example, on the one and only occasion when we received Red Cross parcels a Jew was going around with a sack buying up all the packets of American cigarettes he could get. In a camp where everybody is hungry and starved of amenities, that sort of thing leads to bad feeling, or, to put it bluntly, jealousy, and the less there is of that in a community such as this, the better.

Moreover, the Jews were very much addicted to gambling and frequently got into trouble both with the Japanese authorities and our own officials over the quarrels and fights that rose over their gaming tables. As a community they were regarded with distrust, aversion and contempt — distrust because of their black-market connections, aversion because they seemed to be interested in nothing except making money, and contempt because they were such gross and unscrupulous profiteers, taking advantage of our wretched conditions with utter shamelessness. But are these generalisations fair? The leaders of the group comported themselves with dignity and judgement. One recalls an admirable lecture contributed by one of their number to the "Modern Thought" series at Changi. And the young men of their group pulled their weight in fatigues, and took an active part in sport. Probably it was only a minority which carried on the gambling, profiteering and black-market activities that were so distasteful to the rest of us, and the reputation of the group as a whole suffered from the goings-on of the few.

On the professional side we were probably as varied and comprehensive a body as has ever been assembled into a prison camp in any part of the world, for we included practically the entire personnel of the senior ranks of the former government services in Malaya, and also a very large number of non-government people among whom was represented every branch of commerce and industry and every profession in Malaya.

Taking first the government element in the camp, we had with us practically the entire cadre of the Malayan Civil Service, other than the younger men, who were in the volunteer forces, and members of the service who were on leave when the Malayan campaign began. Here then, were the men who had formerly governed the country, in the key positions of administration and finance and in the specialised posts dealing with the Chinese and Indian immigrant communities.

Beneath them was bracketed a group of judges and legal officers, members of the colonial legal service, most of them having transferred to that service from the M.C.S. Then we had an astonishing variety of professional and technical officers of the government service: doctors, surgeons, health officers, civil engineers, electrical and irrigation engineers, schoolmasters, policemen, forest surveyors, agriculturalists, customs officers, scientists from the museum, colleges and research institutes, printers, dispensary chemists, post-office officials, prison warders, even executioners… and also the European staff of the Singapore municipality. On the unofficial side we had a large number of merchants and other businessmen, representing among them almost every British firm in the country. The planting community of Malaya was very well represented, some of its most senior members being with us; and there were also numerous groups of mining men, including someone who had managed to get away from southern Siam a few hours ahead of invaders. An assortment of professional men of all kinds completed the unofficial ranks.

Another distinctive group was the clergy. The Japanese interned all those members of the Catholic missions in Malaya who were of British nationality, so that we had quite a large group of priests and teachers from the Brothers' schools in the camp. The Protestant churches were also well represented. All the clergy of the Church of England were there, two of them having remained, with fine courage, at their posts in Penang and Malacca respectively. For over a year the Japanese allowed the Anglican Bishop of Singapore, the Reverend Wilson, to remain in Singapore with two of his clergy and carry on pastoral work, but the entire nonconformist ministers were interned from the beginning. They included six members of the American Methodist Mission (one of whom had stayed behind in Kuala Lumpur after the European evacuation), two Presbyterian ministers, the entire British staff of the

Salvation Army (two of whom had remained in Penang and Malacca respectively when the Japanese forces moved in), and the Malay Secretary of the British and Foreign Bible Society.

Then there were the "Asia boys." It was easier for them than for us, accustomed as they were to dark and overcrowded quarters, narrow gangways and ladders, and hard living. These were merchant seamen, mostly from Liverpool, who had been employed on the Canadian Pacific liner *Empress of Asia*, which was bombed, set on fire and abandoned while bringing troops to Singapore a few days before the fall. About 100 members of the crew, all belonging to the catering department of the troop ship, were left behind in Singapore when the city surrendered and were interned with the British civilians. They had previously done very good work at the General Hospital during those last terrible days when the sights and sounds there were too much even for professional orderlies of the R.A.M.C. Not all of the "Asia Boys" were boys: some of them were middle-aged men, but the majority were lads of an age rarely seen in the white community of Malaya in peacetime. Most of them came from Liverpool, and some apparently, from the toughest dock and riverside districts of that seaport. Belonging almost without exception to the British working class, they formed a very distinctive group in the camp and one which contrasted strongly with the generality of British internees from Malaya. At first they were never without a chip on the shoulder; they realised that the accident of war had thrown together the first-class passengers and the stewards, so to speak, and at first they were expecting to be treated in a snobbish spirit. When they were treated on exactly the same footing as everybody else, and realised that the attitude of the middle-class Malayan internee was a friendly and interested one, they settled down and cheerfully took on a great deal of the heavy and dirty work of the camp.

For our part we were at first inclined to make hasty and unfair generalisations about the "Asia Boys," judging them a crude and loud minority. Having spent all our adult life in Malaya, and being very largely out of touch with life at home, we were amazed and disgusted by the primitive obscenity of the language that assailed our ears in

Changi Gaol. In particular the use of that dreadful word f—. Occurring as it did in the conversation of some youths from the slums of Liverpool, it became a standard Changi joke. Gradually, as we got to know each other better we realised that about 10% of the "Asia Boys" were really tough, and the remainder very decent chaps, the older men being quite sober, hard-working individuals, with a wide and interesting experience of the world. Most of the youngsters were harmless, decent lads. As for the tough minority, they made us realise, if we had not done so before, how thoroughly unjust and evil the social order of Britain is in some respects, when it can retain the slum environment which had made these individuals what they were. And we could not help noting the contrast between them and the Norwegian seamen who we had in the camp. These merchant seamen were not the only ones in the camp; there were also men from other ships, making quite a large group in all.

There was another group which had a label of its own in our camp terminology. Had you been in Changi Gaol in those days you would often have heard internees speaking of the "older men." These were a separate group of elderly men who, while not actually ill, were bedridden or otherwise too infirm to look after themselves and endure the conditions of life in the dormitories and in the cells. They were given a special yard of their own, with a staff of orderlies to do all the domestic work. These men had nearly all been living in retirement in various parts of Malaya, having chosen to settle down in the country when they reached the end of their active careers, instead of following the conventional course and going home to settle down at Bexhill or Worthing. They formed a considerable addition to our communal responsibilities, and some of the younger internees were inclined to criticise them for not having got away from Singapore while they had the chance (for all had voluntarily decided to stay and take whatever consequences the Japanese occupation might bring). But, like the rest, they were quite unable to realise what internment would be like, still less how long it would last, and they had very good reasons for not wanting to start a new life in some other country. They had lived in

Malaya so long that it had become virtually their own country, and most of them had invested the greater part of their savings in houses and land here. Many of them had been living on small estates of their own in quiet corners of rural Malaya; many, too, had married Eurasians or Asiatic wives, who would have been very reluctant to leave their relations and would have been miserable living as refugees in England or Australia. They had hoped, not unreasonably, that in view of their age and obvious inoffensiveness the Japanese might allow them to go on living in their own homes, and the Japanese did do so in some cases. For a long time after we moved into Changi Gaol we kept on receiving old residents of Malaya who had retired to the Cameron Highlands, Penang and elsewhere and had been left undisturbed by the local Japanese authorities, but eventually they were all rounded up. In most cases they had been treated quite considerately, for the Japanese like the Chinese, have a deeply ingrained respect for age. But most internees in the elderly and retired class had been in Singapore at the end of the Malayan campaign, having left their own homes in the general European evacuation of upcountry, and consequently had to endure all the hardships of the early days of internment, which were the worst of all.

By no means all of them had to live in the old men's ward. We had many elderly men among us who were perfectly fit and active and who lived a normal life, "normal" judged by the highly abnormal standards of Changi Gaol. But there were about 50 old and infirm men who could not live in the cells or dormitories, and they had to spend the long, dreary years of captivity as a separate group in the special ward provided for them. One always felt in the old men's ward that there the wretchedness and sadness of the internment reached their lowest depths, for however kind was the attention given, those internees were at an age of life at which the comforts, affectionate atmosphere and familiar personal interests of their own households meant everything; and here they were, spending their last years in the bleak and bare environments of Changi Gaol. The one thing that sustained them was the hope of happiness again after release, but the names of many of these old European residents of Malaya will be found in the long obituary list of the internment. In the old men's ward Keats's lines took on a new and special meaning:

> quiet coves
> His soul has in its Autumn, when his wings
> He furleth close; contented so to look
> On mists in idleness — to let fair things
> Pass by unheeded as a threshold brook.
> He has his Winter too of pale misfeature,
> Or else he would forego his mortal nature.
> ("The Human Seasons")

Finally there are the children. We had among us some 40 boys of ten years and older, boys under that age being permitted by the Japanese to stay with their mothers in the women's camp. These youngsters in the men's camp simply ran wild, and their natural high spirits and noisiness were extremely trying to adult internees in these congested corridors, yards and dormitories.

If an internee gave way to exasperation and punished cheekiness with a box on the ears the father would later come storming out, uttering such remarks as "You ———— leave my son alone," and "If there is any correction to be done I will do it," etc., etc. But in practice the parent did not do it, nor would he allow even the camp policeman to do, so with the result that for three years these lads lived practically without discipline. What effect there will be on them in later years remains to be seen, but it will certainly be hard to go back to normal home and school restrictions again. The schoolmasters and clergy in the camp took a special interest in these boys and they were perturbed at the conditions under which they had to live, not the least being constant contact with the coarse and the base types of humanity that were to be found in our community; but there was not much that they could do to improve the conditions. There was a special dormitory proposed but the parents opposed this on colour grounds. Perhaps it was unfair to blame the fathers too much, for the boys were all over the camp all day long, and it was physically impossible for the fathers to keep an eye on them in the vast rabbit warren of a place. One could not help feeling sorry for these youngsters, spending the precious years of youth in such a place, for the very worst of one's own memories of miserable and dreary moments in an English public school at its bleakest were not comparable with the environment in which these Malayan youngsters were living. But they did not seem to feel the confinement, or the ugliness of their surroundings, not even the monotony and often the scantiness of the food. On the contrary, they seemed to positively enjoy life in Changi Gaol, perhaps because of the free and wild life they led and the absence of proper discipline.

The camp authorities did what they could to safeguard the health and welfare of these youngsters. A school with regular daily lessons was conducted by staff drawn from the many professional schoolmasters in the camp. Extra and more nourishing food was always given to the children, so far as our scanty resources permitted; special arrangements were made to their feeding and bathing; and football, cricket and other games were organised for them. After the move to Sime Road, where they were able to roam over 150 acres and live outdoors all day long, they were able to live a much healthier and more normal life and to work off the overflowing energy of boyhood without getting on people's nerves as they inevitably had done under the utterly unsuitable conditions of the Changi Gaol. So perhaps the internment will not have done the boy internees so much harm after all.

So far we have been considering only the men's camp, which contains six-sevenths of the internees, but the greatest of our communal cares and responsibilities was not in our camp but in the women's camp, with its entirely separate and strictly segregated community of 500 women and children. There the racial proportions were quite different, there being nearly as many Eurasian and Asiatic women as Europeans, while the proportion of children was also very much larger, there being about 100 children of all ages from infancy up to the age of ten, including several babies who entered this vale of tears during the early days of internment. The complexities of the women's camp can easily be imagined by anyone familiar with social life in pre-conquest Malaya; they are discussed in the later chapter on the internment as it was experienced by the women internees. It suffices for the present to say that the welfare of the women and of the large number of young children in their care was always our first consideration, in the allocation of food and comforts, the provision of conveniences and amenities, and the arrangement of fatigues; and from first to last we did all we could to ameliorate the conditions of life in the women's camp, realising that the internment was in many ways a far worse ordeal for women that it was for men. Looking back on it all, it is a matter of genuine satisfaction that the principle of women and children first was applied so consistently and with such unquestioning and unanimous support by the men's camp throughout the internment.

Enough has been said to show what an extraordinarily mixed population it was that filled Changi Gaol and later the camp at Sime Road during the occupation of Malaya. For one thing, the reader now sees what a wealth of specialised skill and experience was available to us in tackling the practical problems of our communal life. In particular, the presence of so many members of the Malay Medical Service and private practitioners was simply invaluable. One shudders to think what our medical, surgical and dental facilities might otherwise have been. The presence of over 100 medical men among us not only enabled us to carry on those services but to provide expert supervision of camp hygiene and make the most of our food resources. But for the constant care of our medical advisers, we should undoubtedly have suffered much more from vitamin and other nutritional deficiencies than we actually did, particularly during the second and third years, when our diet became not only more scanty but more and more restricted. Again, the presence of the experts of the Department of Agriculture was very helpful to us with the vitally important work of growing our vegetables. We were very thankful to have amongst us the officers of the Veterinary Department (the least known of government departments in peacetime) when we were suddenly called upon to carry on a pig and poultry farm after the move to Sime Road.

Again, the galaxy of engineers of all sorts in our community, particularly those accustomed to dealing with water, sanitation and electric light services, was invaluable. Whenever a new need arose in the camp, we always seemed to be able to find an expert to deal with it (although the provision of the required materials and equipment was another question). Did we need yeast to make bread? A chemist promptly came forward to make it. The same wizards produced a medicine for stomach ulcers out of wood ash. Time and time again one was reminded at Changi of one's boyhood reading of *Swiss Family Robinson*, the story of a family which was cast away on an uninhabited island and discovered the most ingenious and improbable ways of solving its problems.

The cultural side of this galaxy of professional knowledge and talent was equally valuable, as will be apparent from the latter chapter on "Changi University." In the government section of the camp we had experts in all the Asiatic languages spoken in Malaya; we had the scientific and academic staffs of the research institutes and colleges of Malaya — the Institute of Medical Research, the Rubber Research Institute, and the two colleges of Singapore, the College of Medicine and Raffles College — and we also had scientists from the Malayan Museums.

The staff of the education department was also helpful, particularly in catering for the literary interests; and the group of clergy in the camp not only met the religious and denominational needs of the camp but made distinct contribution to its cultural life. To sum up, we had men among us who were competent to lecture on, and to teach, practically any subject; and this was of the greatest possible value in adapting ourselves to captivity and making the best of it.

Lastly, it will be apparent to the reader, from the outline of our community given above, that we had peculiar social and racial factors to deal with, and social responsibilities which were no slight burden in circumstances such as those.

It is impossible to close this chapter on our community without a passing reference to those who were taken from us by death. Some of the oldest, most senior and best-known members of the former European community of Malaya ended their days during the internment, as well as many others not so well-known. Over 100 men and women died during the internment, the death rate increasing markedly during the latter days at Sime Road, when the strain of the long period of captivity and dietary difficulties made itself felt more and more, particularly among the older men.

[7]
Life in the Sun

The picture of the internees at work given in the last chapter was startling enough to the imaginary visitor because, it is assumed, he had known those said internees in the social and professional roles that they had filled in the former British regime in Malaya, set in authority over staffs of clerks and coolies and artisans, with Chinese cooks and houseboys to do all their domestic work for them, never doing any manual or menial labour whatever, travelling everywhere in motor cars, occupying spacious, comfortable houses in spacious compounds, and in many cases living a sedentary suburban life in the towns of Malaya, with no more physical exercise other than they got on the golf course out of office hours.

But it is only when viewed in the Malayan perspective or, for that matter, in that of the foreign communities in the Far East in general, that the everyday scene in Changi Gaol during the war is so remarkable. Had the camp been in Germany or any other white man's country the sights we saw on our tour would not have been remarkable at all, for in those countries every kind of manual work is done by white men as a matter of course. It is only because the white man in Malaya did not work as a labourer or an artisan that our imaginary visitor was astonished by what he saw during this tour of the Changi internment camp. But after all, the Japanese could not be expected to provide cooks and "boys" and "tukang ayers" for us: it was perfectly reasonable to make this large body of able-bodied men do all its own work, even if they were white men working in an equatorial country. Moreover, from the viewpoint of the white internees the doing of all this unaccustomed, unconventional, and, if you like undignified work, could be regarded as no more than an adjustment to purely temporary conditions, done because it was necessary for survival and because they had no choice in the matter. What was really remarkable, novel and of lasting significance in the internment on Singapore Island was the radical re-adaptation of the white man to the environment of Malaya which took place as a result of the conditions under which he lived in Changi Gaol and later in the Sime Road camp. Those internees whom we saw in our tour of the camp in Changi Gaol were living as the white man has never lived in Malaya before, or perhaps in the entire equatorial belt of this planet. In Changi Gaol and later in the Sime Road camp we came right down to the lowest levels of human life in Malaya, with the exception of the jungle tribes and the slum population of Singapore.

Quite literally, we lived like the Malay peasant, the Chinese coolie, the Indian state labourer and the Malay peanut-farm worker. The work we did, the food we ate, clothing we wore, the quarters in which we ate and slept, and, above all, the outdoor life we led. All these conditions of our internment on Singapore Island were no better, and in some respects actually worse, than those under which the labouring classes and peasantry of Malaya live. We did that for three years, and, except for those who were organically unsound or too old to stand so abrupt and drastic a change, we maintained our energy and health, not indeed at an ideal or even a normal standard, but sufficiently to keep the vast majority of us out of hospital and fit enough to do all our own work and produce a large part of our own food. Thin and hungry as we were in the later stages of the internment, and as widespread were the signs of vitamin deficiencies and insufficient calories and protein, the vast majority of us were still able to work six hours a day in the broiling sun in the vegetable gardens of the Sime Road camp, and if that is not a test of physical fitness for a white man in the climate of Malaya, one would like to know what is. During those three years this body of white prison internees, most of them middle-aged or elderly, worked, fed and lived like coolies, and if they had only had slightly better food one could honestly say that they would have positively thrived on it. One cannot stress too strongly the fact that this amounted to nothing less than a revolution (even if it should prove only a temporary one) in the manner of life of the white man in Malaya and one which may have far-reaching effects on the traditional ideas, attitudes, prejudices and habits of the European community of this country in the future; for this experience of ours of the internment showed conclusively that the adaptation of the white man to the climate and the diet of Malaya can safely and beneficially be pushed very much farther than had ever been supposed. Indeed, one is inclined to go farther than that, and say that our experience during the internment proved that the white man in Malaya can do anything that the Chinese or Indian coolie can do, on the same food, and do it for long periods with no serious impairment to health.

It had always been known that white men could and regularly did do strenuous outdoor work in much greater temperatures than are ever known in Malaya, for example in the Middle West of the United States and in Queensland, but it was assumed that this was because it was a dry heat in those regions, and that the very high humidity in Malaya would make similar work for white men impossible. In parenthesis, it may be added that the experience of the white prisoners of war in Malaya during the Japanese occupation was even more convincing than ours, for we were required to do only our own domestic work whereas they were taken out of the camps to do all kinds of heavy manual work for the Japanese, and in spite of poor food, poor by the standards of the labourer in a white man's country, they seemed to do the work quite as well as gangs of Chinese or Indian coolies would have done and kept fairly fit so long as they were in districts free from malaria.

On the other hand the British and Australian troops were young, fit men, specially trained for active service under tropical conditions, whereas we were a body of middle-aged and elderly civilians, most of whom had been leading a sedentary life before the captivity, so in one way the evidence of re-adaptation and more radical acclimatisation afforded by the internment is even more remarkable, even though we were not worked so hard as the soldiers.

These are large claims that are made above. Let us examine in more detail the evidence for them. We have already seen what the living and sleeping accommodation in the internment camp was like. The Chinese mining coolie in his "kongsi" house or the Tamil estate labourer in his coolie "lines" does not live harder than we did in Changi Gaol or in the crowded huts in the Sime Road camp. We have also seen the various kinds of work which the internees did.

Let us now consider particularly those changes in our manner of life, which may be considered as an entirely unprecedented adaptation to the Malayan climate. I refer to changes from indoor to outdoor life, from the conventional dress of former days to the scanty garb which I shall presently describe. Food also played an extremely interesting part in this compulsory mass experiment in "going native," to use an unpleasant but expressive term used in the white community of Malaya before the captivity to describe individuals of their race or colour whom they regarded as social pariahs. But food was the subject of such absorbing interest to the internee that it will have to have a separate chapter all to itself. In this chapter we will confine ourselves to a series of glimpses of the internees living and working in the sun.

By way of contrast, let us first recall the traditional ideas with regard to the climate which these white residents of peacetime Malaya took with them into internment. All of them, except the youngest, could remember having been solemnly warned of the danger of sunstroke when they first came to the country as young men. They were told that they must always put on a topee (sun helmet) when they went outdoors, even only for five minutes, and that the light on the dull, overcast day was even more dangerous than blazing sunshine. The back of the neck was said to be a particularly vulnerable spot. It was believed that one could get sunstroke through the eyes, and a peculiarly horrific form of this menace which was brought to my notice in my early days was "sunstroke through the spine," in consequence of which I always felt somewhat uneasy when sunbathing on Sunday mornings at the Singapore Swimming Club until I finally decided that either my spine must be particularly well-protected or that there was no such thing as sunstroke through the spine, and thereafter I worried about it no longer.

In later years the general belief in sunstroke as a danger of the

Malayan climate gradually faded out among the white community, the lead being given by the younger school of medical practitioners in Malaya who, supported by personal experience and observation of the lay community, none of whom had ever actually seen a case of sunstroke in Malaya, although everybody had heard a lot of talk about this mysterious and undefined malady. The general belief that whatever might be the case in certain other parts of the tropics, notably those such as in India, where the temperature is much higher and the humidity much lower at certain seasons than in Malaya, there was no such thing as sunstroke in Malaya, in the sense of a sudden, serious physical collapse of some sort attributable to some mysterious deadly element in the tropical sunlight. With the abandonment of this belief the topee gradually went out of fashion. Planters and others who had to spend the greater part of the day out of doors continued to wear the topee (or the specially thick and broad felt hat known as the double terai) as a protection against the heat and glare, but among the European mercantile community and other office workers the topee disappeared almost entirely. Nevertheless, the attitude of the white resident towards the climate in general was one of caution and distrust, and also unappreciative of the temporary exile, everlastingly harking to the pleasures of the temperate climate and the beauties of its changing seasons which he had left behind. He never allowed himself to forget that he was a European in an Eastern land, a product of a temperate climate, a white man in a land that was emphatically not a white man's country, and never would be.

That was the white man's vision of Malaya and his own relation to the country, and it resulted in an ultra-cautious attitude towards the climate; it prevented him from wholehearted and unreserved enjoyment of the glorious golden sunshine that floods the green land of Malaya all year round. He might have come to regard the belief in sunstroke as nothing more than a picturesque local legend; he might play his Sunday golf during the full heat of the day; he might play cricket all day or take part in an all-day tennis tournament; and to that extent he had modified the tradition that the only proper times for physical exercise in this climate were in the coolness of the early morning and late afternoon. But your modern white resident in the years before the Second World War played his games in the heat of the day rather as a devotee of the British colonial fetish of regular daily exercise, and because he had been inoculated with the game's tradition at his public school, than because he wanted to be out in the sunshine. He, as it were, braved the sunlight of Malaya on these occasions, and if anyone exposed himself to it in ways not sanctified by social and sporting traditions he was inclined to be critical. For example, the very few members of the white community who experimented with cycle touring in Malaya or indulged in cross-country walks during the heat of the day were regarded as being somewhat eccentric and as doing something odd and possibly dangerous to health.

Moreover, although the topee had been largely discarded among the white community of Malaya, the habit of keeping the head covered out of doors during the hot hours of the day had not. In recent years a bareheaded vogue had been noticed among some of the younger men of the white community of Singapore, having spread there from Batavia and Surabaya, but most men continued to wear a felt hat of the European trilby type, and if they indulged in sun-baking at a swimming pool they took the precaution of swathing their heads in towels.

As for dress, the only concession to the climate made in the regulation office costume of the European in Malaya was the wearing of a white duck suit. This was cool, compared with the European or even the palm-beach type of suit, and it had the merit of being washable, but how many accessories went with it! Let us look back for a moment, remembering that these words are written in the Sime Road camp in 1944, at the typical European resident of Singapore setting out for his office after breakfast any day in 1943. From head to foot his body is encased in one or more layers of clothing. On his head he wears a felt hat, a memento of his last home leave. Round his neck there is a collar and tie. True, it is a soft collar, instead of the stiff collar worn in Singapore 30 years ago, but later in the day that collar and tie will form a tight, hot, uncomfortable band around the sweating and protesting neck of this victim of convention. Next we find that the upper part of his body is swathed in two, and sometimes, three layers of clothing.

Starting from the outside, we find first a white coat; inside that is a shirt; and inside that again there is often a singlet next to the skin. Below this abdominal cocoon we come to a pair of long trousers with short pants underneath them. Finally we find the feet of our specimen European encased in socks and stiff leather shoes. A total of nine separate articles in the costume of a man about to do a strenuous day's work four degrees from the equator. The only parts of his body on which the fresh air was allowed to play were the face and hands. If it had been a planter or miner that we were observing, the sartorial scene would have been less complicated: he could have been wearing an open shirt and khaki shorts, while knee-length stockings would take the place of socks, and a topee instead of a felt hat.

Now let us look at those same Europeans as they appear during the internment on Singapore Island. White suits and all other kinds of suits were put away from the beginning, and we got into open shirts and shorts. In the early days in the temporary camps at a time when everybody suddenly found himself under the necessity of having to wash his own clothes, there was a water shortage, and it was necessary to reduce washing to a minimum, so people began to go without shirts. The next step was to discard the singlet and go bare to the waist. Topees and hats continued to be worn for some time, until internees found that they could do without them with no ill effects, and then they were put away too. The last step was to discard socks and shoes. Many internees were only provided with one pair of shoes and soon saw that it was necessary to conserve them.

Of course, there were certain occupations, such as the carpenters and wood cutters, in which it would have been dangerous to go barefoot; and there were always some internees who continued to wear shoes and socks, either because they did not care to run the risk of stepping on a nail and so on, or because they could not bring themselves to descend this final step to the level of the peasant and the coolie. But many others had no such feelings, or soon lost them, and a barefoot vogue spread rapidly in the camp. The constant walking on concrete and trudging over hard roads on outside fatigues wore out footwear quickly, and materials for repair were very scarce, so most internees eventually reached a point at which they were forced to put away their last pair of shoes or face the prospect of having no footwear when the great and well-nigh unimaginable day arrived when we would walk out of the camp for repatriation (as we hoped in those days) or to go back to Singapore after the war.

And so these former members of the most self-conscious and conventional social castes in the world jettisoned all their former habits of dress and came to wear nothing more than a pair of shorts from morning till night, or a pair of bathing-drawers if they had them. Some went further and made themselves a pair of lap-laps or a G-string in which they went as near complete nakedness as the primitive tribes dwelling in the Malayan jungle. Bareheaded, bare to the waist, and barefoot, the white man in the Singapore internment camps wore no more than a peasant working in his paddy fields, the Chinese coolie in the tin mines or the Tamil coolies sweating on the asphalt roads of Singapore. And they did this not just for a few days or a few weeks at a time, but continuously for three years, until it seemed almost second nature to them to live half-naked in the sun, and it seemed incredible that there had ever been a time when they had gone to the office wearing a white suit, collar and tie, shirt and singlet, socks and shoes, and they wondered whether they would ever be able to do so again. Incidentally, it is interesting to note how deep-rooted the sense of decency was. I saw only one instance of an internee venturing to go without clothing altogether. He was digging in the vegetable gardens at the time, and despite the fact that our clothing was wearing out rapidly by that time, the social reaction against this experiment was so prompt and emphatic that the would-be nudist noticed at once and abandoned it. "We may be living like coolies, but we haven't become animals yet," was a general comment. Moreover, for fatigues, shirt and shorts were compulsory, and for outside fatigues near the camp at least a pair of shorts. Half-naked or virtually naked, then, we lived in the sun.

In the prison yards at Changi people would sit reading for a whole morning in the full sunshine, a thing they would never have dreamt of doing in their own gardens in ordinary life. In this dress they worked in the vegetable gardens, carrying logs on rubber estates, hauled firewood carts along the roads, or walked to the beach in the days when we were allowed a sea-bathe once a month. And we wore the same dress indoors as well as outdoors, never bothering to put on a shirt except in the cool of the evening, and often not then. The simple life indeed!

Sometimes, when going to a concert in Changi Gaol which involved no more than picking up one's stool and walking to the laundry, it was amusing to look back on the complicated sartorial ritual one had had to go through in order to go to a concert in the Victoria Memorial Hall, Singapore, in one's former life. The thought of putting on an ordinary white shirt made one feel positively hot in our internment life. The reader can imagine what the social uniform required for concerts and formal dinner parties seemed like in retrospect.

Of course, we got too much of a good thing. The compulsory hours of work required of us by the Japanese eventually increased to six hours a day at the Sime Road camp and we worked those hours every day of the week except for the half-holidays on Wednesdays and Sundays. This was unquestionably too much, especially as we were on "Tokyo time," which was two hours ahead of the sun, so that the afternoon working hours from 2 p.m. to 5 p.m. were really from noon to 3 p.m., the hottest part of the day, when even the Malay rice farmer stays at home in the shade. Some of us, too, were never able to accustom ourselves to sitting in the full sunlight when reading or studying, although we could stand it with ease when walking or doing physical work. As to the six-hour working day, I am convinced that the younger men at the camp could have got through that without the slightest difficulty, and in fact positively enjoy themselves, had they been able to eat as much rice as they wanted, together with a slightly larger allowance of protein foods. Given sufficient food, it was no hardship for a fit man to wield a changkol on the bare hillsides and in the sun-baked valleys of the Sime Road camp, but rather a real physical pleasure.

The results of this revolution in European dress in Malaya were extremely interesting. To begin with headwear, we never had a single case of sunstroke or anything that could be considered as heatstroke. Some people found that they could not comfortably go without hats, but the vast majority went bare-headed without the slightest ill effect. In my own case example, I'd never gone on a country walk during the hot hours of the day without wearing a topee and very dark sunglasses and even then I often had the penalty of a headache for the rest of the day. But in the internment life, I ceased to wear either the topee or dark glasses and found I could spend an entire morning in the sun without any trace of a headache.

As to shirts and singlets, we look like boiled lobsters for a day or two after we discarded garments but after one bad sunburn we had no further trouble and felt a sensation of coolness and comfort such as we had never had in our peacetime life in Malaya. Our bodies took on a healthy tan, and this became so universal that if one saw amongst the crowd bathing in the laundry of Changi Gaol, one of the rare individuals who continued to wear a shirt and lived in his cell by day, one felt a shock of repulsion at the unhealthy appearance of the white skin. Among all these tanned bodies the cell-dweller looked like an enormous pallid white ant.

The barefoot fashion resulted in our stubbing our toes and getting little cuts and abrasions at first, but eventually we acquired that new consciousness of the feet and that automatic caution which are necessary in order to go barefoot with safety, and the soles of our feet became well-nigh as tough as those of a Tamil coolie, though I would not go so far as to say that any of us would have been willing to volunteer for the annual fire-walking ceremony in Singapore! We had one sad case of a young man dying as the eventual result of stepping on a rusty nail, but otherwise we were lucky in that respect. And we rediscovered something we had never known since we were children: the physical pleasure of going barefoot. Everyone knows the delight in which children take off their shoes whenever they are allowed to, on the beach or beside a stream or in a grassy meadow, and that same sensation came back to us as adults in our Singapore internment. We knew for the first time in our conventional Malayan lives the pleasure of feeling the grass and sun-warmed earth under one's feet; and one also became conscious in an entirely new way of one's feet as the beautifully modelled and exquisitely balanced organs that they are.

Many of us found that the itchy complaint known as "Singapore foot," which we had never been able to get rid of in normal life, cleared up like magic once we exposed our feet to the sun and air. Once one got used to going barefoot, it was a positive discomfort to put on shoes and socks again, except in the cool of the evening. There were some people who could not bring themselves to take what they more or less subconsciously regarded as the final step in the process of "going native," or who felt that it was not worthwhile taking a risk, but a very large number of internees went barefoot and once they had done so they never wanted to go back to socks and shoes again.

But above all this complete change in habits in dress bought about a more intense enjoyment of the climate of Malaya, a new appreciation of it, and a new attitude towards it. We became devotees of the ancient cult of sun worship, consciously or unconsciously; instead of fearing the tropical sunshine as a potential menace to ourselves as white men and aliens from a temperate climate, we found ourselves revelling in it and appreciating it as never before. For the first time in our artificial highly conventionalised lives in Malaya, we knew the elemental pleasure of living half-naked in the sun, feeling the kiss of the sunshine and the balmy breath of the wind on our bodies all day long. The freshness of the early morning, the soaking, intense, irradiating sunshine of high noon, and the still air of the evening, the joy of a lively, blowy day with white clouds racing across a blue sky, the indescribable stillness and peace of one of those heavenly mornings we get occasionally in Malaya, when there is not a leaf stirring and the whole world seems intent on listening for some revelation, a revelation that never comes unless the morning itself is it. These things we sensed with heightened sensitivity, responsiveness and delight after we had shed the stuffy trappings of civilisation and lived the simple life.

I often recalled in those days my reaction when I had come upon Fauconnier's novel, *The Soul of Malaya*, some years before, which I read with scepticism not to say incredulity, judging by my experience up to that time, that it seemed to be overdone. I felt Malaya was no country for that kind of life, that the heat and glare were too great, that in cold prosaic fact those white men on a Malayan beach would have been very uncomfortable. But now I knew that Fauconnier was right, for I had known the same thing myself in the infinitely less beautiful surroundings of the Changi countryside and the camp on the fringe of the suburbs of Singapore. We found not only more physical comfort in the climate, but the shedding of dress seemed to make a fundamental difference.

We felt closer to nature in Malaya than we had ever been before, more nearly a part of our environment, more able to enjoy the simple things of life. For the first time we realised the deep, elemental, animal happiness that must be in the soul of the Malay peasant as he walks along the little grassy paths between the fields of waving padi and feels the sunshine and breeze playing on his body. And for the first time we compare, to the disadvantage of the white man, the Tamil coolie working in his loin-cloth amid the dappled shade and sunlight under the rubber trees, and his European boss sweating in topee and shirt and shorts and shoes. We shared too the feelings of the Chinese squatter as he toiled half-naked in the good earth of some quiet Malayan valley, for had we not done the same thing? In a word, we enjoyed the climate of Malaya as we had never done in our former peacetime lives in this country.

Is it too much to suggest that from that experience will be born a fundamental and lasting readjustment of ourselves to our Malayan environment, with all that that implies of a new and more contented acceptance of our lot, a less restless spirit and a deeper contentment, a less exclusive and more inclusive social consciousness, a closer relationship with the peoples to whom Malaya is their homeland, than we had ever thought possible in this beautiful but alien land?

[8]
Rice, Rice, Rice

Food deserves a chapter to itself in this story of the internment, for it was of great interest from several points of view. This was the first time in the history of Malaya, and probably of the Far East in general, that a body of several thousand Europeans had to live continuously for years on a rice diet. It was the first time in the lives of most of those internees that they had to live on an almost purely vegetarian diet. It was the first time in the lives of these white residents of Malaya that they had to live almost entirely on the food of the country, as distinct from imported produce. It was as radical a revolution in their traditional and conventional ways of life in Malaya as the doing of manual labour and the change in dress. And, from the point of view of the individual internee, rations were a matter of absorbing interest and paramount importance, so much so that would be impossible to give the reader who spent those years under more normal or more fortunate circumstances an adequate account of what life was like for these white residents of Malaya during the internment on Singapore Island unless we accord to the daily menu the prominence which it had for the internees themselves. Looking back on it now, it seems almost comic to recall the part which food played in our conversation in Changi Gaol. That solemn appraisal of the day's vegetable soup, the detailed account of one's good fortune or the reverse in the all-important matter of "seconds" and so on.

But in truth food took on an altogether new and vital importance for those middle-class British people, so rudely uprooted from their comfortable and secure lives that had been theirs in peacetime Malaya. You might see, for example, a pair of well-known lawyers engaged in absorbed and serious conversation in the Main Yard, really dissecting the knotty question of whether palm oil was better in the soup or the kunji, or the day's seconds. This elementary human need became as pressing and anxious a problem for them as it is for the most poverty-stricken slum-dweller in Britain or the primitive savage never free from the spectre of famine.

Thus the internment was in one sense a unique mass experiment in European diet in the tropics, and one that gave the hundred medical men in the camp plenty to think about; but however valuable may have been the data collected, the internee did not at all relish his enforced role of a guinea pig to nutritional research, and one must admit that he was singularly ill-prepared for it. Let us recall for a moment the typical ideas and habits of the European in Malaya with regard to food before the Second World War. In this matter the British resident was intensely conservative and seemed to take a straightforward and irrational pride in his conservatism. He ate, so far as possible, exactly the same diet that he had done in the totally different climate of the British Isles. He was able to do this because of the remarkable technical progress and commercial enterprise of the cold-storage industry, which imported an astonishing variety of staple foods and luxuries from temperate and subtropical countries.

The beef, mutton, and veal on the European's table came from Australia; his bacon or ham came from England; his milk, butter and cheese came from Australia, likewise the flour in his bread; his potatoes came from countries as far apart as India and Japan, his onions from Egypt, his cooking oil from the olive groves of Palestine, his carrots and parsnips and other vegetables from the highlands of Sumatra or Java, and the apples and oranges which he conscientiously ate in a country abounding with tropical fruit came from California and Australia. Those were just the ordinary humdrum meals that we have been considering, but if the European resident wanted to be extravagant he could eat oysters brought by aeroplane from Australia, fresh strawberries brought in "dry ice" from California, grouse from Scottish moors, Dover soles from England, and dozens of other costly and exotic luxuries in the array of items on his grocer's shelves. Admittedly this generalisation about the diet of the white man in Malaya requires qualification. The British resident ate the excellent fresh fish of the country. He made some use of local green vegetables, and he might or might not eat an occasional banana or mangosteen or pineapple. But in general it is true to say that the typical British resident of Malaya had the same foods in the same proportions, and with the same high contents of meat and other protein in the hot climate of Malaya as he had done in the British Isles before he came out east. Above all, he was not a rice-eater. That was the main difference between the European and the Asiatic in Malaya from the dietary point of view, and the most significant one in relation to the internment. In normal times the European in Malaya ate rice only once a week, when he indulged in a gargantuan Sunday curry tiffin, and that was as near as he ever allowed himself to go in enjoyment of what he called "native food." Of course there were some white residents who had acquired a real liking for rice and ate rice dishes fairly often, but they were a small minority. The staple carbohydrate food of a white resident was bread, which he ate three or four times a day and the fact that the Cold Storage Company had regularly on sale over 22 kinds of bread is in itself sufficient explanation of why rice seemed a tasteless and uninteresting food to the European palate.

There is one other fact that we have to bear in mind in discussing the part which food played in the life of the internee, and that is that very few of those people had ever known real hunger, except in the sense of a pleasurable sharpening of the appetite, with the certainty of being able to satisfy it within a few hours. All their lives they had always had enough to eat, had taken three meals a day for granted. They had never known what it was to be continually underfed. On the contrary, they had, like most middle-class people the world over, consistently even eaten too much.

Much as some internees would object to doing so, it is also necessary to consider the subject of food during the internment from the Japanese point of view. One also has to bear in mind the circumstances existing at the time. Singapore has a population of 700,000, and the staple food of nearly all is rice. In normal times the whole of the rice required to feed that vast massive Chinese, Indian and Malay population is imported from Siam, Burma and Indochina; practically none comes from the Malayan hinterland. The Malay Peninsula is not a cattle or sheep country, having very little grassland for grazing. Singapore imports all its meat from overseas, except for a certain amount of locally produced pork, which is not nearly sufficient to meet the needs of the Chinese population and has to be supplemented by a large importation of pigs from Bali. Singapore is self-supporting in green vegetables, and receives a certain amount of other vegetables and also fruit and minor food products from its hinterland; but here again there is a large importation of vegetables and fruit from the East Indies and other neighbouring countries. The fresh fish landed at Singapore is normally sufficient to meet the needs of the population, but otherwise Singapore may be said to be almost entirely dependent on overseas sources for its food in normal times.

After the Japanese conquest the established, automatic, commercially motivated processes of trade with neighbouring countries broke down, and the difficulty of getting sufficient food into Singapore was presumably increased by submarine warfare and a shipping shortage. Moreover, the Japanese administration adopted a policy of making each of the Malay States a self-supporting area, keeping its own food products within its own borders as far as possible. So Singapore was not able to draw on its hinterland to any large extent. The cutting off of imports from Allied countries also intensified the local food problem. For example, most Asiatics in Singapore had been in the habit of eating bread once a day. When the supply of wheat and flour from Australia was cut off the demand for rice and other carbohydrate substitutes such as tapioca and sweet potatoes naturally rose far beyond the normal level. Again, with no refrigerated meat from Australia or canned foods from the United States, the demand for locally caught fish rapidly rose far above normal. For similar reasons, the demand for locally produced fruits was abnormal. In these circumstances there was bound to be a food shortage in Singapore, especially when there was a large Japanese garrison to be fed, as well as the internees and many thousands of military prisoners.

All things considered, therefore, Singapore was one of the worst places in the East to be interned in, so far as food went. Had we been interned in Java or Siam, countries full of locally produced food, we might have fared much better. Moreover, looking at the matter from the Japanese point of view, one must remember that not merely Singapore but the whole of Malaya presented a very difficult food problem. Malaya normally produces only enough food to feed one-third of its population. Rice cultivation is solely in the hands of Malayans, and they are peasants living on smallholdings and requiring most of the rice they produce to feed themselves. The remaining two-thirds of the population, some 350,000 Chinese and Indians, mostly employed on the estates and mines, depend on supplies of rice imported from other countries. For that reason, and because of the breakdown of the peacetime trade machinery, many people feared that there would be a famine in Malaya after the conquest. But the Japanese did not allow this to happen. They not only took over the rice rationing scheme of the former British administration but saw to it that sufficient rice was brought into the country to stave off famine, particularly before the cultivation of alternative food crops had been developed on a large scale. One mentions this to show that it was not nearly as easy for the Japanese administration in Singapore to get additional food supplies from upcountry to improve our diet as some internees supposed. They had to assume the direct responsibility of feeding not only ourselves but the greater part of the population of the country.

Yet another factor in the situation was the very different standards of the Japanese with regard to food. Their national diet is a very simple and plain one, consisting chiefly of rice and fish, and it was not to be expected that the ideas of what constituted an adequate diet for the internment camp would coincide with those of a body of Europeans accustomed to a much more varied and more appetising fare.

Japanese rations applied to the internment camp comprised rice, meat or fish, vegetables, salt, cooking oil and tea. Unfortunately the meat or fish was a very uncertain factor, and at the best of times was never sufficient for more than two meals a week, while the quantity supplied was but a small allowance for 3000 people, judged by the standards of ordinary European diet. Moreover, the vegetables supplied by the Japanese included no greens, so essential for a balanced diet. That deficiency was accentuated by the fact that for long periods we got no fruit whatever. If we had had to live on the official rations we should have had to become strict vegetarian five days a week, but fortunately we had three other sources of supply. The Japanese allowed us to buy food in town with our own camp funds and also allowed the local representative of the International Red Cross to send in supplies to the camp; and, for a while, there was also the "Black Market." We were fortunate also in that the full rigour of the new regime did not descend upon us all at once. What happened was there was a slow, progressive deterioration in our diet, so that we were able to break ourselves in gradually to living on short rations and unaccustomed foods. The internment fell into two periods from the food point of view: before and after the abrupt change in our fortunes known as the "Double Tenth." On October 10, 1943, the Japanese military police began an investigation into certain grave allegations against the camp, and thereafter our position changed for the worse in every respect and remained so until we left Changi Gaol. But for the first 19 months our food was not too bad, compared with what we had to put up with in the lean times that were to come later, and it is that first period that I propose to discuss first.

When we first moved into Changi Gaol we went through a very hungry time, as was inevitable when cooking and commissariat arrangements for so large a body of people had to be organised, but we soon settled down and within two months we were feeding very well. Had anyone ventured to express this opinion in Changi Gaol at the time he would have stood a good chance of being lynched, for the internees thought they were very badly off indeed; but in the very different perspective of the time and place in which our own present perspective is (these words are written in the Sime Road camp in November 1944), one sees that that assertion is true. It may help the reader to sense the atmosphere at Changi Gaol in those days if I recall my own first impressions of the food.

I happened to come in three months late, having been a patient in hospital outside, where I had been half-starved. What was my surprise and delight to receive for breakfast on the first day a well-sweetened and appetising porridge of rice and sago, a bun made of wheat flour, a thick wedge of cheese, a pat of margarine, and tea with milk in it. For the midday meal a pint of thick, nourishing meat stew and a plateful of steamed rice. And for the evening meal another plate of the same porridge with milk in it this time but no sugar, and again tea with milk in it. What's more, if one wanted a second helping of steamed rice or kunji (rice and water porridge), with four cubes of tinned pineapple in it, all one had to do was to go to the big wooden tongs (tubs) and help oneself. Compared with the rations I had been living on, the meals on that first day seemed a veritable feast, but I found that my fellow internees were far from realising how comparatively fortunate they were. On the contrary, they regarded themselves as being only slightly above the starvation level and many of them complained of being perpetually hungry. One used to see internees very carefully cutting their bun into thin slices, each barely sufficient to provide one satisfying mouthful for a healthy infant, and they would eat the slices at intervals during the day with morsels of cheese to stave off the pangs of hunger, this at a time when quantities of rice were being thrown into the swill pits every day! The trouble was, at that time, memories of ordinary peacetime life were still fresh in the minds of internees; their dietary standards were still those of their former lives. Moreover they had not yet accustomed themselves to a rice diet, to eating a sufficient quantity of rice to provide the necessary calories. Most of the internees still cherished a prejudice against rice as an Asiatic food, and absurdly ill-informed notions as to the real nutritional value of rice were current. One was continuously hearing such remarks as "It's all I can do to get the stuff down," "There's very little food value in it," and so on. Moreover, quite apart from the psychological resistance of the internee, it is probable that his system had yet to adapt itself to the assimilation of a much higher proportion of carbohydrates than he had been used to. The main reason, however, why people felt hungry at that time was not that there was a real shortage of food, but that they were down to a very simple and monotonous diet for the first time in their lives and were missing the varied, well-flavoured and comparatively rich dishes, the sweets and savouries, of a normal European diet.

Actually we were feeding at that time better than might be supposed from the above description, for that was the heyday of the black market in Changi Gaol. The policy of the former British regime had been to stock Singapore for a long siege, which was then the worst that we, in our foolishness and credulous acceptance of our own propaganda, had expected. So the godowns and provision shops of the city were bursting with tinned foodstuffs when the Japanese captured it. During the last few days before the fall, and for day or so afterwards, there was widespread looting, with the result that all sorts of people had tinned foods to sell besides the ordinary shopkeepers. Nearly all the internees in Changi Gaol had managed to bring some money with them, very large amounts in some cases, and the connection between supply and demand was soon established. At that time the campsite guards consisted of Japanese soldiers, and they were only too willing to supplement their meagre pay by bringing in food for the hungry prisoners. This went on more or less openly. One of my first recollections of Changi Gaol is a senior Japanese sentry coming through the archway into the front courtyard in the half-light of the evening with a heavy and bulging sack on his back. I did not see the significance of it at the time, but I soon found out. What I had seen was a consignment of goods arriving to the black market. The Japanese army officers in charge of the camp forbad this practice, and our own camp officials and camp police tried to suppress it, but public opinion was against them, and hunger, like love, will always find a way, so that in those days large quantities of tinned foods of all kinds were coming into the Gaol and were distributed by a network of wholesale agents and runners selling the stuff on commission. By the time that everybody concerned had taken his rake-off, the price was fantastic compared with what that same article had been sold at only three months before: the price of a tin of milk, for example, sold for $6, as against its normal price of $0.30 or $0.40, but it was dirt cheap compared with the utterly fantastic prices of the black market two years later. But the black market was not the only means of supplementing our rations in the early days. The Chinese and Malays living in the vicinity of the Gaol were plentifully supplied with tinned foodstuffs, which they wanted to convert into cash, so when the firewood and other outside fatigues returned, they did so with bulging pockets and a choice array of tinned goods on the cart. There were also perfectly legitimate opportunities of buying extra food at that time, for fatigues were being sent in to town several times a week, and they were always allowed by the Japanese guards to stop at the shop and buy all the foodstuffs and tobacco they wanted. It was a very unlucky internee in those days who did not have a tin of condensed milk or jam to flavour his rice porridge morning and evening, while at the midday meal one would see tins of bully beef and sardines and cheese on every side. Tins of toffee, tins of biscuits, bottles of sweets, pickles… it makes one's mouth water to think of the luxuries that were to be bought in Changi Gaol at the time. But all that belongs to the very early days of the internment. The supplies of tinned foods outside the Gaol soon dried up and Japanese supervision became stricter, so that the firewood fatigues came back empty-handed.

Then, after we had been in Gaol about six months, the Japanese military guard was taken away and replaced with Sikhs, mostly former policeman and warders of the British regime. The behaviour of these new guards was naturally very different from that of the carefree Japanese soldiers, who had regarded their duties in the internment camp merely as a pleasurable interlude in active service. The Sikhs maintained from the first a strict and aloof attitude towards the internees and were far too much in awe of the Japanese authorities to risk any illicit trafficking, so there were no black-market goods forthcoming from that quarter. Thereafter such goods became more and more scarce and expensive in the Gaol, the only new supplies being the very small quantities bought in by fatigues from town and by the internees who worked as lorry drivers. There were always wealthy individuals who managed to feed a good deal better than other people, but for the average internee the time soon came when he had to stop buying in the black market and live solely on camp rations. The rations did not long remain at the relatively high level of my first day in Changi Gaol but soon began to deteriorate slowly but steadily. First the wheat flour gave out, and the daily bun had to be replaced by a dreadful product of amateur bakery, known as a "rice cake," made of rice flour, grated coconut and water; then the daily pat of margarine came to be issued every other day, the cheese became but a happy memory, the sugar in the rice porridge was reduced so much that it would not be tasted, the milk disappeared from the tea… and so on and so on. It became more and more difficult for the camp to buy European foodstuffs in bulk, as the stocks in town dwindled, and we became more and more conscious of the unpleasant realities and potential dangers of our situation.

So much for the first six months. It was a phase in which we tried to cling to a European diet as far as possible and were able to benefit temporarily from the supplies of imported foodstuffs left over in town from the British regime. From then onwards it is possible to distinguish three distinct and successive phases of the internment from the food point of view: the period in which we were still able to draw on stocks of tinned foods and meat in cold storage to supplement the Japanese rations; the period in which we lived on a comparatively varied and nourishing diet composed entirely of Asiatic foods; and the final period, comprising the last half of the internment, in which we lived on an almost purely vegetarian diet insufficient both in quantity and quality.

Resuming our chronicle at the point at which we cast a wistful backward glance at the early days when all the colourful array of a pre-captivity provision shop was represented in Changi Gaol, we enter now a phase in which imported meat and fish still figured in our prison menus. The Japanese continued to send in Australian beef once a week so long as the stocks in town lasted, not much for 3000 people, but enough to give us meat soup two days a week. We were indeed thankful that the Singapore Cold Storage Company had laid in such large stocks during the war. Moreover, the camp had been able to lay in substantial stocks of tinned foods in the early months by bulk purchases in town, made with the permission of the Japanese authorities, so that we always had bully beef or tinned chicken curry or sardines in a midday soup when we did not have beef. It may have been a thin soup — in fact, it got thinner and thinner — but at least it had a flavour and variety, and content of animal protein, that were very welcome to a white community living mainly on rice. And on days when we had a purely vegetarian soup the midday menu always included "Sardine on the Hoof," that is to say, an issue between every six men of one of those tins of large and succulent California sardines which were the favourite luxury of the Tamil estate coolie before the war. When the supply of refrigerated meat gave out the Japanese supplied fresh pork for a time.

By the way, the mention of so odd an article of diet as tinned chicken curry may arouse the curiosity of readers who have not been in Malaya in recent years. Curry is eaten regularly every day by hundreds of thousands of Asiatics in Malaya, but tinned curry was unknown in this country until a few years before the war, when an enterprising manufacturer in Penang began putting chicken curry in tins, ready-cooked so that it only required heating to be ready for use. This product took on immediately, and the internment camp was able to lay in a large stock of it in the early months. It became one of the standbys of our prison camp cuisine, and a very popular one, even though it was used in the soup so sparingly that all that was left of it by the time it reached the individual internees was the taste. No local product has ever received such effective free publicity among the white community of Malaya.

Our breakfast by this time had become the meal of truly monastic simplicity that it was to be throughout the internment, consisting of no more than a plate of unsweetened rice porridge and a mug of tea without sugar or milk. The evening meal was slightly more interesting. The tea was the same again, but the porridge had a little powdered milk in it and therefore it became dignified with the name of rice pudding. To flavour it we received four cubes of tinned pineapple and a spoonful of juice, measured out with meticulous care. We also got the aforementioned rice cake, which by this time had evolved by a process of trial and error into a tolerably palatable sort of bread; and to spread on it we received a small pat of tinted dripping or margarine.

We went on like this until the end of the first twelve months, but then the tinned foods in the camp store began to ran out one by one, until the time came when we ate our last hint of curry chicken, our last sardine and our last pint of bully beef soup. But while our food position was deteriorating in this respect it was improving in others. We were entering now on the phase in which we said a final goodbye to our customary European food and lived entirely on Asiatic food, and lived much better than we expected.

The kunji was no longer the plain rice-and-water porridge of the early days; it had become as tasty and nutritious a breakfast food as any of the concoctions made in America, for by this time it always included one or another of a novel and interesting variety of Asiatic cereals, beans and peas available in eastern Asia. Let us take a typical day in Changi Gaol in the middle of 1943, that is to say after about 18 months of internment. At that time the conditions of the captivity were the best that we ever experienced, not only in respect to food but in every way, and it was a phase that lasted some months. In later days we came to look back on it as a time of comparative plenty. Let us first look at the internees' breakfast at that time. The breakfast menu still comprises only kunji and tea, the basis of it is still rice, but it is thickened with flour made of sago or maze or tapioca. The sago came from the swamps of Borneo, the maize from Java and the tapioca possibly from the Malay Peninsula or half a dozen neighbouring countries, for it grows like a weed in this region. None of these cereals figured in the normal peacetime diet of the European in Malaya, except that sago with coconut milk and palm sugar was the traditional dish which finished off a Sunday curry tiffin, but by the time it was served, one had usually eaten too much curry to be able to appreciate it. There was usually one other ingredient in our breakfast kunji at that time, either soya bean or groundnuts or the small green peas known as "kachang hijau," ground into flour. This was particularly important, because it meant that we were protected against the greatest danger of a rice diet: the serious disease known as "beriberi," caused by lack of vitamin B1. This vitamin is essential for the proper assimilation of rice as a human food; without it the system cannot fully metabolise the rice starch, with the result that poisons are set up and cause beriberi; the more rice you eat the greater the danger. On the other hand, given a sufficiency of vitamin B1, you can eat as much rice as you want without danger. The remarkable thing is that nature has implanted in the rice grain the very constituent that is required by the human body. The outer layers of the rice grains contain vitamin B1, and also iron and other minerals essential for human health. But those outer layers were carefully removed in the rice mills of Bangkok, Saigon and Java, and the vitamins and minerals fed to pigs and poultry in the form of a waste product of the mills, leaving a highly polished rice which is virtually purely starch and much inferior as a human food to what nature made it and a positive danger to health when used as the basis of an otherwise poor and restricted diet such as is eaten by many millions of the poorer classes of Asia. This is an evil of quite recent times; it is only within the last 50 years or so that the Asiatic has acquired a taste for over-milled and polished rice, following on the introduction of modern milling machinery into the Far East. This does not apply to the parboiled type of rice eaten by the people of India which is husked by a boiling process which results in most of the vitamin and mineral content soaking into the grain and thus being preserved. In fact beriberi is rare among the Indian labouring class in Malaya (whose diet is otherwise a very poor one), whereas it is common among the Chinese in this country. But all the other rice-eating peoples of Asia eat the polished rice, except where the peasantry still follow the ancient ways of life, husking the rice produced in their own fields and eating it themselves, but nowadays the Malay peasant prefers to sell his rice harvest to the miller and buy polished rice from the village shop for his own consumption. This ignorant devitalisation of the staple food of hundreds of millions of people will no doubt astonish later and wiser generations, but the taste of polished rice has now become so ingrained that nothing short of dictatorial methods can solve the problems of the present generation whatever propaganda in the schools may do for the next. Before we condemn the Asiatic, however, let us not forget that precisely the same is done with wheat, the staple food of the European.

Well, we have wandered a long way from Changi Gaol, but this digression will show why beriberi was the greatest danger to our health during the internment and why our medical authorities had to be constantly on the alert to contrive to give us a sufficiency of B1, which cannot be stored in the body, but must be replenished. This they did by persuading the Japanese to give us unpolished rice whenever possible, and when this was not available by adding groundnuts or soya beans or some other kind of bean or pulse to our kunji. In the main they were successful, but there were some cases of beriberi in the early months and mild symptoms became quite widespread for a time in the Sime Road camp.

For most of us the soya bean was one of the most interesting discoveries of the internment. It was typical of the conservatism of the European in Malaya in matters of food, and of his indifference towards local food resources, that he made no use of the soya bean before the war. This is the one of the most nutritious beans in the world, unique in its high content of proteins, fats and vitamins. The Japanese make a tinned condensed milk from it which they claim to be almost as nutritious as natural milk, and during the Japanese occupation this soy milk was widely used in Malaya. The soya bean is produced mainly in Manchuria, but there is also a considerable production in the United States. It is imported into Malaya in large quantities in normal times, being used in the manufacture of the Chinese sauce known as "tow-yew," which is eaten with rice, the bean curd which is largely used in Chinese cookery, and the yellow soya cakes which are one of the commonest articles of food sold by hawkers in any Malayan town. After the conquest of Malaya the Japanese saw to it that shipments of soya bean continued to come into the country, for some months they included it in the rations they supplied to the internment camp. Unfortunately they were not able to keep this up, and we got no more soya bean after the end of the second year, but so long as we were getting a substantial quantity of it we had no need to worry about vitamins or the shortage of animal protein in our diet. When ground into a flour and cooked with rice, the soya bean made a very tasty and satisfying porridge, and after living on polished rice for some time we felt an immediate benefit in increased energy and a general sense of well-being when we began to get the soya beans in our diet. Consequently many of us wondered why we had never gone to the Chinese provision dealer for this cheap, nutritious foodstuff in our former lives, and promised that we would certainly do so in the future.

Another of our gastronomic discoveries was the merits of the humble peanut, or groundnut, as it is properly called. This is one of the cheapest and most abundant foodstuffs in Malaya, being produced in the country and also imported, and is largely eaten by the poorer classes, but the European resident never eats it except when it is served, fried and salted, as "kechil makan" with beer or cocktails, or as one of the accompaniments of a curry. Consequently our curiosity was aroused and we were surprised when "peanut kunji" first appeared on the menu in Changi Gaol. The peanuts were ground into a meal and mixed into the rice kunji while it was cooking, and this combination immediately proved highly popular, being very palatable and much more sustaining than the rice alone. Its food value was in fact considerable, the groundnut being rich in proteins, oil, and vitamins, particularly the all-important B1. Here again many of us felt that bitter experience had taught us a lesson. We had bought all kinds of fancy breakfast foods put up in cartons and imported from America, and had never dreamt of using this excellent foodstuff on sale at our very doors. Now, having learned the value of peanuts as food and its possibilities in the recipes of the European household, we added yet another to the good resolutions we made in Changi Gaol. It is safe to prophesy that in some European households in Malaya in future "peanut kunji" will appear on the breakfast table, in spite of its association with bygone hunger and captivity.

If there were no soya beans or peanuts in the camp store or if unpolished rice was not available, medical experts combated the beriberi danger by mixing a type of small green pea known as "kachang hijau" into the morning kunji, again grinding it into a meal first; later they also used for this purpose a type of red bean about the size of the haricot bean which was said to be imported from Java. These latter two ingredients in the kunji were interesting as being Asiatic foodstuffs new to most of us, but they were not sufficiently attractive for us to make a mental note of them to future use, as we had done with the soya bean and peanut. But their food value was considerable in our plight at that time. Actually, it very rarely happened, after the first few months, that we had to eat plain rice-and-water porridge for breakfast: our camp officials always managed to produce one or other of the supplementary foodstuffs to mix with it, thanks mainly to their own purchases in town or the free supplies received from the Neutral Agent.

But we have not yet come to the end of our description of a typical breakfast Changi Gaol somewhere about the middle of 1943. Other things figured in it that were actually novel from the conventional European point of view. Had you been able to visit the Gaol about eight o'clock in the morning (Tokyo time) in those days, you would have found the occupants busily engaged in scraping coconuts, in preparation for breakfast. At that time the Japanese were allowing the camp to buy thousands of coconuts every week from the adjacent Chinese and Malay smallholdings, and these were distributed free to internees. Thus every internee received two or three coconuts a week, and a regular technique was soon worked out for dealing with them. At first we had nothing but pocket knives for getting out the meat, but, in the extraordinary way in which needs were met in Changi Gaol, it was not long before everybody was equipped with a scraper, either the small hand type or the larger type used by Asiatics which we have already seen in use in our tour of the front courtyard. Some people ate the grated coconut just as it was, but the majority went a stage further and made coconut milk. This is not, as most people wrongly suppose when they read stories of the South Seas, the fluid found inside the nut: that is as colourless as water, and not nearly as nice as novelists have made it out to be. The true coconut milk is made by grating the white meat out of the nut, squeezing it, and diluting the resultant fluid with water, resulting in a white, rich milk delicious in flavour. Under the name of "santan" this coconut milk is one of the commonest ingredients of Asiatic food in Malaya. It is made in every Malay household every day, and figures in almost every recipe of Eurasian and Straits Chinese households, while it is also one of the most important ingredients in India or Malay curry. This is possible because coconuts are normally very cheap and plentiful in Malaya, being produced in that thick belt of palms which covers the coastal plain on both sides of the peninsula, stretching ten or twenty miles inland along its entire length. The coconut palm is also found inland around every Malay hut and Tamil coolie line. The coconut is in fact one of the staple articles of food to the Asiatic population, but here again it plays practically no part in the diet of the European resident, except when he has had it in his Sunday curry or served with the sago pudding after the curry. In Changi Gaol, however, we were only too glad to make santan to flavour our kunji, and, having it day after day for many months, we came to like it as well as any Asiatic. It is indeed one of the most delicious flavouring substances in the world, and considering how cheap it is in Malaya and how easily made, we felt that we had been singularly unenterprising in virtually ignoring it before.

We enjoyed our santan in Changi Gaol all the more by reason of the fact that for a long time we were able to buy the Malayan product which is its ideal complement, the brown palm sugar known as "gula malaka." This is made by distilling the sap of the coconut palm or the nipah palm (found in dense thickets along the muddy shores of the tidal swamps), or the kabong palm, which is the least common of these three. In ordinary times Java cane sugar is so cheap in Malaya that gula malaka is not used for ordinary purposes but only in recipes for special sweets made by the Eurasian, Malay and Straits Chinese inhabitants, but during the war sugar was strictly rationed and palm sugar was widely used as a substitute, with the result that it became one of the most thriving village industries and was produced on a scale never known in this country before. Our camp officials were allowed to bring in large quantities from town, and there was an eager demand for it, there being virtually no other sugar in our diet at the time. Taken with the freshly made coconut milk, it made as delicious a combination of flavours for our morning kunji as could be found in the most subtle cuisines of London or Paris. Of course, it was not always available, and never in sufficient supply to meet the demand, while the consumption of it was limited in many cases by the amount of money an internee could afford to spend, but everybody got a certain amount of it, and this product of Malay kampongs was appreciated as it has never been appreciated by Europeans in Malaya before.

There was yet another ingredient in our Changi breakfast at that time which should be noted, and that was red palm oil. This is produced from the African oil palm, the cultivation of which only began as a plantation industry in Malaya after the First World War. This industry finds its markets in Europe and America, in the soap and margarine and tin-plate industries, but attempts were made to popularise the oil for cooking purposes in Malaya. Its special merit is that it is almost as rich in vitamin A as cod liver oil, and very much cheaper, but is also very suitable for general cooking purposes. This propaganda had very little effect among the European Community, who went on using their comparatively expensive olive oil or imported lard or margarine for cooking, and most of us tasted this product of Malaya's youngest plantation industry the first time when it was issued to us in Changi Gaol. Great stress was laid on it by our camp medical advisers as a source of vitamin A and fats, which was seriously deficient in our diet after the meat, dripping and margarine gave out. Palm oil has an unpleasant taste and smell when taken cold, like medicine, but these drawbacks disappear when it is mixed with hot food, as we soon found that it made a most desirable addition to the morning kunji, giving it a rich, buttery flavour and making it much more sustaining as the basis for a morning's work. Moreover, we all found that we never had any trouble with our bowels so long as we were taking palm oil. This was definitely one of the new tastes we acquired in Changi Gaol, and is likely that most of the white residents imprisoned there will go on using palm oil after the war if only because of its mild laxative effect. Later on in we received coconut oil in our kunji and fried rice.

That, then, was our breakfast in Changi Gaol during the best period of our internment; and if there is any more delicious or more nutritious breakfast food than a plate of porridge made of rice and soya bean or peanut meal, flavoured with santan and gula malaka, and given body with palm oil, I have yet to find it. And when we were given coffee for breakfast instead of tea, as we were on Sunday mornings for some time, we reached a peak of gastronomic pleasure, for santan goes unexpectedly well with coffee, giving it a really creamy consistency. I remember reading a story of the South Seas in which a solitary white man had to have coconut milk with his coffee because the boat had failed to call at his island with supplies, and I thought at the time how that must spoil the coffee. But I discovered in Changi Gaol that my sympathy with that solitary white man had been wasted. But gula malaka does not go with it so well. However, we got a pound of sugar a month, and ordinary brown cane sugar plus santan will give you a very nice cup of coffee indeed, or at least we thought so in those days.

The midday meal at this time consisted of rice and vegetable soup, except one or two days a week when we had dried fish as well. On other days we had a purely vegetarian tiffin, literally with no animal food in it whatsoever, and it was much more palatable than you might suppose. One would come back hungry from an energetic morning loading and hauling firewood carts, and sit down to a meal of boiled rice and a good, thick, appetising vegetable soup containing spinach, ubi kayu (tapioca), peanuts, red beans, some cereal or soya or pea-meal thickening, and palm oil, and it was surprising how tasty and satisfying that concoction was, particularly when flavoured with a salty soy sauce that we were all able to buy from the camp shop at that time.

Of course there were individuals totally ignorant of food values who imagined that because they were deprived of meat their health was in serious danger and who kept prophesying the rapid decline of themselves and their fellows, but in fact no such decline occurred; on the contrary, one was struck by the obviously robust health and splendid physique of the younger men in the camp while they were on this vegetarian diet, so long as there was enough of it, and also by the output of energy of the woodcutters and others doing strenuous work (far more strenuous than they had ever done on a meat diet in normal life), working both morning and afternoon in the blazing sun and apparently enjoying themselves. (They must have done so, for they need not have done the work if they had not felt inclined: they were all volunteers.) At this time we received eggs two or three times a week free so we were not entirely without animal protein, and for a time the Japanese supplied dried fish in fairly large quantities, so that we were able to have it fried once or twice a week. But this did not last long: the supplies soon began to dwindle, and it was not long before it had to be used in the most economical form, namely by making a fish paste and doling this out a spoonful at a time. Dried fish is one of the staple articles of the diet of all the Asiatic communities in Malaya, especially among the Malay peasantry and the Chinese and Indian labouring classes, but it was eaten by very few Europeans. The dried fish supplied to us in Changi Gaol was of very varying quality, some of it quite good and some almost inedible. In normal times most of us would prefer fresh fish, since the latter is readily obtainable, but if hard times come it will certainly be no hardship to go back to dried fish again. It should be added that the Japanese also sent in fresh fish from time to time, but usually there was only enough for the hospital, the women's camp and the children: fresh fish was a very rare treat for the ordinary internee.

The evening meal at this time was a comparatively substantial one. True it consisted only of kunji, bread and tea, but the kunji still had milk in it and we got not only a rice-flour bun baked in the camp kitchen but a fair-sized loaf of bread from the bakery in town. This latter bread was a local wartime substitute for ordinary wheaten bread and was apparently a mixture of tapioca flour, sago flour and maize flour, with some sort of oil in it. Whatever it was made of, it was very palatable and filling. For this very welcome addition to our ration we had to thank the Neutral Agent, who paid for it out of the funds at his disposal. There was always something to spread on bread, a spoonful of fish paste or some other concoction made in the camp kitchen or honey. Yes, honey. This was the last thing we should have expected to get during the internment, for there is no beekeeping industry in Malaya and in fact the keeping of bees is unknown, except for an interesting experiment began on Singapore Island before the war. Yet we were getting honey in at Changi Gaol two years after the fall, long after imported stocks must have been exhausted. We could only conclude that it was wild honey collected in the jungle, for there had been a small but regular importation of this jungle honey into Singapore from Sumatra and other islands before the war, though it was known to very few Europeans. At any rate, a teaspoonful of honey once a week was one of the bright spots about life in Changi.

These then, were the typical meals of this period during which we were living on relatively plentiful and almost purely vegetarian food. But the food resources of the internees at this time were by no means confined to the camp rations. Free issues of papayas, limes and peanuts were available. The black market had almost dried out, but the quantity and variety of foodstuffs distributed through the camp shop had greatly increased and was now better than it had ever been or would be again in the remainder of the internment. The camp shop had its retail shops in each of the dormitories, and at this time the internee could buy regularly from his floor shop the following goods:

eggs (in addition to those issued free), bananas and sweet potatoes, dried prawns, dried ikan bilis, vinegar, soy sauce, palm oil (in addition to the free issue), ghee, and curry stuffs. Moreover, the camp was well-stocked with gula malaka, peanut toffee and sometimes biscuits and sweets as well. These things were all made locally and we would have turned up our noses at them in the days when we could buy all the best makes of European, Australian and American chocolates, sweets and biscuits, at our disposal; but in Changi Gaol we eagerly took up our share of these cheap Chinese-made luxuries of the coolie class, and we were very thankful to get them. The peanut toffee was especially popular. This is a local product, very cheap in normal times and on sale in every Chinese coffee shop, but very few of us had ever come across it before. We found it very good and made a resolution to go on buying it after we returned to a normal life. For a time it was available in fair quantities in Changi Gaol, so that we were able to buy two or three packets a week, and there were days when you could buy as much as you wanted.

By this time there were wood-burning cooking stoves in each of the prison yards, the Japanese having allowed us to bring in these stoves from the empty warders' quarters outside, and private cooking had become one of the features of our prison life. At any time of the day, and particularly in the evenings, you would see groups of internees around the Dover stoves in the yards, boiling and baking and frying dishes of their own making, and a surprising amount of culinary skill and ingenuity appeared among dignified gentleman who formerly had never gone into their own kitchens once in six months. Really excellent curries, fried rissoles, fried eggs, fried bread and sweet potatoes, even very toothsome puddings and cakes. There were always many internees who could never be bothered to do any private cooking but lived quite contentedly on the camp rations and the extras they could buy in the shops.

Even now we have not yet come to the end of the ways and means of supplementing the camp rations that existed in those days. The Japanese allowed a daily "parcel post" from the women's camp, and a trolley loaded with parcels came over every day, so that the husbands and relatives in the men's camp were able to enjoy curries and cakes and puddings made by their womenfolk. The women for a long time were allowed much more liberal shopping facilities in town (although ours were comparatively good at that time), and they were able to make all sorts of good things; and of course the opportunity to be able to do something for their menfolk during that time of painful separation was a very welcome one. On the other hand, this custom caused a certain amount of ill feeling, as the women's camp always received favoured treatment both in the quantity of food sent over from the camp kitchen and foodstuffs sent there from the camp shop, so that internees who had no relatives in the women's camp were inclined to feel that our chivalrous policy benefited the husbands rather than the wives. And of course envy was inevitably aroused, particularly at times when food was short.

So for a time we lived pretty well in Changi Gaol, even if the food was not that to which we were accustomed. It must not be supposed, however, that all these extras from the shop were available whenever one wanted them or that one could buy as much as one wanted when they were on sale. On the contrary, it was always necessary to draw out the available supplies and strictly equal shares; and many times one would get no more than two or three small bars of peanut toffee or one or two bananas once or twice a week. On the other hand, these goods did come along at fairly regular intervals and one can remember days when one could buy all the bananas or toffee one wanted. It depended partly on whether money was tight or not, in other words, whether it was near payday, for at this time we were getting an allowance of $5 a month from the camp funds. Sweet stuffs were usually taken up eagerly but for a long time there was never any difficulty in getting extra foodstuffs of private cooking, because there were always many internees who could not be bothered to join the queue at the Dover stoves and lived quite contentedly on camp rations. But this happy state of affairs did not last long. Goods in the shop gradually became more scarce and limited, and by the time the Double Tenth burst upon us it was impossible to buy anything more than curry stuffs, sweet potatoes, and cooking oil, and even those were becoming more and more difficult to get. By this time, too, there was a queue for the surplus rice, by people who were using it for private cooking, which increased as other means of supplementing our rations deteriorated. Even so, I do not remember ever feeling real hunger up to the Double Tenth. I never, for example, reached the point of eating plain rice, as I did, and did with relish, during the latter days in the Sime Road camp. In Changi Gaol at the time we are considering, one could always fill up any empty spaces with a bun and the town-made loaf of bread in the evening.

After the Double Tenth there was a sudden and calamitous change in our food position. The supply of rice lessened, the supply of bread from the town was stopped, all camp buying in town was prohibited, and very little came in from the Neutral Agent. The result was that we very quickly found ourselves down to a level such as we had not experienced since the first days of the internment. A plate of thin, watery kunji at breakfast, a small amount of boiled rice and very thin vegetable soup for tiffin, and a small piece of bread baked in the camp and a mug of tea in the evening with a spoonful of fish paste or some other home-made spread, that was all we had for several months. It was during this time that measured "seconds" for midday rice and the morning and evening kunji were instituted for the first time; no-one could help themselves as before and there was never a grain of rice thrown wasted. The evening meal was particularly scanty. The reader can imagine what it was like to have nothing except a slice of bread to subsist on from midday to nine o'clock the next morning. Gardeners were still turning out to do an afternoon's work with nothing but this bread to last until breakfast time the next morning. They, however, had at least the motive of duty for carrying on, for never were the camp gardens more necessary than during that phase of hunger and scarcity. What was more remarkable was that even when the diet was at its very worst one could still see the internees turning out to play tennis in the morning after the wretched apology for a breakfast described above, or for football or hockey in the evening with practically nothing in their bellies, until the medical advisers stopped this as being a harmful expenditure of energy. After about six months the Japanese gradually relaxed the rigour of the penalties inflicted on the camp, in connection with the enquiry proceeding in town, and such things as bananas and toffee began to be distributed again, but in much smaller quantities, for by this time scarcity was making itself felt in town as well as in the Gaol and it was becoming increasingly difficult for the Neutral Agent to buy the supplementary supplies of cereals and other foodstuffs on which we were solely dependent to supplement the official rations. The rest of the story belongs to the Sime Road camp and is told in that chapter.

[9]

Changi University

Another aspect of our communal life in Changi Gaol that was blotted out by the Double Tenth was the cultural, recreational and educational side. This was extremely well-organised. We were fortunate in having any number of people capable of acting as instructors on almost any subject, and in a short time a curriculum was drawn up which, together with a programme of lectures and concerts and debates, fully justified the expression one often heard on the lips of internees in those days: "Changi University." There were some 60 separate classes meeting regularly. Language study was the main activity; one could study any of the principal languages of Asia, particularly those spoken by the polyglot population of Malaya, and all the chief European languages, as well as Greek and Latin. But there were also classes in a large number of technical and professional subjects. We had no classrooms, in fact no indoor accommodation of any kind where these classes could meet, so that our "university" was exclusively an outdoor one. All over the Gaol, both morning and afternoon, one could come upon classes meeting in the shade of a wall or in some quiet corner, quiet by Changi standards, at least, for one could never get away from distracting noises in that place. The Japanese allowed us to bring in a number of textbooks in the early days, but most people had to carry on as best they could without textbooks and with a very scanty supply of paper. The price of ordinary school exercise books containing only ten pages actually rose to $8 in the camp shop during the third year of the internment, so acute was the shortage of paper in Singapore. One remarkable thing about these classes was the way in which people braved the sun in order to attend them. Many of them met at four o'clock in the afternoon, Tokyo time, which was two o'clock by British Malayan time, the hottest, drowsiest, heaviest time of the Malayan day. If you had asked any of those Changi students three years before to sit in the open on an expanse of sun-baked concrete, with an adjacent concrete wall reflecting the midday heat, and under those conditions give his mind to the study of, say, Malay or accountancy, you would have been regarded as a lunatic. But people did it in Changi, and found that they could endure these conditions, and do effective mental work, much better than they would have believed possible. And if anyone had told me when I was struggling with the loathed and utterly dull subject of English grammar at school that 25 years later I would find myself going all over that ground again and in company with a group of other middle-aged men, and finding it positively interesting, well... I would not attempt to conceive the effect of such a prophecy upon my juvenile imagination.

Our English grammar class met three times a week at four o'clock in the afternoon, in a spot where there was no shade whatever and we had some very interesting and amusing, as well as profitable, sessions, refreshing our schoolboy knowledge of the structure of our language. As the Malayan headmaster who was our mentor remarked, this was the first time in his professional experience that he had taken a class in English grammar that had actually asked for that subject. It was for him a new and stimulating experience to take an adult class, keen, critical, appreciative, and aware of the practical significance of what they were doing, and many other schoolmasters and college lecturers in the camp found the same reward in this adult response, as compared with the schoolboys and college students with whom they had been struggling for so many years.

In addition to the classes there were a number of courses of lectures with a serious definite educational purpose. Many internees learnt for the first time something of the fascination of physiology in a course of lectures conducted by a member of the faculty of the College of Medicine, Singapore, which was particularly popular. One of the malaria research scientists of the F.M.S. gave a course on malaria which drew a keenly interested audience of planters and others whose work takes them into the countryside. I personally remember many a pleasant morning listening to an admirable series on the development of English literature given by a member of the Education Department. Then there was a course in general science which was the most popular of all, even with a total lack of laboratory facilities, and the demand being so great that the class had to be split into three groups, each meeting three times a week; and there, in the small yard known to internees as "the old churchyard," perched on stools in the full heat of a tropical afternoon, would be a group comprising every possible type from Malayan civil servants to commercial men, satisfying a newly awakened interest in chemistry, botany and zoology.

In the evenings, after tea, the recreational programme took the place of the more serious activities of the day. Lectures with a more general and popular appeal were given, and these were extraordinarily varied and numerous. On any one evening one usually could attend two lectures or talks and sometimes had to choose between two given simultaneously. The history professor filled a large courtyard once a week with a series on the 19th century in Europe, the bishop of Singapore drew a large audience for a series on the modern interpretation of the Bible, the intellectuals of the camp followed a series called "Modern Thought," the clergy contributed a very interesting series on the history of the Church, and so on. All kinds of people were catered for and could find something to interest them in these evening programmes, whether their hobby was bird-watching or gardening or travel. The last-named category was a particularly varied and interesting one, for we were a widely travelled community, thanks to the practice of giving Europeans in Malaya long leave on full pay every three or four or five years, so that we had plenty of men among us who could contribute a talk on different parts of the world.

We were particularly fortunate in the quality and resources of music in the camp. Lieutenant Okasaki, the first commandant, had taken a personal interest in the creation of a camp orchestra and had given us facilities for getting instruments and music from town, so that we had a good camp orchestra. The Japanese also allowed us to bring in three good pianos. We were also fortunate in having at our disposal a large stock of records and a good gramophone. Then we had two male voice choirs, both of a quality such as had certainly never existed in Malaya before. The series given by the "Glee Singers" illustrated the development of song from ancient to modern times and was exceedingly well done, and one will never forget the magnificent singing of the Hallelujah Chorus one Christmas Eve, at a time when we badly needed uplift and inspiration.

In the open-air gramophone concerts in "Hudson's Bay" and the choral concerts in the laundry many of us found a new pleasure in music, a deeper appreciation than we had ever had before, in the days when we had merely listened in a desultory way to music on the wireless or turned on the gramophone occasionally, or sat on a hard uncomfortable chair in a concert hall because it was the thing to do. In Changi Gaol, where life was so hard and empty and unsatisfying in many ways, music brought a great elevation to troubled spirits, and it had probably never had more attentive and responsive audiences, certainly never in Malaya, than it had during those evenings when we listened under the stars in "Hudson's Bay" or in the laundry, with the twilight striated by a pattern of iron bars.

The really interesting part of all this is that it beckoned an awakening of intellectual and artistic interests that was something quite new in European life in Malaya. Of course there have always been exceptions, individuals here and there who kept up their reading or music, but in the main it is true to say, and was indeed generally admitted, that a dearth of intellectual and artistic life was one of the outstanding characteristics of the European community of Malaya before the war, as compared with what you would expect to find in a similar group of people, with the same class and educational background, in a provincial town in England. For example, lectures were absolutely unknown in Singapore, one of the most important cities of the Far East, whereas they were a regular feature of life in any English provincial town during the winter; and on the very rare occasions when such a thing was organised there was never more than a bare handful of people willing to turn out in the evening to attend it. Again, the musical public in Singapore was negligible until the great influx of the services for the war increased it to the point at which a fair-sized audience could be got together to hear a visiting celebrity of world reputation. The reading of the average man was apt to be confined to subjects which should not call for any serious intellectual effort — travel, biography and fiction. One came across cases time after time of people with distinguished university records at home who had let their classical or literary or scientific interests slide in the lazy environment of Malaya; and it was very rare indeed to meet people with the active political, sociological economic interests such as are common in any provincial town at home. There was no equivalent in Singapore or Kuala Lumpur or Penang to the meetings of the Conservative and Labour parties, the local branch of the League of Nations Union, the socialist and communist groups, the very wide and intelligent interest in civic or national life, that you find in England. The Malayan environment in general was singularly lacking in stimulants to intellectual and artistic life. Formerly we used to put this down to the enervating climate, to the brain-fag (over-reacting and particularly over-thinking) which most Europeans suffer from through the comparative inefficiency of their subordinate staffs, the keenness of competition in commercial life, the abnormality of family life, making for a restless state of mind and a craving for sport, entertaining and social life generally. But in Changi Gaol we found in ourselves a capacity for intellectual and artistic enjoyment under Malayan conditions that we had never suspected. The lectures broadened our mind and stimulated our interests, the classes gave us a mental discipline totally outside the rut of our professional lives that was refreshing and satisfying, and the musical side of our camp life gave us an insight into the realm of the human soul that many of us had never had before.

Looking back on our past life in those days, it seemed sadly empty, such a waste of precious time, all those boring hours at pahit (cocktail) parties and dinner parties trying to make conversation to complete strangers, all those hours wasted in sitting around tables in clubs, all the time spent in desultory and superficial reading, when there were so many more interesting and worthwhile things in the world, even in this little Malayan world. It is not too much to say that that side of life in Changi Gaol was a revelation of what life might be in this country, a foretaste of what it will be when planned economics have given men security and freed their minds for other things, when a just social order has opened up new opportunities for all, and when a totally different and happy environment will have eliminated that craving for shallow and crude entertainment represented by the cinema and the amusement park. But even though we of this generation cannot hope to be freed from these handicaps when we return to our peacetime lives, it is certain that those classes, concert, lectures and quiet reading in Changi Gaol will have a lasting effect in our personal and private lives. Outwardly we shall be, or we hope to be, pretty much the new government officials and planters and miners and merchants that we were before; inwardly we shall not be quite the same men that we were before we entered Changi Gaol, thanks to the new influences and stimulations that were brought to bear on our minds, and, dare I add, our souls within those grim walls.

But I have forgotten to mention a great part which reading played in our lives. The library, with its 5000 books, has already been mentioned. This was not a very good selection, and the proportion of really solid and satisfying literary fare was very limited; still, so far as it went, it was simply invaluable and there were as well many good books in private hands. The ample leisure, the feeling of being cut off from the outside world in the seclusion of monastic strictness, the lack of other interests and distractions, the impulse to take our minds off our present situation and our personal and domestic worries, caused us to read more widely and seriously than ever before. I personally did more worthwhile reading in one year in Changi Gaol than I had done in ten years outside, and I heard many others make the same confession. History, the classics of English fiction, popular science, the best modern novels, Shakespeare, the Bible, all the books that one had been intending to read for years and had never done so before, in many cases the books that one had had on one's shelves for years and had never more than dipped into.

Owing to the limited range, many an old-fashioned author experienced a resurrection, authors whom one would never think of reading in ordinary life. Dickens and Thackeray were re-read as perhaps they never are nowadays. I personally read *Jane Eyre* with the keenest enjoyment, also *Pride and Prejudice*, something I would never settle down to doing in the restless atmosphere and hurried tempo of European life in Singapore.

But at most it was not more than a third of the camp that benefited by these facilities or showed any desire to do so. There were many who never went to a lecture from one year's end to the other, while the musical programmes naturally always appealed only to a minority. The majority did not take up any study, did not read anything except fiction, and occupied themselves with cards, football in the evenings and gossip. But there was very little conscious highbrowism. One did not look down on these people. These new intellectual and artistic interests were absolutely genuine, spontaneous and unaffected. The whole atmosphere of the place was such that no one would ever dream of going to a concert because it was "the thing to do." One went because one really wanted to go, or one stayed away. The conventions and customs of peacetime social life were completely absent. And we did not look down on people who found their pleasures in other directions. We learnt a new tolerance, and many in fact made the best of both sides, attending a football match one evening and a concert the next.

[10]

The Early Days

It was a depressed and embittered company that found itself facing the conditions in Changi Gaol. They had not yet got over the shock of the British debacle in Malaya. They had been taken in by the smokescreen of propaganda emanating from Singapore over a period of years which apparently was intended to bluff the Japanese but actually left them quite unimpressed, its only effects being to create in the world in general, with the exception of Japan, a grossly exaggerated notion of the strength of the Singapore naval base, and in the inhabitants of Malaya itself a totally false feeling of optimism and security. Consequently the rapid advance of the Japanese army down the peninsula, the powerlessness of the RAF to resist, the unforgettable shock of the sinking of the two battleships within a week of the outbreak of war in the Pacific, the deeply humiliating impotence of the British naval power in the Straits of Malacca and along the east coast of the peninsula, the collapse of the British civil power everywhere, and the hurried evacuation of wave after wave of white and other refugees into Singapore from upcountry — all these experiences were fresh in the minds of that assemblage of British civilian prisoners in Changi Gaol. They felt that they had been let down by the government in London, by the local government, and by the army in Malaya. They did not then appreciate the fact that Malaya had been deliberately sacrificed to meet more desperate demands for aircraft, tanks and men in North Africa and Russia and that the resources of the Royal Navy had been stretched too far to permit adequate protection for Singapore. Moreover, they were full of bitterness against their own troops. They had seen Singapore thronged with deserters — British, Australian and Indian. They had seen the basement of every comparatively safe building in the business quarter of the city crammed with demoralised soldiers. They had seen and heard more than enough to show the state of demoralisation that had been reached in the defending forces after that headlong retreat down the peninsula with no air support to protect them against the ceaseless bombing and machine-gunning from the air, no naval support to stop the enemy landing time after time on the coast to turn their flank, and in the latter part of the campaign no reliable support from the majority of the Indians. The success of the Japanese on Singapore Island, in which 60,000 white and Indian troops were concentrated, had particularly struck the civilian mind. With the exception of the two Scottish regiments, the Loyals and the Ghurkas, the general impression in Changi Gaol seemed to be that no troops had done any fighting at all. But all this was very uninformed (for very few of those civilians had been in the front line) and very unfair.

The truth is that they owed their lives to the troops. Whatever the state of morale may have been when the siege of Singapore Island commenced, and it was admittedly bad, there was some very fierce and bloody fighting once the troops had rallied after the third shock of the Japanese crossing of the Straits of Johor; and if it had not been for the troops maintaining an unbroken line and thus permitting of surrender by negotiation, there is little doubt that there would have been no civilian internees to tell the tale. For no intelligent person believes that if Singapore had been taken by storm, and if there had been fighting in the streets and public buildings, the white civilians would have stood a chance in the face of shock troops maddened with the heat of battle. As it was, the frontline was still five or six miles from the centre of the city when the surrender took place, and the Japanese troops which entered the city were under perfect discipline, so that very few of the European civilians were molested or interfered with in any way, while in some cases the Japanese officers were extremely polite. But there was no disposition to make this acknowledgement in Changi Gaol. They had to find a scapegoat for their humiliation and disappointment, so they concentrated on General Percival. The truth is that there was practically no one who was fully informed as to the military side of the campaign. It was in every case a very limited, individual view that they had; and even though they could not fail to see the overwhelming numerical, naval and air superiority opposed to General Percival, their reason was blinded by their emotions. Later, when there had been time for calm reflection, many internees were much more reserved in their judgements and ready to admit that they had not heard the other side of the case. Perhaps when they have read expert and impartial military accounts of the Malayan campaign, they will feel ashamed of the criticism they expressed in those early days in Changi Gaol, and the only reason for recalling them now is that it would be impossible to convey the state of mind of internees at that time without mentioning it.

Another very curious and marked feature of mass psychology in Changi Gaol in the early days was a hostile criticism of the Australian troops in particular, voiced by a very large proportion of internees hailing from the British Isles. This was in part the continuation of feeling that had been aroused before the Pacific War, when the Australian troops had received a disproportionate amount of publicity through no fault of their own, the reason being that they were the first dominion troops of any kind to be sent to Malaya and had a news value that a British regiment had not. But the result was to give the impression that the Australians were better troops than any others, which remains to be proved. They behaved themselves very well, and had many friendly contacts between them and the white civilians in Malacca and other districts where they were stationed, but this publicity did harm. On top of all this came the fact that the Japanese landing on Singapore Island was made on the Australian front, west of the Johor Causeway, and the counter-attack launched by the Australians the next morning was a complete failure, and one battalion on that front broke and straggled back through the Jurong swamps into the streets of Singapore. Again, there was the undeniable fact that there were many Australians deserters in the city, and these, being by nature more expressive than the stolid British Tommies, talked the loudest of all. Again, a false impression was created by the fact that shortly before the Pacific War the slouch hat was adopted for all white troops in Malaya, so that the turned-up hat which had come to be almost a symbol of the A.I.F. was actually being worn in Singapore during those days by many deserters who were not Australians at all. The greater independence and initiative of the Australian temperament undoubtedly made them more outspoken in their resentment, and more affected by the retreat, than they would have been by a stubborn defence, compared with the British troops, but the truth is that by far the greater part of the A.I.F. remained at the front and that many Australian batteries and infantry units saw some very hard fighting. If they had not done so, it would never have been possible to maintain an unbroken front around the defence perimeter of the city of Singapore. But you could not convince the average internee of this, and as there were over 200 Australians in the camp, many of them decidedly brawny individuals, we had some tense moments. It was all an expression of the anti-Australian prejudice which is so marked and unpleasant a characteristic of the British middle-class mind in Malaya. It is the same in all the new English-speaking countries. Wherever these people go, one hears the same laments, "I loathe the country and the people," and made particularly by the women.

The internees had lost practically everything they possessed. Nearly all of them had sent their wives away on refugee ships with nothing more than one or two suitcases, all they had been able to save of the household possessions. All the way down the peninsula, in the wake of the fleeing whites, there was a trail of empty houses abandoned just as they stood, with all their furniture, clothing, glass and silverware, books. The majority of women had not even had time or space to take their wedding presents. All the cherished and familiar acquisitions of life had gone, and the twice and thrice repeated looting of European houses in Singapore had left no doubt as to what had happened to those upcountry. Many Singapore people had even had the mortification of seeing their houses looted by their own troops before the capitulation. The financial position of most internees was a gloomy one too, for few people had had more than a small amount liquid that could be transferred through a bank to a place of safety. Many internees had invested nearly all their savings in Malayan tin and rubber companies, and Heaven only knew when those securities would yield dividends again. Wives and children had had to leave with only enough money to last a few months, and while government officials could feel reasonably sure that their dependents would be taken care of, there were many men in the camp who had reason to not know how the families would live and had reason to fear that they would be dependent on public relief of one sort or another. Many men too, did not even know whether their wives were safe or not. Some women and children had left by the earlier refugee ships, so there had been time for a reassuring cable back from Colombo or India or Ceylon, but many of those without children had stayed with their husbands until the last moment and their husbands were still in the dark as to whether they had got through or not. Anxiety was especially acute about those who had left on the Thursday and Friday of the last week, for perturbing reports soon began to come through. All the big, fast ships of the liner class got through but the last of those left on the Thursday before the capitulation, and after that there were only small, local slow ships of the coaster class left in the harbour. They were sailed packed with a dense mass of refugees on their decks, nearly all women and children, although there were some men amongst them. By no means all of them where Europeans: many of the Eurasian residents and also some Chinese and Indians sent their own womenfolk away. The husbands, fathers and brothers of many of those refugees were in Changi Gaol, and for some time they suffered acute anxiety, for the Japanese themselves published a statement that they had sunk or captured 26 ships attempting to escape from Singapore and news soon began to come through of this or that ship having been bombed and sunk. Eventually it became known that most of those who left on local ships were in internment camps in Palembang and Sabang, in Sumatra, or in Java. But some husbands in Changi Gaol had the sorrow of finding that their wives were not on the lists supplied from these camps, particularly those who left on the *Giang Bee*, a Chinese coast freighter which was sunk at the Banka Straits, and three small ships which were caught by Japanese bombers in the Rhio Archipelago — about a dozen ships in all so far as we could tell from piecing together stories.

Internees were also bitterly critical of their own government, but the impartial listener could never find out precisely why. Unfortunately the Straits Settlements government had made the blunder of not building public air-raid shelters. This was not through negligence but as a result of deliberate repeated consideration. The water table in the greater part of Singapore is so low that underground shelters were impossible, tunnelling in the hills was advised against by an expert committee, and surface shelters were not built for two reasons: firstly, experience at home showed that brick shelters were easily blown to pieces and secondly, the Asiatic quarters of Singapore are a maze of narrow streets lined with flimsily built houses and inhabited by a dense population, and since incendiary bombs were at that time thought to be the greatest danger it was thought that surface shelters would merely be death traps in a chaos of wrecked and blazing streets; so the official policy was to get the population of these thickly populated areas into open spaces, where they could shelter in trenches. Unfortunately there were areas of Chinatown that were near no open space and in which the inhabitants had to shelter in drains or in their own houses. That, in fact, was what thousands of people did. However, the Japanese did not use incendiary bombs and made no attempt to set fire to the city, and while the shelter trenches in the open spaces were very largely used, there were areas of Chinatown in which the inhabitants had no protection except roadside drains and in some cases not even that. Then in the last week came the shelling as well. There was also the fact that the estimates of probable air-raid casualties given to the civil administration by the RAF were proved to have been greatly underestimated, having apparently been based on the assumption that there would be no daylight raids and that there was nothing to fear except long-range raids from Indochina. Although it is true that air-raid shelters could not have been built in anything like sufficient numbers without putting them in narrow streets and other situations which were impossibly dangerous having regard to the threat of fire, the government undoubtedly made a tactical blunder in not building at least some shelters, for this was seized upon at once by special correspondents, made the most of by local enemies of the government, and the impression created that the most urgent necessity of all had been completely overlooked, whereas in fact it had been under continuous and most anxious review.

But one can easily see how this influenced internees, many of whom had been serving in the Air Raid Precautions and Medical Auxiliaries Services and had seen for themselves the absolute hell in which several hundred thousand helpless Asiatics in the congested quarters of Singapore lived during those last days when they had no shelter except flimsy shophouses against bombing, machine-gunning from the air, ack-ack fragments and splinters and shelling. But apart from this single issue, one could not find in the recollections of internees anything more than the inevitable results of the progressive dislocation and breakdown of the last few days in Singapore, when civilian and military powers were overlapping and not even the organising genius and energy of Napoleon could have prevented the breakdown of liaisons between different departments and authorities, the misunderstandings, the mistakes and the failures that did occur. The element in our community which had to bear the brunt of this irrational and unfair criticism was the M.C.S. This was one of the most unpleasant characteristics of camp internment psychology in the early days, but always confined to a small and loud-voiced minority. In peacetime there had always been feeling against the M.C.S., because it was the supreme authority and had to hold the balance between the rival claims of the technical departments and also private interests, and quashed many a departmental official's pet scheme in consequence. Many of the commercial men amongst us also were anti-M.C.S. because they had been brought under much stricter government control during the war than they were used to and had found themselves restricted and hampered and interfered with in all sorts of ways, and all this had produced an exasperation which had not yet died down in Changi Gaol. For these reasons feeling against the M.C.S. was one of the most unpleasant characteristics in Changi Gaol. And an unfortunate civil servant who had been a district officer in Kuala Lumpur found himself disgraced for some mysterious reason as being personally responsible for the British defeat in Malaya and the sufferings of the internees. There was also intense bitterness among some people against the government for having been responsible for their having stayed and been interned, but this was confined entirely to government officials, the reason being that the latter had received direct orders to stay, with the tacit threat that if they disobeyed they would risk the loss of their pensions and future employment. Whereas the commercial and other non-government people had simply accepted the fact that it was their duty to stay until the fall of the city was certain and after that point had been reached all available shipping accommodation was required for women and children. At any rate one did not find among non-government internees any bitterness against the local government for not having got them away, although they might complain against the Imperial government for not having done so. In the main, it seemed to me that the non-government section of the internees were more philosophic about their fate than the government people, because the latter felt that they had been the victims of their own discipline, whereas the former merely thought that they had been caught in the events beyond the control of any local authority. But there was a much more general feeling among both sections against those who got away, in the Changi term current at the time, those who "ratted," and this, with the inconsistency of human nature, was often voiced by the same individual who complained bitterly because he had not been allowed to get away himself. Here was matter for many an angry argument, into which envy undoubtedly entered. The war was specifically against the whites. The Chinese were also in danger, but they did not go and leave everything behind, they preferred to take their chances, whereas the European would have been glad to get to the UK, Australia, India and elsewhere. It was difficult to believe that many of us were really doing any good there in the internment camp, when we might have been doing some sort of war service in a state of freedom elsewhere. On the other hand, there was the fact that a wholesale flight of British people from Singapore, leaving the local people to bear the brunt of whatever might happen, would have a deplorable effect for generations to come. Moreover, practically everybody was in some sort of emergency service. All the shipping space was required for women and children; it was therefore the unquestionable duty of every fit man to stay and help in the defence of Singapore so long as there was any chance of the city holding out.

There was such a chance up to the beginning of the last week. It was not until the Japanese landed on the island, or, rather, the following day, after the final counter-attack had failed to drive the Japanese back across the Straits that it became clear that our troops were being slowly driven back on the island, that the fall of Singapore was a certainty. After that a man had to decide whether he'd leave with honour, although not with permission. Was he still indispensable? Was it fair to his dependents to allow himself to be interned? What good would he do by doing so? There were many difficult questions. But no doubt, had shipping been available and sea communications open, a large number would have been evacuated in that last week.

In all this was manifested a trait of human nature that one saw time after time in arguments about the war that went on in Changi

Gaol, namely the inability to think objectively, to take into account impersonal factors, the outcome being a craving for a human scapegoat, some individual on whom the disgruntled person could vent his personal grievances. Thus the explanation of the British defeat in the Malayan campaign was popularly ascribed to the professional deficiencies of the commanding general, Lieutenant-General Percival. Yet it was plain to the veriest tyro in military matters that Napoleon himself could not have prevented that defeat or materially slowed down or altered the course of events. The decisive factors in the campaign were obvious to anyone: the overwhelming numerical superiority which the Japanese were always to bring to bear at the point of attack, throwing in wave after wave of fresh troops against the two tired divisions which were all that General Percival had between the northern frontier and Johor; the fact the Japanese were war-hardened, experienced troops, toughened by years of actual fighting in China, whereas very few of the white troops had ever been on active service before; the unreliability of some of the Indian troops in the latter stages of the campaign; the use of light and medium tanks by the Japanese, whereas the defending forces had none; the ability of the Japanese troops, accustomed to guerrilla fighting in China and to a scanty diet, to infiltrate enemy territory far ahead of the frontline, with nothing but a bag of rice and salt, while the white troops were all accustomed to moving in large bodies with all the traditional systems of cooking camp kitchens and supplies; the almost total lack of air support for our own troops and the miscalculation of the Japanese air strength, the enemy being able to attack communications and troops from the air with practically no resistance; and the absence of British warships in Malayan waters, enabling the Japanese actually to come down the Straits of Malacca in sampans in broad daylight and turn our positions on the mainland time after time.

All these factors were well-known; if anyone was to blame it was the home government, for leaving Malaya so weakly defended. But such considerations could give no consolation to the disgruntled internee. He found a queer satisfaction in bitter criticism of General

Percival, the implication being that if only we had another general all of this would not have happened. The fact that General Percival, in the face of enormous difficulties, had succeeded in engaging the enemy for two months — two months that were doubtless very precious ones for the purpose of strengthening the defence of India and Ceylon — was allowed no weight whatsoever. The British troops had suffered a crushing defeat at the hands of Asiatic troops whom they had come to regard as fit for nothing better than service against ill-armed and untrained Chinese guerrillas. They had to find an explanation for this, and so they put all the blame on the Australians. That salved their wounded national pride, and they went about repeating with a peculiar, spiteful malice, a popular remark that the Australians were like the daffodil: "tall, thin and yellow." If one retorted by asking them who did the running between Kedah and Johor, a stretch of 400 miles, they became too angry to give a coherent answer.

Again, these people were embittered because they had been captured and interned, so they found solace in railing at Sir Shenton Thomas. In the eyes of the uneducated type of internee, Sir Shenton was the cause of all their troubles. If only someone else had been at the head in charge, everything would have been different. Again, they had been humiliated by the collapse of the British civil authority in Malaya, so the obvious scapegoat was the M.C.S. The M.C.S. had made such "a mess of things," they had made all sorts of blunders (conveniently unspecified); it was so much more satisfying to pour out a stream of invective of this sort than to reflect upon the situation soberly, fairly, and objectively, which did not relieve one's feelings at all.

This, then, was the bubbling cauldron of talk and argument that went on in Changi Gaol as people looked back on their recent experiences, brooded upon their personal losses and troubles, and became more and more conscious of the plight in which they found themselves in the hands of Japan, with no assurances as to how long the war would go on. But, as always it was only a minority that talked in this way. The majority of internees took their misfortunes quietly, philosophically and cheerfully, and spent little time in blaming the military or civil powers for their plight; instead, they found a job of work to do, or a course of study to pursue, and got on with it, leaving the grousers to themselves.

There was in the early days intense curiosity as to who was with us and who wasn't. The British community in Malaya is a small one and, except in Singapore, everybody knows everybody else, at least by sight. During the first three weeks we had been segregated in three separate camps and it was not until we found ourselves in the Gaol that we came together as one body. Then began the process of sorting ourselves out, finding out who was there and who wasn't. On every hand one heard the question, "What happened to so-and-so?" or the remark, "So-and-so got away." Then people had a great deal to talk about, going over their experiences, some of which were very remarkable. One could hear some amazing tales of adventure and escape in those days, when the experiences of the retreat down the peninsula and in the seizure of Singapore were still fresh in people's memories. There was a captain of an oil tanker who had dived into the sea covered with blazing oil and spent months in hospital with burns; there were merchant seamen who had been on board a great liner when she was set ablaze by bombs; there was a Dutch planter who, with extraordinary courage and self-sacrifice, had stayed on his estate in the Rhio Archipelago and allowed himself to fall into the hands of the Japanese in order to stand by his Javanese labour force. There were 16 British electrical engineers who had kept the main power station of Singapore going through all the bombing. When a Japanese officer entered the station he said, "Sixteen brave men." There was a man who had seen the *Giang Bee* go down with over 100 on board and clung to a raft for four days until he was picked up by a Japanese destroyer, taken to Saigon and sent back to Singapore. There was another man who had swum to a small island from a wrecked steamer, set off again in a junk and eventually had to give himself up in Sumatra. There was a man who had been afloat in a dinghy in the Malacca Straits for two days, made his way up to Palembang (in Sumatra), only to find that it was already in the hands of the Japanese. There were Norwegians who had made one of the largest open boat voyages in history — 88 days; there were other Norwegians who had been torpedoed in the Sunda Straits. There were Dutchmen who had seen the fighting in Java and had been taken up to Burma. There was a tin miner who had been caught behind Japanese lines in Kedah, and been taken before General Yamashita himself, and given a safe conduct pass to walk back through Japanese lines. There were other miners who had had hair-raising escapes in Siam, making their way into Malaya, only to finish up in Taiping Gaol. There was a Dutch civil servant who had remained, a solitary white officer on a lonely island to await and hand over to the Japanese, with the uncomfortable knowledge that he had obeyed the orders of his government to carry out "scorched earth" measures and might have to pay the penalty for doing so.

These are just a few typical stories out of hundreds that might be heard in Changi Gaol in those days. Everyone had his adventures in the siege of Singapore. Many people from upcountry had only left their homes when the enemy was only a few miles away. If ever there was a community that illustrated Lord Northcliffe's remark that there is one first-class news story in every man's life, it was true then.

There was also intense curiosity in those early days as to what was happening in the town under the new regime. People coming back from fatigues in town were eagerly questioned as to their observations and impressions, as also were the municipal and government officials who came in one after another as the posts were filled by Japanese. But gradually this curiosity waned, until we became indifferent to what was going on in Singapore and lived in a self-contained world of our own. The *Syonan Times*, which was supplied to the camp by the Japanese authorities, was closely read with the same motive.

We were also very curious about the POWs, but knew very little about them, although their barracks were only three or four miles away. We were strictly kept away from them and could only catch a glimpse of them on firewood fatigues or perhaps get a word with one of them on a fatigue in town. This curiosity was natural, for many internees had relatives in the volunteer camp.

But gradually people got over the shock and settled down to their new life. Many of them found in regular work a blessed anodyne.

Others realised what a unique opportunity this was for reading and study and were determined to make the most of their leisure. There was a general process of adjustment. The spirit of the camp was on the whole remarkably good. There was a social convention of cheerfulness. Even if one did not think that the war situation was promising, that things weren't going well, one pretended that they were. But this cheerfulness in the early days was based on an estimate of the probable length of our captivity that seems incredible in the light of later events. The majority of internees, even intelligent and well-informed, confidently expected to be free men and back to work again in six months. They based this on the belief that the Americans would retake the East Indies and Malaya as quickly as the Japanese had done. They did not then know that the American battle fleet in the Pacific was under the waters of Pearl Harbour and in spite of what they had seen in Malaya they still hopelessly underestimated the war strength of Japan. If anyone had told them in those days that three years later the Japanese would still be fighting stubbornly all over the southern Pacific, standing the full weight of American industrial strength, he would have been dubbed a madman.

[11]
Within the Walls

The reader now has the background of our life in Changi Gaol: our work, our manner of life, our food, recreation, our society. But I imagine that what the reader really wants to know is what life was like during the internment, how we felt about it, what the atmosphere of the camp was like — in short, what newspapers call the "human interest" of the situation.

When the citizen of Singapore in years to come motors past Changi Gaol and looks at those grim walls and buildings, he will probably think that the people who spent two years inside those walls during the Second World War must have suffered greatly from the confinement, accustomed as they were to a free life. And no doubt it is for a convict in peacetime. But our viewpoint was very different from that of the convict. Those walls from the inside appeared to us not as restraints on our freedom, as barriers shutting us from the pleasures of normal life, but rather as defence against a hostile and dangerous world. It was no hardship to be imprisoned at that time, for we felt comparatively safe in the camp, whereas we knew that for us Singapore had become a different place, one in which we had no part, where we were regarded with the utmost suspicion, our whole environment had changed; we seemed to be living in a new Asia called "Syonan." New internees coming in after completing their work in the essential services in town told us that, while they were reasonably well-treated by the new regime, they were never free from a sense of uneasiness and tension. As they put it, "you never knew where you were," "you never knew what might happen next." So they were sincerely glad to give up the greater comforts and better food of life outside and settle down to the comparatively peaceful life of an internee. For this reason none of us ever had the slightest urge to escape. In the literature of this war Changi Gaol will provide no sensational escape stories. With the exception of one case in the early days, who was caught by the Japanese and dealt with more leniently than we had expected on the grounds that it had been the first offence, nobody ever tried to escape. For one thing it was far too dangerous: a European wandering about the town would have been spotted at once. And if anyone dreamed of more ambitious adventures, all he had to do was to remind himself that he stood not the slightest chance of reaching the frontier of India 2000 miles away or of threading his way undetected through the countless islands of the East Indies in an attempt to reach Australia. One might have managed to remain free so long as one remained within the borders of Malaya, but on the other hand one could not have done so without depending on help from the local inhabitants, and one would have no right to jeopardise their lives, even if they had been willing to help, which was by no means certain. And beyond the borders of Malaya were Siam and Burma in the north, occupied by Japan, and to the south the countless islands of the East Indies, again in enemy occupation almost to the coast of Australia. We knew that merely local escapes would be far too dangerous, and attempts to reach British territory quite impossible, so, in those circumstances, were content to be within our own little world in Changi Gaol.

It must be remembered that our position was not the same as that of war prisoners in Europe. We felt that we were in the hands of a strange people, whose ways were not our ways, whose minds did not follow the same pattern as European minds, whose attitudes and feelings and actions were unpredictable and often incomprehensible from the European viewpoint — something of the grimness and starkness and other characteristics of the mediaeval mind. Throughout the captivity we never felt that we really understood the Japanese, and they probably felt the same about us. Moreover, we realised that there was a clash not merely of rival imperialisms and nationalisms, as between Britain and Germany, but a definite clash of colour, a head-on conflict between two fundamentally different civilisations. It was the declared aim of the Japanese to end the white domination of Asia, to put the slogan of "Asia for the Asiatics" into practice. And, temporarily at least, they had succeeded. All Asia east of India was in their hands, except for a spark of revolt still smouldering in the remote interior of China. And there we were, a small community of white captives in the midst of this vast new empire of Greater East Asia.

It is no wonder that we felt it incumbent on us to walk very circumspectly, and that we always had at the back of our minds, seldom voiced but always there, the feeling that we never quite knew what might happen next or what might happen in the future. One might momentarily forget our situation on a sunny, serene morning in the courtyards of the Gaol, but we were always vaguely aware of unvoiced fears and vague but menacing possibilities outside the walls. We might feel that we knew our own camp officials fairly well, but above them was the Japanese High Command in Singapore, and above that was the Japanese government in Tokyo, and those were little-known and unpredictable factors from our point of view. But within the walls of the Gaol we lived in a little world of our own, we saw little of the Japanese, and created a world that had all the familiar racial and cultural components, and so long as we were there we felt as secure as we could in the circumstances. We felt that there was safety in numbers, that the fact that we must be one of the largest prison camps in the occupied territories ensured that it would be administered in a systematic, responsible and organised manner, with proper supervision by the higher authorities, whereas the evidence of people who had been interned in Penang, Kuala Lumpur, Taiping and Malacca showed that we were getting very much better treatment in every respect than people who happen to be interned in very small groups and were solely dependent on the local authorities. So, for a long time, there was no sense of claustrophobia within the walls of Changi Gaol, no homesickness, no desire to read anything Malayan, to talk about Malaya. Lectures on the local birds, natural history, forests, etc., were avoided; there was a desire to forget one's former pleasures. All this made it easier to settle down to our new mode of existence.

On the contrary, there was at first, after we had got over the preliminary hardships, made ourselves as comfortable as possible, organised a communal life, and settled down to a routine of work and recreation, a very pleasant sense of relaxation of the strain under which we had been during the siege of Singapore and the Malayan campaign, and even after the novelty of our new life wore off and we began to feel the monotony, dreariness and sadness of it all, we still had a sense of security inside those walls which compensated to a large extent for our loss of freedom. Strange as it may seem to a peacetime reader, we looked upon Changi Gaol with a certain affection as our home in a hostile world, as the country man does when he sees the light of his cottage on a night of howling wind and pouring rain. But when we were outside, a sudden yearning for freedom would certainly well up in us, bringing with it a well-nigh unbearable sadness. I remember days when I was out with the firewood fatigue in a rubber estate on the Tampines Road, looking at the road dipping and rising and curving away through the rubber until it vanished over the sky-line half a mile away, and feeling an almost unbearable longing to walk along that road as far as one wanted, at any time one wanted, on and on and on, alone, without an Indian guard armed with a rifle forever at one's back — in a word, to be free again. But we never had the same feeling when we went on fatigues into Singapore. As we looked over the sides of the lorry at the familiar streets and buildings and the everyday scenes of life in Singapore, we felt that we no longer had any part in that life, that we no longer belonged there, and it was with a feeling of relief that we turned back in the direction of Changi Gaol.

After some months, though, we began to feel a definite and growing sense of claustrophobia within the walls, living in small concrete boxes. The fact that one's eyes were brought up short wherever one looked by those eternal, blank, grey walls, that nowhere in the camp could one get an open view, making it an actual physical pleasure to allow one's eyes to stray over hill and dale or over the sea to the line of the remote horizon, was one factor. I often had the same feeling when I paused by the kitchen and looked out through the front courtyard at the vista of the sunny, peaceful, quiet landscape seen through the Main Gate, a picture of living green in a frame of massive concrete. People used to allay the craving for a view, for the ocular relief of far distances, by looking out from the very few big windows at each end of the cell blocks, which commanded views on one side of rolling country, rubber and coconuts and the jungle of Bukit Timah Hill in the background, with a faint blue mass of Gunong Pulai rising from the mainland in the far distance, and on the other side of a glorious panorama of sea and coast curving into the eastern end of the Straits of Johor.

One of the sights in Changi Gaol that has remained most sharply engraved upon my memory is that of the row of faces, wan and ghostly against the interior darkness, with hands clutching the bars, that might be seen at any time of the day looking out through the big window in the second floor of C block, which gave a view of the sea. The picture of those ghostly human figures peering out of the great grilles high in the prison block, looking longingly and silently at the world of freedom and beauty outside has haunted me ever since. But the time came when we were forbidden to look out from any of the upper floors.

The confinement was beginning to be felt at the end of the first twelve months, but then came a very valuable boon. The camp was then under the control of Mr Asahi, and he granted us the concession of going outside the walls three evenings a week. He caused an area all round the Gaol to be wired off, and within this fence there was a small space to go for a stroll or read or talk in pleasant and restful surroundings with trees and grass around us instead of the eternal concrete. The greater part of this extra space was broken up into vegetable gardens, so an additional 200 internees were enabled to go outside the walls during the day as well. These evening walks brought great relief, and as long as they continued, together with the walks to a rubber estate twice a week to fetch wood and the monthly sojourns to the beach for a sea-bathe that we were then allowed, we were able to stand the confinement very well. But this privilege was withdrawn after the Double Tenth, as was the sea-bathing, while all opportunities for work outside the camp were also drastically cut down for a time and then the confinement really did begin to oppress our nerves and spirits.

By then it was not merely the more rigorous restrictions imposed upon us but the duration of the captivity that was beginning to tell. We had been 20 months in Changi Gaol at the time of the Double Tenth, and we were becoming thoroughly tired of the place. Then we found ourselves compelled to remain within the walls from morning to night, with no relief and change, and no means of exercise except to pace up and down the sandy stretch in the Main Yard parallel with the outer walls. Then we began to feel a definite claustrophobia, intensified, I think, in the case of those who lived in the cells. Sadness, frustration, memories of the past against the palette of the sunset sky began to take their toll. I grew to hate B yard, a shining boiler-house with a giant stovepipe, and the profile of walls and the towering wall of the block, with a rectangular pattern marking the rows of the cells. And the concrete benches around the walls, the elliptical loop of concrete in an expanse of sand around which the convicts used to exercise, one behind the other, like animals parading in a circus. The same faces, the same voices every morning, the same cranks, the same types, the same slum denizens spitting in the paths where internees walked with bare feet, the same queue at the lavatory, the same unceasing process of urination, the same ugliness and dreariness and dullness…. And it was no use going elsewhere, for one yard was just like another. One became more and more conscious of the appalling ugliness of the place: the greyness, the blankness, the bars and concrete, the darkness, the jostling in the corridors and the floors. Sometimes one would go for relief to the inside vegetable garden, where one was at least among green things and pace up and down the sandy path between the beds of spinach and sweet potatoes. There was surprisingly little quarrelling or signs of nerves, but the weight began to press down on our spirits more and more. There was a sort of weary apathy and dullness. But we never realised how much we hated the place until we knew we were going to leave it. Then all the subconscious feelings that had been suppressed in the unconscious came to the surface, and we realised that we had been suffering from a subconscious claustrophobia to a much greater extent than we had realised. The last day in B yard, one felt the bliss of having the yard all to one's self, of knowing that one was about to leave the detested place.

[12]
Three in a Cell

For most of us overcrowding was much harder to bear than the confinement. However the walls and all that they stood for may have affected us in the subconscious levels of our minds, the hardship that we were most conscious of, that was a continual, unceasing strain on the nerves, was the overcrowding. Anyone who has made a long sea voyage knows that after only a month he feels that he has seen quite enough of the majority of his fellow passengers and more than enough of his cabin mates, if he has had to share a cabin with strangers. Most people are not capable of more than a certain amount of sociability, and in order to achieve even that they must have frequent spells of privacy and relaxation. But in Changi Gaol we were far more crowded than passengers are on a liner, than soldiers in barracks, than Chinese coolies in a kongsi house. Imagine the population of a small town in England crowded within the walls of a prison built for 700 convicts, kept within the walls from morning till night, and you will have some idea of the overcrowding in the yards, corridors, stairways, dormitories and cells. It was impossible to get away from people anywhere in the Gaol. No matter where you went, you could never get away from other people's voices. If you were in one of those moods in which you felt that you must get away from your cell (for with three men living together month after month in a small, dark, windowless cell, such moods are common in the most harmonious trio), and you found a quiet corner in the yard to settle down, no sooner would you have settled down with a book than someone would come along and start a conversation or, worse still, an argument within a few feet of you… and then you would spend the rest of the morning trying to concentrate on your reading or your study with those voices boring into your ears, on and on and on, until you felt like shrieking to high heaven and gave up in despair. This annoyance was intensified by the remarkable acoustics of the concrete walls. Having no chairs, we always found a wall to lean against, and sound travelled along those walls in a remarkable way, so that a conversation going on 50 feet away could be heard with perfect clearness. Often people had no idea of how far their voices were carrying, with the result that it was rare to attend a class or a lecture that was not disturbed by a drone of conversation around the corner or voices in an adjacent corridor. Under these conditions the need for quiet became urgent to a degree that can scarcely be imagined by people living a normal life. In the dormitories and on the upper floors one could hear at any time of the day the shout of "Quiet!" The understanding was that in these places people should avoid noise as much as possible, otherwise life would have been intolerable in such packed, jammed masses of humanity. People got so sensitive to noise that they would shout "Quiet!" at the slightest provocation, without discrimination and as a sort of reflex action, until this cry got on people's nerves nearly as much as the noise that provoked it. In the block in which I lived there was a little yard known as "The Sanctuary," a sort of narrow little canyon lying between high walls, in ordinary circumstances a depressing place; but the rule of silence was enforced there, and it was a blessed relief to read there.

So intense was the craving for silence that one of the pleasures of going to the weekly concert of classical music was that on that one occasion in the week you could be among what was the novelty of being in a group of perfectly silent people, although even there you had to put up with the distractions in the environs of the outdoor concert hall, the perturbing irritation caused by people on the fringe of the audience who merely wanted music as a background to conversation. The laundry was no better. There one had to listen to the music to the accompaniment of people washing dishes or cleaning their teeth or bathing at the taps outside. We certainly listened to music under difficulties in Changi.

The overcrowding was worst of all in the cells. There you had three men, who probably were unknown to each other, living in a small, dark, concrete box, with no outlook on the outside world. We take windows for granted in ordinary life, and it is not until you live in a prison cell that you realise how much pleasure you unconsciously get from them. I used to think of the vista of Malayan gardens glowing in the sunshine that I used to see from the interior of my own house, framed in a window, or moments at Fraser's Hill when one looked out of a room at beds filled with English flowers, or vistas of the sea at Port Dickson seen through a bedroom window, or views I had had from skyscraper towers in American hotels. That is the kind of picture that comes before the mind's eye when you sit and face a blank concrete wall six feet away, day after day, week after week, month after month, year after year. It is one of those elemental pleasures that you do not fully appreciate until you have been a prisoner. One puts down these comments here in the hope that others may profit by our experience and realise how rich life is if only one has eyes to see.

At first people were jumbled together anyhow in the cells. Later there was a certain amount of reshuffling, as people discovered their incompatibilities, but this was not possible in many cases and people acted on the principle of "Better the devil you know than the devil you don't." So that all the way through the great honeycombs of concrete which were the cellblocks, an extraordinary jumble of social classes, temperaments and interests was exhibited. Generally speaking, you would find a colonial civil servant, a product of Oxford or Cambridge, sharing a cell with a winch-man from a Malayan tin dredge, speaking broad Glasgow, and a pantry boy off the *Empress of Asia*, born and bred in a working-class district of Liverpool. You might find a judge of the Malayan bench living with a clergyman and a shop assistant from one of the big department stores. Drawling, supercilious university accents mixed with every county dialect of England. The public school, the grammar school and the elementary school rubbed shoulders for the first time in their lives. The former habitué of the most exclusive European circles in Singapore slept side by side with a Eurasian foreman and a prison warder. An insular middle-class Englishman, incapable of appreciating any country except his own, would find himself a stable companion of an Australian and a Dutchman.

Generally speaking, class and racial differences caused little trouble. People soon discovered the human being beneath the superficial differences, and in many cases internees who had eyed their fellows with suspicion and reserve at first, because they had never worn the old school tie or because there was a strain of Asia in their blood or because they were so unfortunate as not to have been born in the British Isles, came to look upon their cellmates with real affection and to realise that in the important things of life, internment life, anyway, they were superior to themselves. Undoubtedly this experience in Changi Gaol broadened the minds of many people and gave them a deeper understanding of other types and greater tolerance. One saw many cases of friendly relationships developing between individuals who would have been separated by an impassable gulf in an ordinary British community. The man who had always been lucky enough to travel first class might find himself working and living next to a P. & O. steward, and both would find they met for the first time on a basis of equality and talk as human beings. This was particularly true in the case of Eurasians. But honesty compels one to admit that in the main, birds of a feather flocked together; there was not much mixing. The public-school class, trained beyond redemption to divide all men into commissioned officers and other ranks, kept to itself pretty much, professional men consorted together, the merchant seamen formed a group of their own, the lower ranks of the former European community of Malaya retained their identities. There was equality in the distribution of food, the allocation of work, and other essentials, but in social life the strata of the pre-war social caste system were preserved.

Some idea of the conditions existing in the big dormitories on the ground floor has been given already in the previous chapters. In the former workshops and dining rooms on the ground floor the internees were so tightly packed that there was just enough room for a camp-bed or a mattress three feet wide, with a suitcase at the head of that. The internee was literally within arm's length of his neighbour on either side. In front of him, on the other side of the passageway, barely wide enough for men to pass, were more beds, and also behind him, unless he was lucky enough to have one of those coveted sites next to a wall. So that the internee, accustomed to a house much more spacious than is customary for people of corresponding station of life in Europe, and to a domestic life which is abnormally silent and solitary compared with the home standards (for there are no children over kindergarten age in the typical European home in Malaya) found himself one of a tightly packed mass of humanity, with people as close as possible to him on every side. Under these conditions one lived in the most unrestful atmosphere imaginable. In order to live at all under such conditions the internee had to be continually on the alert not to tread on his neighbour or to knock over his or his neighbour's pots and pans or to blunder into other people's beds or belongings or persons as he threaded his way through the room. Apart from the sheer physical discomfort of it, there was perpetual noise and movement in the room, except for little movement during the two-hour siesta after the midday dinner, and any attempt at reading or study had to be carried on with conversation going on close by the whole time.

In the cells of the upper floors of the prison blocks it was worse in some respects. In the big workshops, where one was one of a hundred or so, it was paradoxically true that one had more privacy than if one was one of three in a cell. Conversation in a workshop was impersonal and diffused, whereas in a cell it was always the same two voices, the same two personalities, the same opinions and ideas.

You had three men living in a concrete box twelve feet long by eight feet wide, dark, gloomy, dank and chilly in wet weather, ugly and depressing beyond belief. At night the occupants were even closer together than the tenants of the workshops. The two that slept on the floor were in danger of catching the kneecap a crack on the side of the sarcophagus, a feature of moving their knees incautiously, while the one that slept on the sarcophagus was in danger of rolling off it onto his neighbours. During the day it was utterly impossible to read or do anything requiring mental concentration if a conversation was going on within the cell, for within those blank, high concrete walls it was impossible to detach oneself or think of anything else. If in addition the personalities jarred on each other, if the ideas and opinions and attitudes constantly expressed in the conversation of the other two were irritating, then a really unbearable situation developed, and the distraction of conversation became intensified tenfold to the point of mental agitation. The secret of successful living in a cell was to observe silence as far as possible, talking only at meals or at other suitable times, and if you got a trio that was agreed on that point, life in a cell was not only tolerable but actually pleasanter, the upper floors being free from mosquitoes and flies and more easily kept clean, besides affording a measure of real privacy for a well-assorted trio, than in the big workshops. The same held good where you had three men who were all talkative and gregariously inclined, so that they could each talk and entertain their friends in a cell without annoying the others. But where, as usually happens, you had one person of quiet tastes, and two of whom were forever arguing about the war, or talking over camp gossip, the conditions were quite unbearable for one party or the other. In practice, most people lived in their cells as little as possible, for in the best-assorted trios they got very tired of each other and felt that they had to have a change of scene and company between meals. But when they went outside their cells, conditions were still very trying.

The result of living under these conditions was that one developed almost morbid craving for solitude and quietness, and neither was to be found within the confines of the walls. There being no recreation rooms, the only place to which you could go to read or study or play a game of chess was one of the exercise yards, and there you would encounter other internees all over the place, particularly in any shady place. The only place in the camp where one could get away from people was the inside vegetable garden, where one could be almost alone in a wide and sunny space clothed with living green, and many a time one has found solace by walking up and down the little sandy, grass-verged paths between the beds of spinach or sweet potatoes. But in the garden you are a trespasser unless you are a gardener, and you could not read a book or go there too often. Then there was the girdle road, and there you really could read in quiet. Some of the best hours I spent in Changi Gaol were spent under the shade of a papaya tree under those two high walls. But soon the girdle road was out of bounds, by order of the Nipponese, and that refuge ceased to be available. Otherwise, the only way to find solitude was to go and pace up and down the Main Yard in the heat and silence after tiffin, or stay up late at night, and in fact it was under the stars or in the moonlight, when darkness cast a veil on our surroundings, that we mostly found relief from the noise and friction of the day.

Perhaps those who are accustomed to find solace in nature suffered from those conditions more than the type which normally finds its relaxation chiefly in social life, in clubs, hotels and entertaining. You could have all the company, conversation and bridge you wanted in Changi Gaol. The man who found his pleasures chiefly in the world of nature, in his garden and in the countryside found the Gaol an abomination of desolation. When we first went in, the only living things in all that desert of concrete were the vivid rectangles of turf in the exercise yards, with the loop of concrete in the centre round which the convicts used to walk for exercise every day, in single file, silently, like animals parading in a circus ring. But this greensward soon vanished beneath the tread of the new occupants of the Gaol, for each of the big yards had to serve eight or nine hundred men, and it was not long before there were only two or three small yards where the eye could find rest in a pleasant plot of greensward. There was not a tree in the prison. (Trees are one of the joys of life in this country, so numerous and varied are the number of species and so infinite the interest and pleasure to be had from them.)

There was, at first, not a flower in the prison. In peacetime the warders had lived outside, and the convicts were not allowed to enjoy beauty in any form, so there were no gardens within the walls. Garden-lovers among the internees soon got to work and planted flowers where they could, but very little space was available. The most successful effort was a little garden between narrow walls in a courtyard we used to call "Hudson's Bay." These could see hibiscus, zephyranthes, balsams, cosmos, marigolds, cannas, the Honolulu creeper, the blue ternate creeper, bachelor's buttons, orange lilies and other flowers. A regular patchwork quilt of flowers. The surroundings were ugly enough: a concrete path on either side, a concrete wall beyond each path, and iron grille lining the passageway at one end, a view of the double exterior walls at the other. But the very ugliness of the setting seemed to enhance the beauty of the flowers. A background of stone always does that anywhere, as the European in Malaya, accustomed to compounds lined with bamboo and hibiscus hedges, rediscovers when he goes home on leave and sees the beauty of a cottage garden with flowerbeds framed by old stone walls. In that little garden in Changi Gaol the flowers seemed to glow with a new intensity of light and colour, so that there were mornings when a great blood-red hibiscus flower, the commonest of flowers in ordinary life, or a clump of orange Jerusalem lilies springing out of the sandy soil, seemed to be the loveliest things one had ever seen. Many an internee found peace and solace in that garden in the worst moments of the captivity and looked back to it with peculiar gratitude and affection. I do not suppose that there has ever been a time or place in Malaya where flowers have given greater pleasure. In these circumstances one began to take on new interest in wild flowers and one got to know the dozen or so species of wild flowers to be found within the confines of the Gaol. It was there for the first time in 20 years that I suddenly saw the fairy beauty and delicacy of the pink pom-pom plant in the cool of the morning, dusted with yellow pollen and gemmed with sparkling points of dew. Then there was a rambling plant which grows low in the grass and gives it a misty purple tinge with its pattern of tiny, four-petalled flowers. But mostly the wild flowers of the prison were tiny, inconspicuous flowers, of the sort that grow in crannies of walls or tangled in the grass, so inconspicuous and lacking in showy qualities that one would hardly look at them twice in ordinary life, unless one's approach to wild flowers was not aesthetic but rather botanical; but in Changi Gaol, there were so few living things except mankind, one got to know them all.

Needless to say, the bird-lover was equally out of luck in Changi Gaol. There was plenty of time for bird-watching, but very few birds in the garden. The sparrows were everywhere and one got quite fond of these perky little chaps, they always seemed cheerful when nobody else was. One found a pleasure and interest in watching the sparrows that one never had in former life. Then there was a tailor bird in the inside garden which patiently wove its dangling nest to a spinach plant time after time, only to lose it when the bed was cropped, colonies of grackles high up under the roofs and in the angles of the outer walls, the sunbird in the "Hudson's Bay" garden. But the highlight of bird-watching in the Gaol was the kingfishers. There were always two or three about in the inside garden or the Main Yard and they soon became astonishingly fearless. One pair made a nest in the side of a deep swill-pit in the Main Yard and would go on with the process of excavating the hole quite unperturbed, with a dozen internees interestedly watching close by. Even experienced bird-watchers pronounced it as a unique sight. Without the slightest attempt at concealment one could stand and watch the bird come out and perch on the edge ten feet away, a living crown jewel, burnished turquoise shining in the intense sunshine on the tawny sand. Every minute or so it would appear out of the hole in the bank like that, and this would go on for hours. This is certainly one of the few impressions of beauty that I saw within the walls of Changi Gaol.

But there was compensation in the intensified appreciation of nature outside the walls. Who will ever forget his first Singapore fatigue? The delight of riding through the countryside, seeing the familiar trees again, the Honolulu creeper on the old plaster walls at Katong, the angsana tree in bloom at the entrance to the airport, the flame trees, the flowering trees planted by the roadside. Then those walks with the firewood cart. To hell with thoughts of humiliation. It was all too exhilarating to let it spoil one's pleasure. The lalang blazing with a magical green and gold. The roadside flowers, the despised sendudok, the wild passionfruit, the blue speedwell by the brook, Bromeliad orchids under the rubber trees, the beauty of a rubber estate, the smell of the leaf mould, the rich chocolate brown of the earth, the curious markings of the bark, the surprising amount of birdsong in the rubber trees (and one had always thought there was little birdlife in a rubber estate). Some of one's best and yet saddest moments were spent in that quiet little valley beside the Tampines Road. There we used to meet the POWs also pulling firewood lorries and sometimes caught a glimpse of a friend or relative.

[13]

Our Health

Most of us experienced a marked and early improvement in health on the new diet. One had a feeling of internal soundness, well-being and positive health that one had never had while living a sedentary life outside. In my own case I had arrived at middle age from sedentary life, I rarely ate hotel foods, drank very little, ate very little meat but did eat a good deal of fruit. In those days one had been uneasily conscious of a number of clear symptoms in the abdominal region. In my own case I was beginning to get pains across the small of the back which indicated that all was not well with the kidneys. I managed to keep out of hospital, and rarely saw a doctor, but I always felt below par, as though serious disease may not be very far away. I was also beginning to get headaches rather often. I never had that feeling of confidence, unconscious, untroubled health which one sees in really healthy people. But after I went on a rice diet, with only a little protein, I felt as if the system was being cleansed of accumulated poisons. I had a feeling of internal cleanliness and soundness. For the first time since I was a boy, I found myself taking health for granted, never giving a thought to my body, and this was the general experience. Most people confessed that they had better health in Changi than they had ever had outside. Bad colds were common as were very troublesome skin infections and beriberi at first. Dysentery and malaria were also common but on the whole, internees felt better than they had done for years. We took regular, plain meals and there was no temptation to overeat. We were soon waking up with clear eyes, a clear head, a clean tongue and without a bad taste in the mouth.

Most of us felt that we had been eating far too much protein food and poisoning our systems. We were forced to this conclusion when we looked back at our former diet, eggs and bacon for breakfast, fish or meat again for tiffin (sometimes both), fish and meat again for dinner and perhaps cheese as well, and butter at every meal. And now here we were, getting no animal protein except in meat soup at midday and in the later months half an ounce of fish paste every day or so. Sigh as people might for the joys of a mixed grill, they learned how little protein they could live on and still keep fit and feel fit. Indeed, many men who had had office jobs in peacetime were actually expending more energy in Changi than they had ever done in normal life. The younger men looked in splendid condition, and men doing such strenuous work as woodcutting worked morning and afternoon without difficulty. It was a revelation of what could be done on a cereal and vegetarian diet and of how little animal protein was really necessary. People complained that they had not the strength they used to have, but this must have been mostly imaginary, for the time was to come when they were to be forced to do much harder work on much less food, and yet keep reasonably fit.

Some people felt a craving for meat, and used to talk longingly of the joys of a mixed grill, but I must confess that I had a sense of internal cleanliness on cereal and vegetarian food that was very pleasant, and I found it no hardship to live without meat. But that undoubtedly was not the general experience. Perhaps one reason why we felt healthier in Changi than outside was the general absence of constipation after the first shock of captivity was over. This was perhaps the most important lesson of all that we learned here, that it is easily possible to find and live continuously on a mildly laxative diet which will ensure regular and easy elimination of waste matter, and that that is in the main the secret of physical health and mental clear-headedness in civilised life.

We found that while we were taking santan with a little palm oil or coconut oil with our kunji, together with more oil in peanuts or soya beans, we never had the slightest difficulty with the bowels. And all those constituents of our diet are normally dirt cheap in Malaya so what excuse is there for constipation? In my own case I knew two remarkable cures of chronic constipation. One man had never had a natural motion since boyhood: for 30 years he had used an enema or laxatives every day. He managed to bring his array of drugs, etc., into Changi, but within three or four months he found himself having natural motions more and more frequently, and it was not long before he was perfectly normal in this respect. I knew of another cure that was almost equally remarkable. This was not the universal experience — there were men who suffered from severe constipation, the rice diet not agreeing with them — but it was the general experience. However, during the periods when there was very little oil in our diet, we quickly began to suffer severely from constipation. I make no apologies for drawing on the subject, for it seems to me that in Changi we found the answer to one of the most serious evils of modern civilisation, at least as far as Malaya is concerned. One has only to recall the slot machine selling laxatives and purgatives that one had seen on the streets in London, New York, Sydney and elsewhere, to realise how far this evil has gone in the life of the city-dweller. And it stands to reason that this perpetual clogging of the bowels and consequent poisoning of the system must have serious results in the long run. May it not be one of the causes of the appalling increase in diseases of the alimentary tract that every doctor has noticed during the last 40 years? Yet here you had 3000 white people who with a few exceptions were totally without this trouble so long as they had a little vegetable oil, a minimum of protein and lived mainly on cereals and vegetables. Surely the lesson to the European in Malaya is plain. It may be a rash guess for a layman to venture, but I'm convinced that if that body of middle-aged and elderly men could be persuaded to continue with their Changi diet, with a slight increase in the protein content, there would be far fewer cases of serious abdominal trouble among them in years to come.

But this was not the only way in which health improved in Changi.

There was a general loss of overweight. This was phenomenal in some cases. The record was actually 158 pounds, but there were many cases of four, five, six stone and up. The profiles and waistlines of many prominent figures in pre-war Malayan society took on a positively svelte line, and they felt very much the better for it. Falstaff may be amusing on the stage, but in real life he is more often than not gross and disgusting. That was the thought that occurred to one when one looked at men who had been walking barrels of fat and now looked lean and fit. And here came in another of the valuable lessons that we learned in Changi, and that was that much of the discomfort which the white man feels in the climate of Malaya is largely due to his being overweight, as nearly everybody is in ordinary life. If you carry fat in this climate you feel the heat much more than you do if you are lean, and you sweat more. Have not all seen the common European type, red of face, with his neck standing out in rolls of fat round his collar, and sweat pouring off his brow and complaining of the heat? We found that we felt the heat much less, could stand it with greater comfort and do all sorts of unusual things in it, and sweated very much less, partly due to lack of clothing but also due to the reduction of fat.

Another interesting feature of the diet was the virtual deprivation of sugar. The Japanese ration was six ounces every ten days, and sometimes even that was not forthcoming. At times one was able to buy gula malaka, but not much, and there were long periods when this was not available. Moreover, after about nine months, no sugar whatever was used in cooking. In general, it is true to say that, except for a period of a few months in 1943, the amount of sugar in our diet was negligible compared with what we had consumed in cakes, puddings, sweets, chocolate, tea and coffee in normal life. How this affected others I cannot say, but my own case may be interesting. I had always been a heavy sweet-eater and had heavily sweetened tea and coffee, and had been fond of cakes. And for years I have suffered from very bad colds, at least one a month, and the slightest draft would start me off; I was highly susceptible to drafts and always sneezing. On the majority of days throughout those three years of internment, I ate no sugar whatsoever. In Changi I gradually got rid of my susceptibility to colds, until finally I was almost entirely free from colds, although living in draughty, dusty huts, exposed to every breeze that blew, and wearing very little clothing. I found I was always more susceptible to chills than the average internee, who could go bare to the waist after sundown where I could not, but certain it is that my system seemed to have been purified of the poisons that were causing my colds before, and I put that down to having continually and habitually eaten an excess of sugar. The lack of sugar in our diet also proved to arrest tooth decay — only two cavities in the three years of confinement. But I did feel a strong craving for rich, sweet things, and many other people did too. Yet on the infrequent phases when we had all the rice we wanted, I lost that craving and one also found that sugar was one of the causes of overeating. If you have only rice and salt, you each eat no more than you need.

Of course the improvement of health was partly due to the total deprivation of alcohol. Within a week of the capitulation every one of those thousands of men had perforce to become a teetotaller. This was one of the most drastic changes in their habits, for nearly all of them had been accustomed to taking whisky and soda regularly every evening, besides beer, and aperitifs and the liqueurs at appropriate occasions. Alcohol played a very large part in social life in Malaya before the war. It was almost unknown to sit down for a conversation without drinks. It was the most characteristic feature of Malayan clubs. In homes the evening stengah (whisky and soda) was a recognised institution. Some of the men in Changi had been notoriously heavy drinkers, many had thought nothing of taking several stengahs every evening, besides a pahit or two before tiffin or dinner, and beer and gin slings on Sunday mornings. (Consider the amount of alcohol at dinner parties and pahit parties, and some people went out three or four evenings a week.) In the internment these people suddenly found themselves totally without alcohol; they had to cut it right out of their lives, and the remarkable thing was that they felt no craving for it, and while one could not say that they never missed it, they would have liked a drink if they could have got one, still, they found it quite easy to be teetotal. The absence of alcohol did not affect their nervous or mental balance in the least, except for the better, and their physical health was greatly improved in the case of the excessive drinkers. One expected in such cases symptoms similar to those which occur in an opium victim when he is deprived of his drug, but nothing of the sort was seen. The explanation no doubt was a psychological one: they knew that there was no possibility whatever of getting drink, the Japanese were extremely strict about this, and it was never smuggled into the camp, and so they simply forgot about it. The psychological conflict which goes on in normal life when a man tries to give up alcohol, with the stuff available at every street corner, was not present; it was no doubt a blessing that alcohol was not available in the camp. At all events, the internment certainly added five or ten years to the lives of some elbow-lifters. Some men who one would not have expected to do so vowed never to touch it again, but no doubt this was not general; but many admitted that they felt much better without it. It was extraordinary how men could enjoy life and carry on animated talk without this stimulant. Mild stimulants were very welcome when we could get them. Many of us were very glad to brew coffee or tea when we could get a supply.

It is interesting to speculate whether the tobacco habit would have been shed as easily, but the test was never made. During the first year internees with money could buy plenty of locally made cheroots, cigarettes and a peculiarly potent and coarse variety of pipe tobacco known in Changi as "Sikh's Beard." Thereafter tobacco continued to come into the camp throughout the internment. The supply was not nearly equal to the demand (the amount that the camp was allowed to buy in town being fixed by the Japanese), and smokers frequently ran out of supplies altogether, but it came in at sufficiently frequent intervals to keep the habit alive. There was only one period of any considerable length when the camp was without tobacco, and that was after the Double Tenth, when the camp was not able to bring in tobacco for a month or so and there was a veritable tobacco famine. During those weeks the effects were marked, in frayed nerves and angry outbursts, and on the evening when a supply eventually did come in the rejoicing in the camp was astonishing. One might have thought that the news had come that we were about to be repatriated, such was the atmosphere of cheerfulness and relaxation that suddenly displaced the general gloom. As a non-smoker myself, that was a revelation to me of the hold which this habit gets on people and the unpleasant results which follow if the craving by any chance cannot be satisfied. I remember on that evening when the famine ended hearing an "Asia Boy" exclaim outside my cell, "There's tobacco in, they're issuing it this evening. There'll be murder if they don't." I could not help thinking that if that was the grip that smoking had on a 20-year-old youth, he would be much better without it, and I thought the same when I saw grown men, once of a prosperous station in life, ranging the prison yards with their eyes on the ground, looking for dirty, spittle-soaked butt ends that others had thrown away. Smoking undoubtedly eased people's nerves, and perhaps allayed the cravings for food in hungry times, but smokers had to pay for this on the many days when they had no smokes left; whereas the non-smoker felt no discomfort whatsoever, so that I felt very thankful that I have never acquired the habit. Certainly in those circumstances, when you got just enough to keep craving alive until the next lorry came in from town, it seemed better to be without it.

How will the experiences of the internment change the dietary habits of the internees after the war? One thing is certain: many people will take away with them a more intelligent and better-informed understanding of nutrition than they ever had before, thanks to the lectures they heard, their contact with medical men, and the practical demonstration of theoretical knowledge about vitamins, carbohydrates, proteins and fats which they gained in Changi. Never again will they show the indifference to the vital question of the nature of the fuel taken into their own bodies that they felt before. But some people will go out into the world again just as ignorant as they were when they came in.

All that has been said above applies to the period when the diet was still good and there was a plentiful supply of rice, even if the diet consisted mainly of cereals, pulses, green vegetables and vegetable fats. Later there was a serious loss of weight and deterioration of condition, but more of that later.

[14]
East and West

East is East and West is West
and never the twain shall meet.
— KIPLING

If ever this tag was falsified, it was in Changi Gaol, where the traditional ideas of the East met those of the West, with an inevitable result in misunderstanding and at the same time, on our part at least, a deeper understanding of Japanese ideas, beliefs and ways of thought. It was at all times a difficult situation, but there was no serious friction between us and our camp officials, and their attitude towards the camp was a reasonably helpful one.

In that curious way in which nations at war bestow a half-humorous, not-unfriendly nickname upon the enemy, just as the Germans in the last war were not "The Hun" to the fighting troops, but simply "Jerry," so the Japanese were "the Nips" to us. This nickname seemed to come into use naturally and dates from the first days of the internment. It is difficult to say how it arose. Perhaps the explanation lies in the fact that at first the Japanese insisted upon the use of the name "Nippon" instead of "Japan" and always used this name in the local newspaper. "Japan" is a purely foreign word, the name used by the Nipponese themselves being "Nippon." Later they seemed to drop this rule, no doubt because "Japan" had become the established name among other peoples.

Our first contact with the Japanese was not reassuring. The first officer appointed to take charge of us was Major Kato, and in an address to us on that day when we assembled on the Padang, and also in several later addresses at Karikal, he expressed great bitterness against the British and Americans, and in general seemed very hostile. He said that when the Japanese troops took Davao, in the Philippines, they found that some of their own civilians had been killed by American troops. He said that the Japanese would not treat us in the same way, but we should have to be very careful indeed as to how we behaved. It was at Karikal too that several internees received summary punishment, for living in huts outside the camp and being apparently inattentive to an address. But Major Kato's attitude gradually changed as he realised that we intended to carry out the Japanese instructions to the letter and to cooperate fully in running the camps, and by the time he left us the meetings between him and our executive committee were being conducted in a much more friendly atmosphere. He had been at first very much on his guard and suspicious of us, but his manner changed as he got to know us better. With regard to our treatment at this time, it must also be recorded that although conditions at the temporary camps were very hard, we were allowed by the Japanese High Command quite liberal facilities for obtaining what we needed in town, and our lorries went to town every day and came back loaded with food and other urgently needed goods.

When we moved to Changi our first camp commandant was Lieutenant Okasaki, who had as his second-in-command Lieutenant Taikuda. (It puzzled us that officers holding a rank that in the British Army would be a very junior one should be placed in charge of so large a camp.) Lieutenant Okasaki was a good administrator. While strictly correct in his relations with us, he was fair and well-intentioned. He was a Christian, a member of the Presbyterian denomination, and a man of character. He was interested in music and we were particularly indebted to him for his assistance in organising the orchestra and getting the instruments and also pianos from town. He actually requested that the orchestra play "Home Sweet Home."

We soon became aware in Changi of the difference between Japanese and our own etiquette. For example, there was a matter of bowing. From the first we were required to remove our hats, if we wore them, stand at attention and bow from the waist downwards when we spoke to one of the camp officials or when Japanese officers visited the camp. Later this rule was extended to include bowing when we passed the sentry outside the guardroom and the sentries at the Main Gate, so that when you went out, attached to the ropes of a firewood cart, you had to bow twice before you left the Gaol, while the procedure for getting to see one of the higher officials upstairs in the tower involved bowing three or four times at different stages. When the Japanese military guard was replaced by Sikhs we also had to bow to them so long as they were on sentry duty and also bow to sightseeing parties. For example, if you had business in the women's camp, you had to bow to the Sikh on duty at the entrance. At first this bowing order was not obeyed with feelings of pleasure, being so foreign to our own ideas, but the Japanese explained that according to their ideas every officer in the service represented in his own person the Emperor, and therefore must be honoured accordingly. Moreover, we knew that the Japanese code of etiquette was a strict one, that they were above all a polite race, the bowing was part of their traditional ideas of courtesy, and we saw for ourselves that they accorded this courtesy to each other. So why should they not exact it from internees? We soon saw that it was plain common sense to see the matter from their point of view, and our own camp officials impressed upon everyone the importance of strict observance to this rule. "Paying compliments," as it was called, continued to be a cause of friction throughout our term in the Gaol, the Japanese authorities alleging from time to time that we did not show sufficient respect on frequent occasions when parties of Japanese officers and men visited the camp, apparently as part of a sightseeing tour. But if there was any substance in these complaints, it was not intentional on our part but due to oversight.

But so far as bowing to the Sikhs was concerned, honesty compels one to admit that the conservative type of internee never got used to this, by reason of the position which these guards had occupied relative to themselves in peacetime Malaya.

After we had been at Changi for some months the camp was placed in charge of a civilian, Mr Asahi, who was particularly well-qualified for this post in that he spoke English well, had spent nine years in London as Japanese Consul-General there, had seen the world, and was accustomed to dealing with Europeans. He had charge of the internment camps in Sumatra and Malaya, and he silenced the grouses in Changi Gaol, or gave them something to think about, when he said that he had inspected over 20 internment camps in that region and nowhere were there permanent buildings and essential services as good as ours, and, further, that if we went on complaining in letters to the High Command, we might easily find ourselves in a much worse place, for there had been several attempts to move the camp, in order to make the Gaol available for military purposes, but so far he had successfully resisted them. Mr Asahi never deviated from an attitude of strict reserve and correctness, but he did generally do his best for us. It was during his regime that we were given a very valuable concession of taking walks outside the walls in the evenings, extending our gardens outside the walls, that regular meetings between relatives in the men's and women's camps began and that a radio was installed in the front yard to give us the musical and news broadcasts from the Singapore station.

After Mr Asahi went we were placed in the charge of a retired Army colonel, who seemed to be very much the same sort of person as the retired army colonels one sees in Bath and Cheltenham. He was very insistent on tidiness and issued an instruction that our quarters were to be in "barrack-room order" for inspections. To appreciate the irony, you have to know what the crowded and jumbled state of those quarters was like. But his attitude was a decent and not unfriendly one. He even provided a friendly handshake when he met with the Men's Representative.

In the early months we saw very little of the Japanese authorities. No sentries were posted beyond the guardroom, and the camp was not even patrolled, so that in the main part of the camp you might go for weeks without seeing a Japanese at all. Later, however, regular patrols by Japanese and Sikh guards were instituted, so that at any hour, in the corridors or yards or on the upper floors you might meet a patrol and have to stand at attention but not bow except to an officer.

We soon became aware of the difference between the Japanese methods of discipline and our own. For example, among British people a slap in the face is a mortal insult, not tolerated in the services nor among civilians. But among the Japanese it is common thing and treated lightly. It is indeed a favourite form of lenient punishment. If you are caught smoking in a forbidden place, or if you fail to pay a compliment, or you break the rule against speaking to a woman internee, you got your face slapped. And it is easy to imagine the indignation this aroused in a gentleman whose ordinary manner was a pompous one, a former manager of a mercantile firm, a senior civil servant, and so on. But we observed that this was not a special punishment applied to ourselves and was not even intended to be insulting as we viewed it. Their own non-commissioned officers and men, and even apparently commissioned officers at times, were liable to be punished in this way, and we even saw the more junior members of our own Japanese officials receive this sort of reprimand. But it certainly was disconcerting to Europeans at first. Eventually we got used to it; and anyway it was a rare occurrence, and if you did not want to get your face slapped, all you had to do was to obey the rules.

Another form of punishment that was new to us was being made to kneel for some time. For example, on one occasion when the Japanese considered that the occupants of a certain workshop had failed to show proper respect during an inspection by a high official, all the occupants of that room, over 100 men, were ordered to kneel on the concrete of the tower terrace for several hours.

At times, too, some official or other would show what we thought was a perverted sense of humour, as on the occasion when the camp orchestra was found rehearsing in a quiet corner of the girdle road which commanded a view of the gate leading into one of the women's courtyards. "You like looking at the women?" enquired the official, "Very well, you take your instruments and go on top of the tower." So to the top of the tower the musicians had to go, and spend the night there in the bracing night air, apparently to cool their passions.

After a time discipline became stricter and more severe punishments were occasionally imposed. Later we realised that at that time we were coming under suspicion and the Japanese attitude towards us was consequently hardening. During this period summary punishment became more frequent, and corporal punishment was imposed on several occasions, while a few internees twice had to spend a week in the guardroom. But here again one has to remember that Japanese discipline is at all times severe. When the Japanese occupied Singapore we were astonished time after time of the severity of the punishments that we saw meted out by officers to their own troops, something quite unknown in our own army, but accepted by the Japanese soldier as a matter of course. Even the severest punishments at Changi meant nothing more than that we were being put under the same discipline that was enforced in the Japanese army. Moreover, strict discipline was necessary with nearly 3000 men and only half a dozen officials in a small guard-house, but there was no promiscuous brutality, nothing like our expectations. Many internees went right through the internment without so much as a slap in the face.

After the investigation in town had proceeded for some time, and the military police had apparently satisfied themselves that the gravest suspicions entertained against the camp were unfounded, the regime in the camp became milder again. Our commissariat arrangements were taken over by Sergeant Major Tanaka, whom we always found obliging and courteous. It was at this time to that we found ourselves for the first time under an officer of the rank of General. General Saito took control of the camp and from the first showed a friendly and helpful attitude towards the internees, while at the same time maintaining strict enforcement of the rules. But we felt that it was an advantage to have an officer of his seniority to deal with, as an intermediary between the camp and the High Command.

The relations between the internees and the Japanese officials in Changi prison were very different from those prevailing in German prisoner-of-war camps, judging by the books about life in such camps published after the last war. They became better, more natural and more cordial, in the latter part of the internment, but so long as we were at Changi they were at best formal and at worst, strained. Even under ideal circumstances it is difficult for Europeans to understand the Japanese, and presumably vice versa. In ordinary peacetime life Europeans living in China feel that they are able to get over the barriers of race and culture and language much better than they ever do in Japan. How much more difficult must this be in wartime, in a conquered country, with the former British governing class of the country overthrown from their higher state and held as prisoners by the Japanese army? The possibilities of mutual misunderstanding arising from the wartime situation, the difference in traditional ideas and standards, racial feeling aroused by the war, and the suspicion always present on both sides of the colour bar, need no emphasis. As a matter of fact, we never felt that we really understood the Japanese. In my own opinion and that of some others in the camp, we made the position more difficult than it need have been by the attitude we adopted during the early days. The frigid reserve which emanates from the British upper and middle classes during the first few days on the P. & O. liner is nothing to what we thought it proper to display in the early months in Changi Gaol. The accepted notion appeared to be that it was our patriotic duty to avoid showing even the slightest hint of friendly or cordial feelings. Anything in the nature of "fraternisation" was frowned upon. Well, I only saw one instance of fraternisation, and I could see no harm in that. It happened when I was living in a room near the main gate. One evening Japanese guards and a group of internees got to talking in pidgin Malay, then to chaffing each other, and finally one of them challenged one of our number, who was of generous proportions round the waist, to race down the girdle road. This was arranged there and then and the race took place amid roars of laughter. I was struck by the contrast between the spirit prevailing on that episode and the cold reserve and artificial hostility that convention prescribed in the camp. Certainly a little more of that sort of thing would have done no harm, and probably some good, in Changi Gaol, during the first year of the Pacific War. Judging by books published after the First World War, friendly and informal relations often developed between German officers in charge of prison camps in Germany and British prisoners, so far as the limitation of the situation allowed, and one could not see why the same thing should be frowned upon in our camp. The view which the prisoner of war took of this question was quite different, judging by what we saw on the outside fatigues and particularly during the day when they were coming into Changi Gaol and we were going out. The relationship between them and their guards seem to be much more friendly, free and easy, illustrating the saying that the war is waged between governments, not between individuals. Of course the feelings of the POWs were different from ours. They were strangers to the country, brought there to do a job of work, and that was all; whereas we had a sense of immense personal loss as well. Moreover, there was camaraderie between soldiers that did not exist in our camp. Even so, if the men who'd done the actual fighting saw no reason why they should feel hostility towards individual Japanese officers and guards with whom they came into contact just because the two countries were at war, there was no reason why the civilians should not have done the same.

But for a long time we continued to act the part the of tuan besar, the taipan and sahib in relation to our captors, and of course that was the very thing, in its political, economic and social implications, that the Japanese had set themselves to eradicate from the Far East, and nothing was calculated to annoy them more. For example, when Mr Asahi came out to the camp to say goodbye on his transfer to another post the attitude of our camp officials was so markedly reserved and cold, in spite of the fact he had done more for the camp than anyone else, that he commented on it afterwards. A little more cordiality would on our part have gone a long way in Changi.

This feeling was more noticeable among the older men, who had spent many years in Malaya in positions of power and authority, than among the younger men. Some of the older men seem to find the position as one of special humiliation. They would not even avail themselves of the opportunities to go outside the Gaol, such as the delightful monthly walk to the beach or the fatigues in town, but condemned themselves to unrelieved confinement within the walls for that reason. Euphemisms were used in the camp. For example, the surrender was never the surrender, it was the capitulation; the Gaol was the camp; and a cell was not a cell, it was a cabin.

When all is said and done, however, those of our camp officials who had to maintain contact with the Japanese officials over us had a difficult task. For one thing, there was the language difficulty. Discussions were carried on in Malay, which one party or the other might not be fluent in, or in Japanese, translated by one internee who had a fair but not perfect knowledge of the language, so that there was always a possibility of misunderstanding. Tact, patience and a quick intelligence was necessary in these relationships, and special gratitude is due to those who took upon themselves the heavy responsibility and the very real contingencies of Men's Representative, fatigue officer and quartermaster.

Allowance had also to be made for the fact that the camp staff were not independent but worked under the strict control of the High Command in Singapore. In matters of discipline in day-to-day administration the Japanese practice evidently was to give the man on the spot a free hand, and there was never any question of appeal to a higher authority, but the general policy in relation to internees was decided by the High Command, so that many questions raised by us could not be settled by our own camp officials but had to be referred to Singapore.

As to the attitude of the High Command, so far as we could judge it, and our treatment in general, it could hardly be said to be generous, but on the other hand it might have been a great deal worse. We would have had a thin time if we had had to live solely on the official rations, but there was a real food shortage in Malaya and we were probably better fed than the people outside; also we were given full facilities for buying supplies in town. Moreover, the Japanese allowed us to keep all the money we had in our possession when we went into internment, and that in the aggregate was a very considerable sum which enabled the camp fund as a whole to go on buying supplementary foods for many months, apart from money retained by individual internees for private buying. (As the Japanese themselves pointed out to us, when we arrested the Japanese civilians living in Malaya and interned them, we did not treat them in that way but took all their money away from them.) There was a puzzling strictness of segregation between husbands and wives during the first year; again, we felt we might have been better treated in the matter of bedding and other supplies, but we were allowed to go into town and buy whatever we could find. We were undoubtedly overcrowded (as previously discussed), but the Japanese had 60,000 other prisoners to look after in Malaya beside the internees. The camp was never visited by an International Red Cross representative, but the agent of the Red Cross in Singapore was allowed to send us a wide range of supplies and to render services that were simply invaluable. The punishments were occasionally severe according to our ideas, but there was no promiscuous brutality. If I had allowed myself to think of such a fate before the fall I would have visualised a herd of dreary, wretched people behind barbed wire, struck with rifle butts, prodded with bayonets, kicked with heavy boots, urged on with brutal blows and threats, barely kept alive. Nothing of that sort ever happened at Changi. There was never any brutal treatment on fatigues, the Sikh guards were not permitted to strike us, and the average internee came through the whole internment without so much as a slap in the face. To sum up, it might have been better, but it might easily have been worse, and it was not nearly as bad as most of us expected it to be.

[15]
Ugliness

The sheer ugliness of the place — unrelieved, ubiquitous, unescapable ugliness — that is one of the memories that brings a foul taste into the mouth when one looks back to those days in Changi Gaol. The whole place was one vast maze of concrete and iron. Everywhere you looked, everywhere you went, you saw nothing but concrete walls, concrete floors and ceilings, even concrete beds in the cells. Every window was striped with iron bars, from the little windows high up in the cells to the great windows at the end of each floor of the cell blocks. If you lived in a ground-floor workshop or dining room you had barred windows shutting you out not only from the yards outside but from the interior corridors. When you walked along those dark, tunnel-like corridors you had iron grilles on either side, affording the view of a workshop on one side and the daylight on the other. Even the windows of the hospital wards had bars. There was only one room in the whole prison where you could rest your elbows on a windowsill and look out at the sunshine without your vision being obscured by iron bars, and that was the mortuary.

The universal grey monotone was deepened by the poor lighting, particularly in the interior of the cell blocks. In the passages and stairways inside these huge, high boxes of reinforced concrete we moved in a gloomy half-light on the sunniest day, and those unfortunate beings who lived in the inner space between the cells were like veritable cave-dwellers. On the ground floor it was not so bad in fine weather, but on a rainy day the whole prison was the dreariest place imaginable, while the brownout lighting restrictions gave the passages a ghostly appearance every night, with dim figures moving about.

Outside, in the yards, it was not much better. Each of the exercise yards, where we spent most of our leisure time, was dominated by a cell block, towering up like a great concrete cliff pierced by lines of little windows and displaying a rectangular pattern showing where the lines of cells were set in the steel framework. On the other side of the yard the eye rested on long concrete walls, with ugly streaks of black along the top and in places decorated with a fringe of downward pointing iron spikes. In other directions you saw the kitchen block with a boiler-house chimney sticking up into the sky like a giant black stovepipe, and the prison tower rising above a complex of sharp, straight profiles, bare walls, and grey rectangular masses of all sizes that looked as if a giant had been playing a game with children's wooden blocks.

When we first moved into the Gaol this universal greyness and ugliness had one curious and interesting effect. It intensified our appreciation, and in some people evoked a quite new appreciation, of the beauty of the sky, its colouring and cloud effects. We saw the yards as the grey frames of the picture that changed every day and every hour. Put for the first time in our lives in an environment totally devoid of beauty of colour or line or form, the great white cloud masses sailing across the sky took on a softness and yet a majesty such as seemed never to have been seen before; the glorious blue of Heaven on a fine Malayan day, the long savannas of the blue, brought a new and intense delight. "Pure colour is rest of heart," wrote Richard Jefferies as he lay on the chalk downs of Sussex and looked up at the summer skies, and we realised what he meant as we looked at the "blue and shining dome of Heaven" above the grey walls of Changi Gaol; and above all, in the evening, in the last hour before the disappearance of the sun, the infinite variety and delicacy of the colouring and the deep, serene, mystic depths of the sunset sky bought rest to our souls. It was partly the reaction from what we had just been through during the siege of Singapore, the sense of relief and relaxation, that bought a new sense of thankfulness to be alive, of the contrast between the loveliness of the world of nature and the horrors of the world of man, but mainly it was the ugliness of the setting of this new life of ours that aroused in us this intense delight in the beauty of the sky, something that we had taken for granted, or rarely been aware of except in moments of rare intensity in our ordinary lives but now had with us day after day. Nor was this confined to a few aesthetes; it was the general experience at the time, and was confessed by human types that ordinarily would never dream of being articulate about such things, even if they were conscious of them. No lecturer had a more sympathetic audience, one more in rapport with himself, than an artist in the camp who gave a lecture in those early days in which he described his own sensations at finding himself in that dreadful desert of concrete and the joy he had received from the intensification of the beauty of the sky above a grey and ugly setting in which we now saw it. Tags of poetry long cherished came back fraught with a new meaning in them those days:

scarves of clouds…

thy dewy fingers draw the gradual dusky veil…

for ever in joy…

Higher still and higher,
From the earth thou springest,
Like a cloud of fire;
The blue deep thou wingest,
And singing still dost soar, and soaring ever singest.
   (Shelley, from "Ode to the Skylark")

Is that not a description of the spirit of the internee immured in Changi Gaol at certain precious moments in those days? Some of those who listened to the artist's lecture felt that it was true of him, and perhaps in certain precious moments, themselves too. In my schooldays I was forced at the age of eleven to learn by heart the "Ode to the Skylark," and was consequently never able to appreciate it for a long time in adult life, but the intense feeling of the beauty of light and colour and space in the sky in that poem was revealed to me as never before in those days. But this awareness faded, as these things do, and as the monotony, the irritation, the frustration, the unhappiness of our life grew upon us, it was only in very rare and heavenly moments of release and distraction that we saw the sky as we had seen it in the early days.

As a rule, the physical discomforts of life in prison did not worry most of us unduly. It was hard on the elderly and the old, who naturally found it very difficult to adjust themselves to such conditions after the conveniences and comforts of their own homes, but the majority of the internees were able-bodied and in sound health, and it was no great hardship for them to "rough it." It is wonderful what you can get used to when you have to, and there is even a certain satisfaction in reducing life to its simplest components and finding that you can still get a surprising amount of enjoyment from it. Once you get down to that level you feel that you have allowed yourself to become unduly cluttered up with possessions in the past and you are glad to have made the discovery that you can do without them. You feel much more prepared to face hardships and adversity in the future, if it comes. Be that as it may, most of us soon ceased to dwell on the contrast, so vividly present to our consciousness in the early days, between the comforts of the past and the wretchedness of the prison, and accustomed ourselves surprisingly well to living in a space of seven feet by three feet, with a corresponding reduction in personal possessions. After all, these discomforts were nothing compared with what people were suffering in the bombed cities of Great Britain and Europe, what many millions of men were enduring on active service, and what we ourselves would in many cases have had to endure had we been free and able to play our part in the war. At the same time, these considerations did not make us like Changi Gaol any better, and there were moments when we felt an utter loathing of the sordid mess and crudity of the conditions of life there. To wake up in the dank, dark, depressing cell at dawn, to try to dress without falling over the other two troglodytes, to wash over a stinking urinal, to wash your eating utensils after breakfast over that same urinal, that was a start for the day that was liable to give you that "Monday morning feeling" on any day of the week. There was also the everlasting standing in queues. You stood in queues for everything, for meals, for the library an enormous queue, for concerts, for the water tap in the yard, even for the lavatory.

Then there were the bugs. Soon after we settled down in the prison we found that the place was infested with bugs, left there by the convicts. It was impossible to get rid of them altogether, for they lived in the crevices of the walls and floors. They got in to all our possessions, even books and shoes and typewriters, so regular debugging became part of the routine of life in the Gaol. This made us feel the squalor and indignity of our manner of life more than more serious troubles. The bugs were harmless but had an unpleasant smell, particularly when squashed, and because they were associated in our minds with the dirt and squalor, we found them the most disgusting features of life in prison. I remember in the early days overhearing an elderly internee, who had just gone through the revolting procedure of debugging his bed and mattress for the first time, muttering to himself in a tone of intense bitterness, "To think that I should have ever come to this." That was how we all felt about it at first. Providentially our peacetime sensitivities gradually underwent a certain coarsening, otherwise, this and many other things in Changi Gaol would have been unendurable.

Another of the trials of life was the absence of chairs and tables. Sitting on a small stool gets very tiring after a while. One does not realise how much the back is supported and rested in ordinary life by chairs and settees and so forth, until one has to do without these things. In Changi Gaol one had to sit in a huddled posture on a stool, preferably with one's back against a wall, and if you wanted to write you did so on a board on your knees. In the cell you sat in still more hunched-up posture, if your place was between the wall and the sarcophagus. There were times in Changi Gaol when in one's dreams, it seemed the acme of luxury just to sit in a decent chair again, and rest one's elbows on a desk, and write or read in comfort. And if that chair and desk were in perfectly empty, quiet room, well that was a dream of paradise.

But above all it was on wet days that one loathed Changi Gaol and longed for the amenities of civilised life. If there is anything in the world more dreary and dismal and depressing than Changi Gaol as it was on a wet day during the internment, with 3000 people herded together and most of them sick of the sight of each other, one would like to know what it is. It used to remind me of my most miserable moments in boarding school in England, the same long, concrete corridors, the same rain-swept yards, the same bored individuals wandering around with nothing to do. Another impression of my boyhood that came back to me in Changi Gaol was that of a workhouse in a provincial town that I visited once or twice, for some reason or other. The greyness and dreariness and sadness of the workhouse made a deep impression on me, even at that buoyant and thoughtless age, and it came back to me when I found myself a prisoner in Changi Gaol. I realised then what life must have been like for those old people ending their lives in those dormitories and those ugly yards, particularly when one visualised the cosy little homes which many of them had known in better days. They don't call them workhouses any more, but one wonders whether there is more happiness in them now than there was then. If the internment does nothing else, it should at least make us more aware of such suffering inflicted by middle-class complacency and insensitivity, and make us more sensitive to such things. Since a very large number of the Malayans immured in Changi Gaol will probably serve on public bodies of one kind or another when they settle down on retirement in England, they may bring their experiences to bear on the running of public institutions. (Heavens what tripe but I can't get the fog out of my brain 16.12.1944.)

Now to return to Changi Gaol. With no rooms set aside for recreation, the only place to which you could go on a wet day was the narrow shelter running round two sides of the block yard, where you sat knee to knee with a herd of other depressed-looking humans. And if you could not find room there, or were forced to retire indoors by driving rain, you had perforce to go back to your cell or workshop and there strain your eyes by reading in bad light and your nerves by trying to concentrate with talk going on five feet away. When that became unbearable, there was only one thing left to do. As a last resort, in the most literal sense, you could go and try to read amid the wetness, noise and confusion of the laundry! What a difference the concession of a quiet, spacious recreation hut would have made at Changi! Worst of all was a wet evening. During the day you could at least try to read in the cell, but in the evening, with the brownout lighting, you could not even do that, and when you had had enough of wandering around the corridors, or had inflicted your company on your friends as long as you decently could, all you could do was to go to bed; and there you lay in the semidarkness of the cell, in the narrow space between the wall and the sarcophagus, listening to the same trivialities of camp gossip, this same endless speculation as to whether we would be released by exchange or not, the same amateur animadversions on the war, the same idiotic rumours from the outside world, all this, as likely as not, carried on in a spirit of acrimonious argument. And when at last "lights out" came, and the hundred or so occupants of the floor settled down to sleep, the relief of darkness and silence was beyond description.

One of the worst trials of life in Changi Gaol was the complete separation from our wives and families. The Red Cross arrangements for the exchange of mails between Japan and Allied countries were apparently a long time in getting organised, and throughout the first year we got no mail whatsoever. Then letters and occasional radio messages began to trickle through, but it was not until we had been interned for 18 months or so that the receipt of letters began to be fairly general in the camp. When they did arrive they were very old, dating back to the early months after the fall of Singapore, and their staleness was increased by delays resulting from the difficulty of censoring such large quantities of mail. Nevertheless, it was an immense relief to get them. We ourselves were allowed to send postcards quite early in the internment, and later on, radio messages as well. Moreover, we several times filled out forms giving particulars of ourselves which we presumed would be used for notification of our next-of-kin through the International Red Cross, but we knew that it would take some time for information to get through and for some months we had to endure the distress of knowing the anxiety our wives and relatives must be suffering not knowing what had happened or what was happening behind the impenetrable curtain of silence that had fallen on Singapore, not knowing whether we were dead or alive. Eventually we learnt that they actually had to wait 16 or 17 months before they had any news of us whatsoever, the official notification reaching them somewhere about the middle of 1943; and our first postcards, written in four months after the fall, took 15 months to reach the British Isles. We also learnt that a considerable number of our radio messages were picked up in Australia, India, Great Britain and elsewhere, but for the most part not until 1943. A few of the letters were read with wry expressions, for they showed that people at home thought we were still living in our own houses and carrying on with our ordinary vocations, while others thought we were in some sort of pleasant seaside camp, with all sorts of amenities. It requires no effort of the imagination to realise with what feelings that information was discussed in the yards of Changi Gaol. Then there was the wife who wrote to a husband from South Africa, "People are saying here that any man of courage and initiative could have got away from Singapore, so why didn't you?" That to an unfortunate husband who had loyally obeyed the order of his government to stay. But of course the arrival of letters brought immense relief and joy, and the day on which we got our first letter, after the long silence, will ever be remembered as one of the brightest spots of our life in Changi.

Another of the trials of life was the sense of isolation from the outside world, of being in the dark while the events of tremendous import were going on outside. The Nipponese authorities gave us the Singapore paper, the *Syonan Shimbun*, and later they also gave the evening programme of the Singapore broadcasting station to a packed audience in the front yard every night through a loudspeaker, but of course this only gave us the progress on the war from the viewpoint of the other side, and we always felt that we were very much in the dark about the war and that our view of it was but a very limited and partial one. The result was that the camp was a hotbed of rumours. Indeed, rumour was a study in itself in Changi Gaol. If one had taken the trouble to keep a record of all the rumours that circulated in the Gaol during that period it would be a most fantastic document, a revelation of human gullibility and credibility, a reflection of one of the most curious aspects of internment-camp psychology. How they started one could never find, but one was forced to the conclusion that many of them were deliberately invented. In a crowded place like that any sort of story spread from end to end of the camp like wildfire, and it would have been as perfectly simple for some person of abnormal mentality to put false rumours into circulation just for the perverted satisfaction of hearing other people eagerly discussing so-called "news" which had originated in his own brain. Again, we probably had among us those same officious fools who in Singapore before the fall thought it was their business to cheer us up. No doubt this explained why on that first Christmas there was a sudden crop of highly encouraging rumours all of which we later realised had been without foundation. The rumours reflected were of an obviously absurd character. If Germany collapsed once, she did so a dozen times according to the Changi rumour-mongers. But it would be boring and unnecessary to try to recall the nonsense we listened to, and talked about for want of something better to talk about in those days. One of the most extraordinary things was the way in which people would be inflated by false news time after time, would undergo subsequent reactions of disillusionment and depression, and yet the very next wave of rumours would find them willing and gullible victims once again. More often than not, indeed, disillusionment did not bring depression, for by that time the people had forgotten what they had believed a month before, and the time-lag thus enabled them to concentrate on a fresh crop of rumours without learning the lesson of the past, and they did not want to learn anyway.

One was struck time and again by the limitations of the untrained mind, limitations of those who did not have to think in their work. They could not repeat accurately anything they had read or heard an hour before, they believed what they wanted to believe, and they were incapable of weighing and analysing rumours. But the influence of wishful thinking on consciously intellectual types, persons who prided themselves on their reasoning powers, was also evident. If ever that famous prologue in Shakespeare's *Henry IV*, and particularly its contemptuous reference to the gullibility of the mob, took on a new meaning in a modern setting, it did so in Changi Gaol:

> *Enter* RUMOUR, *painted full of tongues.*
> RUMOUR: Open your ears, for which of you will stop
> The vent of hearing when loud rumour speaks?
> ... Rumour is a pipe
> Blown by surmises, jealousies, conjectures,
> And of so easy and so plain a stop
> That the blunt monster with uncounted heads,
> This still-discordant, wavering multitude,
> Can play upon it. But what need I thus
> My well-known body to anatomize
> Among my household?

Because we knew so little of what was going on, and realised that a great deal of what we heard was hopelessly garbled and unreliable, we naturally spent a great deal of time in speculating and arguing about the war. Amateur strategists were in their element, laying down the law as to what was happening or what would happen on the various fronts. The interesting thing about all such discussions, looking back on them now, is how utterly and hopelessly wrong even the best-informed and most intelligent people were. The staying power and willpower and cohesion of the German people was hopelessly underestimated. We were constantly assured that "Germany cannot last another winter," that her people were on the verge of starvation and revolt, that the Nazi regime was cracking, that the Germans would never start bombing as the British had done.... All this far back in 1942 and 1943. The same underestimation was observed with regard to Japan, only more so, and it was only gradually that people realised how long the war in the Pacific was likely to last. But gradually it dawned on the most optimistic that we were likely to be interned very much longer, much longer than we had foreseen, and that realisation did not help to keep our spirits up.

Another effect of this sense of isolation, of being cut off from the outside world, was that the happenings of our little world behind those walls took on quite disproportionate interest and importance. One's ears were assailed by the trivialities of camp gossip all day long. Who was the new leader of C block? What was the latest scandal in the kitchen? What had that afternoon's lorry brought in? What was the incident that occurred in the morning's firewood fatigue? And so on and so on. Everybody went over the day's gossip at least once, but some people went over the same dreary, trivial stuff a dozen times during the day.

Of course the main question in our minds was how long the internment would last. How long would the war last, if we were to be held prisoners until peace came? This gave an additional incentive to the endless speculations about the war and acerbity to the rebuttal of any suggestions that were not robustly optimistic. But what we really hoped for was release through exchange. The Singapore paper published news from Tokyo several times that negotiations were going on for the exchange of British internees in the Far East, and our hopes rose high, almost reaching the point of assured certainty in some cases. But it was not to be. Twice we had the bitter experience of seeing exchange ships pass through Singapore, and leave us behind. In the case of the *Teia Maru* we could actually see her lying at anchor off the coast, and we knew that she was full of Americans from Japan, China and the Philippines on their way to freedom. It was a peculiarly bitter moment for the Americans and Canadians in the camp when the ship resumed her voyage to Goa without them. For a long time our spirits were sustained by hopes of exchange, but when a year passed, then another six months, without anything happening, we began to give up hope. But up to that time exchange was the most debated topic in the camp, and some of the theories and rumours attaching to it were truly fantastic. What so-and-so was supposed to have said, some perfectly trivial and meaningless remark dropped by some subordinate official, some sign of unusual activity in the front offices, even utterly unrelated happenings — the taking-over of the first outside garden, the building of huts in the Main Yard, the issue of number plates (cards), the painting of names on baggage — anything was sufficient to start a fresh exchange rumour. How many times did we hear that two or three repatriation ships had left Shanghai, that others had left England or Goa? Who started these lying and cruel stories? We never knew. But the time came when the word "exchange" merely produced a cynical and weary smile… although some people never gave up hope and such stories continued to crop up even in the third year of the internment, after we had been plainly told that we were there "for the duration."

[16]
Human Nature in Changi

By now the reader will have realised something of the strain under which we lived in Changi Gaol and he must be wondering how human nature reacted to it.

In one way, the incarceration was a social experiment such as has never before been made in the history of this country. Although European society in this country is predominantly middle-class, there are a number of subtle gradations in it. Different salary levels correspond more or less to differences in education and social background and the different strata tend to keep apart. There is mixing in the smaller upcountry clubs, but underneath the surface there is a good deal of snobbery. There is a well-known story about an advertisement which appeared in the upper-country newspaper as follows: "Assistant wanted for rubber estate. No public schoolboys need apply." The following day another advertisement appeared: "Assistant wanted for rubber estate. No Scots coolies need apply." It is a nasty story and probably an untrue one, but the mere fact that it could be invented and gain currency shows the snobbish feelings that existed under the surface in the planting districts. It reflects the contrast between two common types of planter: the man who comes from a country family, with a landowning tradition, and the more unpolished but competent Scottish planter. In Singapore the social cleavages are open and unashamed, and the same is true to a lesser extent in Kuala Lumpur and Penang. Moreover, one must remember that the European in Malaya was able to live a more exclusive, indeed definitely aristocratic, existence than he would have been able to do, in most cases, had he stayed at home. There is none of the travelling in trains and tubes and buses during the rush hours which forces your upper-middle-class man at home to rub shoulders with common humanity. The European in Malaya travels to and from his office in his car and rarely rides in the bus; until recent years in Singapore he never did so. Moreover, his suburban life is much more spacious and private than it is at home; there is none of that neighbourly chatting over the garden wall that you get in a London suburb. Your European in Singapore, living in a house surrounded by a large "compound," probably does not speak to his neighbour from one year's end to the other.

Now imagine all those people, with the social prejudices and habits and manner of life, suddenly scooped up by the hand of destiny and thrown higgledy-piggledy into Changi Gaol, there to live together in the closest possible proximity, shuffled and jumbled together with no regard for the class, cultural and economic distinctions which had formerly kept them apart, required to live for the first time on a basis of absolute equality and to be members of a community in which everyone had to do his share of the dirty work, and to be treated in the matter of food, accommodation and the rest of it, exactly like everybody else. How did it work out? Well, there was undoubtedly a gain of mutual understanding. Men learnt to see each other as individual personalities, not as social types with labels attached to them. Many a chance conversation or contact broadened a man's outlook and made him ashamed of his former intolerance and tendency to judge by merely external characteristics. On the other hand, one noticed that there was not much habitual mixing: birds of a feather tended to flock together. Moreover, there were obvious possibilities of friction when such different social types found themselves living cheek by jowl, under conditions both material and psychological which imposed constant strain. It only required a little touch of snobbery on one hand or hypersensitiveness on the other, of condescension and aggressiveness, of intellectual superciliousness or social snobbery, to start trouble. But in general the result was an increase in tolerance, and people soon learnt to see the real personality beneath the superficial characteristics imposed by environment.

A more serious cause of friction lay in temperamental incompatibility. People were under constant strain and tempers were often on a hair trigger. Even when there was goodwill, the conditions, in the cells particularly, were inhumanly difficult.

On the whole, however, there was not nearly as much friction as might be expected, certainly very much less than we ourselves expected when we first realised the conditions under which we would have to make this experiment in communal living. Once people had settled down, and settled disputes over boundaries and worked out a domestic routine, there were surprisingly few rows. The atmosphere was easier in the dormitories than the cells. The really bad cell was hell on earth. However, at the worst people achieved a sort of weary and wary tolerance, at the best something very much better. One came to loathe the egotistic faults and arrogance, but that was only one side of the picture. It would be a strangely misanthropic internee who did not collect many memories of considerateness, interested kindness, generosity and unselfishness. Many people, forced to realise how self-centred they had been in their former lives, found themselves making a definite effort to show kindness and act considerately towards others, and to cultivate a greater awareness of other people's needs and feelings.

In some ways, it was like being back at school again, with the same prefects, the same arbitrary rules, the same faults coming out. In other ways it was like living in a monastery. Sex was much less of a problem than you might suppose. The diet was a low one, of course, but the main factor, I think, was the total absence of the innumerable aphrodisiac influences of everyday life, the cinema, the cinema hoarding, the novel, etc. Another factor was our total separation from women, perhaps the most important factor of all. One curious point I noticed was that there was very little of the smoking-room story element. Had the number of men been crowded together under such boring conditions in normal life, there would have been an endless stream of more or less salacious talk. But, while it was not absent altogether, there was remarkably little of it. And when one did hear it, it seemed in that monastic setting to strike a jarring note even to ears that could not be accused of prudishness. I myself put this down to the fact that the men's thoughts were with their wives and families and the coarser side of life was repellent to them. To what extent we were affected by the absence of wives, women and children it is difficult to say. There must have been a certain coarsening, indeed, a certain amount of that was necessary if we were to endure the life at all. One realised as never before what the influence of women and children means in a man's life. Sometimes one would sit in one's cell and listen to the children playing in the women's camp, invisible but audible. Again, on the very rare occasions when we were allowed to see the women there was an immediate and perceptible taming of tone, a feeling of a return to normal and wholesome living, a realisation that our monastic society was empty and unreal. This was very evident at the first Christmas at Changi, which was an unforgettable experience. It was the first time since the fall that wives and husbands had been allowed to meet, and an atmosphere of happiness pervaded the whole Gaol. Never had such a spirit been seen within those grim walls and perhaps never will be again.

But with all this, one cannot deny that one became aware of the ugly side of human nature as we never had in our secure and prosperous and refined pre-war society (cultivated but not cultured). There were the bad hats among us, the sneak thief, the tough. No proper system of discipline. The flogging rule was unpopular and never enforced. Insistence on conducting our own disciplinary affairs, with the result that a man might behave like a thief, a tough, and a gangster, and get nothing more than deprivation of shop privileges, which his friends promptly made up for him. There were other unpleasant types, those who were coarse and vulgar, the mutilators of books, the cranks, the sexual perverts, the psycho-pathological cases, the exhibitionist, the excrementalist. Then you had the grown-up child, who would have his own way and went into tantrums if he didn't get it. If he refused to do his share of the work and live in a spirit of communal co-operation, there was very little you could do to him. Then there were the rackets in the kitchen, the carpenters' shops and elsewhere.

[17]
Under the Stars

But above all the relief from strain came when darkness fell on the Gaol; the dark veiled its ugliness, replaced the harsh and glaring light of the day with restful darkness, and alleviated that sense of being herded together with other humans. It was then that people went to sit under the stars in the moonlight. This was another of the novel features of our life in Changi. In ordinary life very few of us had ever enjoyed the balmy Malayan nights, had sat outdoors in our gardens after dark. In particular, how many lovely moonlit nights had we let slip by? Of course in one's own garden we would probably have been plagued with mosquitoes, whereas in the yards inside the walls of Changi Gaol there were very few. Anyway, most of us spent more time under the night sky in the Gaol than we'd ever done in our lives before. One result was a new interest in astronomy, and many people took to star-gazing for the first time.

It was one of the regular institutions of Changi life to meet in little groups in the hours after dark to talk and argue. In every yard, and especially in the big Main Yard, one saw these peculiar little groups, looking rather like a "huddle" in an American football game, seated on their stools with their heads towards the centre. The custom was to go over the day's camp gossip, with a due attention to the day's menu, then hash over all the latest rumours, most of which had already been discussed ad nauseam during the day, and then go on to more serious topics. Each member of the group made his contribution, and the common pool was solemnly gone over. One must remember that in this place, living in a little world of our own, trivial matters assumed a disproportionate importance. There was the continuous stream of gossip. All this was gone over in the evening discussions. Usually the members of these groups were the same. The same people met each other night after night, and not infrequently got on each other's nerves after a while.

Sometimes one would not join a group but be in a mood of solitary reflection. I found it extraordinary in Changi Gaol how some people found escape in reverie and how one could sit for hours neither talking or reading, whereas others could not sit for 15 minutes without reading or turning on the radio or doing something or other.

Another change in one's psychology was the way one lived in the past. This was to a large extent an unconscious process: it was as though the unconscious mind was turning over the pages of one's past life, and this was going on without any conscious effort, so that suddenly, while one was thinking about something entirely different, some memory of the past would suddenly come before the mind's eye. Of course this happens to some extent in normal life but it was very much more pronounced in Changi, perhaps because there had been such a complete break with our past lives and all our circumstances prompted retrospection and mental and spiritual stocktaking. The future was too remote to think about: return to normal life seemed too remote to be real, and the circumstances under which one would resume a normal life impossible to imagine. The present was at times unbearable. So the mind turned to the past. This may not have been so in the younger men but it was with the middle-aged and over. A further point was that not only was it largely an unconscious process but the unconscious seemed to be delving deeper and ever deeper down into the strata of memory, so that one found oneself going back to people and events and scenes of one's childhood that one had completely forgotten. One learnt then the lesson, but if one had had one's life over again…. Fortunate indeed is the man in such circumstances whose memories are mainly happy ones. He will be thankful for that store in days to come.

In this mood of reverie, then, it was an infinite relief at times to sit alone under the stars and relax the overstrained nerves under the silence and lose the sense of confinement under the vastness of the night sky. Or one might meet a friend for a talk, and we would talk quietly until midnight and then walk back through the dark corridors, with the sounds of restless and unhappy humanity coming through the workshop grilles and then up the dark narrow stairs to the cells, our boots clanging softly on the iron stairs, and so with a whispered good-night part company to our dark little cells, thanking Heaven that another day in Changi Gaol was over.

[18]

The Women

This will have to be a short chapter, because I was never in the women's camp at Changi and all I know is secondhand, what I've heard from friends who had relatives over there.

To begin with, there were about 200 white women and 250 non-Europeans, of whom about 80 were children. Some internees in the men's camp were inclined to criticise these women for having stayed, and to assert that the former government should have compelled all women to leave the country, as was done in Hong Kong. But actually 200 was a very small proportion of the number of white women in the country before the fall. Almost all of them did go away, and of those that stayed the majority were nursing sisters or volunteer nurses in the Medical Auxiliary Service and so were justified in staying, if they were willing to take the risk. As for the Eurasian and other non-European women in Changi, Malaya was their home and it would have been quite wrong to compel them to leave it. In many cases such women were allowed to stay out for quite a time, but after a time a more rigorous policy was apparently brought into force with respect to the Eurasians. The white women, who at first were in the majority, became a minority. There is no doubt that the women's camp was a heavy responsibility and that an internment camp is no place for women. One is glad to say, however, that the men's camp generally did its best for the women.

When all is said and done, however, it was a wretched life for women in Changi Gaol, much worse for the women than for the men.

A woman missed the quietness, privacy and refinements of her own home much more than a man does. The ugliness, the bareness, the bleakness of the surroundings were bound to affect the women more. Moreover, women cannot get along together as well as men. They are far less tolerant, less accustomed to mixing with all types and adjusting themselves to different types. They are also afflicted with an intense colour feeling, one of the strongest and most unlikeable characteristics of the white women in Malaya, even the nicest of them. It requires little effort of the imagination to understand how difficult social life must have been in the women's camp, particularly as the women were very varied types, some coming from very poor homes and some from relatively luxurious ones, some belonging to racial groups which, so far as their womenfolk were concerned, had no contact with the white community of Malaya in normal times. All these women had to live in close contact, share their food and other supplies, and maintain some sort of organised communal life. So far as one could gather, from echoes reaching us in the men's camp, life there at times was very trying indeed. Snobbery was evident in most detestable forms, and a strange capacity that certain types of women have for being utterly cool to others makes life miserable for everybody, while on the other hand, kindness, tolerance, patience, self-control, and gentleness were never more precious nor put to a harder or more prolonged test. The fact that there was a much larger proportion of children in the women's camp also increased the tendency to irrationality, under those conditions, where everybody was hypersensitive to noise.

[19]

The Last Six Months

So far we have been considering conditions in Changi Gaol when it was at its best, that is to say during the first 19 months. Then came an abrupt change. The investigation by the military police began, and the camp came under grave suspicion, with the result that all contacts with the outside world came to a sudden end, all fatigues, or outside gardening, and walks to the beach, etc. The cultural and recreational programme finished altogether. There was nothing in the shop, the food suddenly and seriously deteriorated, as a result of not being allowed to purchase supplementary foodstuffs. No longer were we supplied with newspapers, and the broadcasts in the front yard came to an end.

For the first time, queues of hungry people lined up for rice and kunji, and these were quickly put on the official "seconds" lists. The midday soup became a thin brew, with little in it except green vegetables, the bread from the outside bakery no longer came in, and through time the evening kunji disappeared, so that all we had at that meal was a small piece of soya bread. Even then, the outside gardeners went on working in the afternoons (inside now) and games like bridge went on so long as they were allowed (but not the recreational programme).

Gradually there came relaxation. The outside gardeners were permitted to work again, the outside firewood fatigue was resumed, shop goods began to come in again, but in smaller quantities (a little toffee or sweets and also tobacco). The evening kunji was restored, but rations remained at a comparatively low level and we really did learn what hunger was in those days. We particularly felt the absence of vitamin B and the loss of vegetable oils; there was a very marked loss of weight during this period.

The tone of the camp went down quite dramatically. People felt more depressed and dispirited than ever before. We were all living within the walls very much more than we had done and began to feel the confinement and be conscious of the ugliness and wretchedness of the place as never before. The pathological brooding became worse than ever. One noticed an apathetic, dull, strained expression coming onto people's faces. Men ceased to speak to each other in the corridors. And no indications of how long this strain was to go on for. We had given up all hope of repatriation and for all we knew we were really in Changi Gaol for the duration.

Then came a startling change in our situation. General Saito was put in charge of us, and soon after taking over came out and addressed us. He told us that it was not known why our governments has left us here so long, but anyway we would have to stay until the war was over, and in the meantime it was up to us to carry on the good work we were doing, for which he thanked us, and look after our health, until the day came when we could rejoin our wives and families. It was altogether a friendly and sensible speech.

But so strong was the obsession with repatriation even then that many internees refused to accept the general's plain statement that we were there for the duration. It so happened that at that time rumours were current of an impending move, and somehow or other these people managed to link those rumours with the general's speech. Excitement reached fever pitch when we were officially informed on the evening of the general's visit that we would shortly receive good news and that it would be "banyak, banyak baik" (much, much better). Of course this could only be repatriation. That was the conclusion to which the majority of the camp jumped, although there were some who predicted a move to Formosa or Japan.

It came as a shock and a bitter disappointment to be told that we were indeed to be moved, but not off Singapore Island, only to another camp on Singapore Island. However, when we had got over the initial shock, a sense of infinite relief at the prospect of leaving the Gaol dawned on us. "Anything for a change" was the general feeling and it was only when we knew that we were leaving the Gaol that we committed ourselves to know how much we hated it, that the repressed loathing of the place came up out of our subconscious minds.

The task of shifting the community of 3400 was no light one. We stripped the entire Gaol and left it there as we found it. All shelves, all boxes and stools, all our pots and pans and bits of string and wiring, nails and sacking went with us. It was the most extraordinary collection of junk one had ever seen. In ordinary life it would have been consigned to the incinerator, but to us at that time it meant all the difference between relative comfort and extreme discomfort. So the columns of lorries came in during four strenuous days, taking out wave after wave of the internees, and meanwhile the POWs came in while we were moving out, strict segregation being maintained during that phase, until the day came when the last party of internees left Changi Gaol and we were all in our new camp.

[20]
Sime Road Camp

Our new home was a camp adjacent to the Bukit Timah Golf Course, in the angle between the road leading to the clubhouse and Sime Road, from which it took its name, and situated about six miles from the city. The camp was originally built for the Royal Air Force and their headquarters had been there during the fighting. Apparently the Japanese were aware of that, for the camp was heavily bombed and almost entirely destroyed. Very few of the original huts had survived when we moved in, nearly all the huts having been built by POWs since the surrender. The frontline had swept beyond this area towards the end and evidences of the fighting were to be seen all over the camp, every one of the original huts remaining being perforated with holes made by bullets and shell fragments, while the concrete floors of the huts and concrete paths showed many signs of the shelling and bombing. There were two small cemeteries in the camp containing the graves of British and Indian soldiers whose bodies had been found there after the surrender, and there were also a number of single graves scattered around the camp, both British and Japanese. The Japanese graves were marked by a low white post surrounded by an enclosure of about four feet square.

Here we found ourselves in a totally different environment. Instead of being cooped up in an enclosure of twelve acres, the camp spread out over 150 acres of several low ridges and valleys, with long huts built of planks and attap and linked by concrete paths and flights of steps.

When we first moved in, these huts stood in the midst of a sea of thick lalang. The POWs had evidently been too uncertain at the tenure or had been called out on outside fatigues too often to be able to do much in the way of tidying up the camp, and some parts of the camp had apparently not been occupied for some time, so that we had a strenuous month's work cutting the lalang and making the huts weatherproof and generally tidying up.

We soon made up our minds that our friend in Changi could be forgiven for having raised our hopes unduly with his "banyak banyak baik," for it really was very much better than Changi and indeed a totally different life. True, we were worse off in certain respects. In wet weather the camp was a very depressing place for instead of permanent, weatherproof buildings we had rather ramshackle huts which were anything but dry when a "sumatra" tore through them; instead of the indoor kitchen and laundry, we had to bathe, wash our clothes and use latrines in the open air and fetch rations from distant kitchens, no pleasant duty in wet weather; and in the huts we were just as crowded as we had been in Changi Gaol. But after all there were not many wet days, and on balance we were only too glad to give up some of the amenities of Changi Gaol for the compensations offered by our new home. Above all, we were out of that arid, artificial environment of concrete and iron, and in touch with nature again. The hypersensitivity of our senses to nature when we first moved into Sime Road was a thing never to be forgotten. That first morning when we woke to see living green grass and rubber trees outside the hut, when we smelt the freshness and the scents of the early morning and heard the birdsong, when we saw the sun rise above an expanse of open country instead of over a concrete wall, was something that brought intense happiness.

> The meanest floweret of the vale,
> The simplest note that swells the gale,
> The common earth, the air, the skies,
> To him are opening paradise.

Again, to see the stars through a filigree pattern of foliage, to see the moonlight on glistering foliage, even to hear the bullfrogs after rain, a feature of Malayan life one had almost forgotten. And the open hillsides clothed with grass, the little wooded valleys on the boundaries of the camp, the rich variety of foliage in the orchard area, and the views…. Imagine what it meant to us, after more than two years in the Gaol, to have a view! In one direction we could catch a glimpse of the reservoir gleaming a dull silver with the richly wooded banks on the other side, to the west an expansive, rolling forest country culminating in the Bukit Timah ridge. Moreover we felt we were more in touch with the everyday world here, for we could see traffic moving along Bukit Timah Road and outlying houses of the suburbs where some of our fellow internees had themselves lived in happier days, and the tower of the Cathay building outlined against the sky in the far distance, and even a glimpse of the white façade of Government House half-hidden in its setting of fine old trees. It was a thrill to see these familiar sights again, after having been isolated at Changi for so long.

The sense of imprisonment was also not nearly as strong here, for apart from these wide views and the spaciousness of the place, the boundary fence was nothing more than a low wire fence which we could easily have stepped over in places had we wanted to.

There was also the happiness of walking along little sunny earthen paths winding through the grass under the rubber trees. And there were all the trees in the camp, the rubber trees, the orchard area, the semak belukar (undergrowth) in the little ravines, the distant views of the jungle and all the familiar flowering trees: flame trees, jacarandas, tulip trees, bougainvillea and many others… all the old friends of our Malay gardens were there.

Crowded though we were so long as we were inside the huts, it was at least possible for us to spread out and get away from each other. Each of the former messes of the Changi camp now found itself in a hut to itself, separated by wide spaces from any other hut, so that they became separate little communities, and we soon began to take an interest in our hut gardens and flowering gardens. After a few months some delightful little flower gardens and borders and lawns were to be seen around the huts. It was at last possible to go for a real walk: one could go for half an hour's stroll when one felt the need to get away from one's own hut, and see a different view and a different part of the camp. And it was easy to find a quiet and pleasant spot for reading.

The Japanese authorities proved helpful and reasonable in this camp, and appreciative of our own efforts to help ourselves. General Saito visited the camp frequently and our relations with all the Japanese officials were very satisfactory. We particularly appreciated the efforts of Sergeant Major Tanaka helping us with regard to food supplies, at a time when the food position outside was becoming more and more difficult. In every way it was a milder regime. The boundary fence was regularly patrolled by the Sikh guards, but patrols inside the camp were much less frequent than they had been in Changi, and apart from the officials supervising work in the gardens, we saw little of the Japanese authorities.

We had to work harder than we had had to at Changi. With all the vacant land available it became possible to undertake food production in real earnest. We inherited 16 acres of vegetable gardens in the valleys from the POWs, and we now set about digging up the hillsides, and this was done with such a will that within six months we had increased the area under cultivation to 50 acres. The whole camp represented one vast market garden. Our main crop was the sweet potato, and it is certain that this crop has never received such an intensive study before. In normal times it was eaten only by the poorer people when they could not afford to buy rice and was grown mainly for leaf by the Chinese market squatters as pig food. The potato could be separated out into at least seven distinct species. It was our main leaf vegetable but we also grew it for the tubers. Many Europeans had never tried it in Malaya before the war, and many people acquired an interest in the sweet potato and an appreciation of it that is likely to last as long as they live in Malaya.

The working hours were hard, from 9 a.m. to 12 p.m. and from 2 p.m. to 5 p.m., with half an hour's break and a mug of tea in each three-hour spell. This was a severe trial on a scorching afternoon, but the people stood it remarkably well. Actually this enforced work was a blessing in disguise: many men who had done nothing whatever at Changi now went out into the open air every day and were all the better for it. It made the time go more quickly and gave them an interest in life. For many of them, it was the first time since they had come to Malaya that they had actually worked in the soil with their hands. Rations were now discriminated, so that the full-time worker, the part-time worker and the non-worker came on to different scales (different serving sizes according to work output).

The food position did not improve, but we could not expect that it would. After about six months we ran out of cereals and substitutes to cereals, and pulses, altogether, and at times lived entirely on rice, but fortunately our consumption of green vegetables per head was very much larger than it had been at Changi, and we produced a fair quantity of tapioca and sweet potato tubers as well. Hungry though we were, it amazed us how much work we could get through on such rations and still keep reasonably fit.

There were some sensational losses of weight for a time, many people looked really alarming, but after a while this improved. On the other hand, the position in the camp hospital became more and more distressing, owing to the exhaustion of supplies of invalid foods and drugs, and the most unfortunate people in the camp were those with stomach ulcers and kindred complaints who should have been living on milk except they had to endure the misery of living on rice and coarse vegetable soup. In the main, however, people did manage to keep remarkably fit, despite their thinness and loss of energy.

Permission was given after a time to resume concerts and entertainments. Gramophone concerts in the Glen all helped to keep up our spirits. In all a very marked improvement in the tone and quality of life at the Sime Road camp. People became more sociable, cheerful; a more normal attitude was felt everywhere. Deliveries of mail greatly improved, an average of 300 letters a day in the first six months. The black market revived in full vigour, supplies of gula malaka, coffee, soya milk, eggs and palm oil resumed through the Jews, and we realised that we had been suffering from claustrophobia at Changi much more than we had previously realised.

On the other hand, the nearness to Singapore in a way actually increased our restlessness and impatience to return to our former life, and the long-drawn-out nature of the internment began to tell on us more; it dragged on and on at times and we felt as if it would never end.

Well, we have come a long way from that first topee hat of mine that I bought 20 years ago, and the well-meant warning about invisible dangers lurking in the glorious Malayan sunshine; but I think the reader will agree that the European in Malaya has come a long way too.† So what were the results of this "social experiment"? Surely this experience will colour the whole attitude of the European in Malaya towards his environment after this war; surely it will make him a less alien, restless, ruthless, exclusive element in this land, less prone to utter that slogan of cynicism and social selfishness so often heard in this country, "I'm not out here for my health," meaning "I'm out here solely to make money, and then get out." Are these anticipations far-fetched? I think not, for surely they are inherent in the capacity for a simpler, healthier, more natural, more contented life in Malaya, which the European will take out with him from his internment: the lessons learnt from deeper friendships formed, the appreciation for food, music, nature and study, the knowledge of human nature and one's own nature, the stock-taking after the complete break from our former lives, and the relief of the gift of the occasional human moment.

† [The author had several notes for the ending of his manuscript, but did not write a definitive ending. This paragraph has been put together by myself from his notes. — ED.]

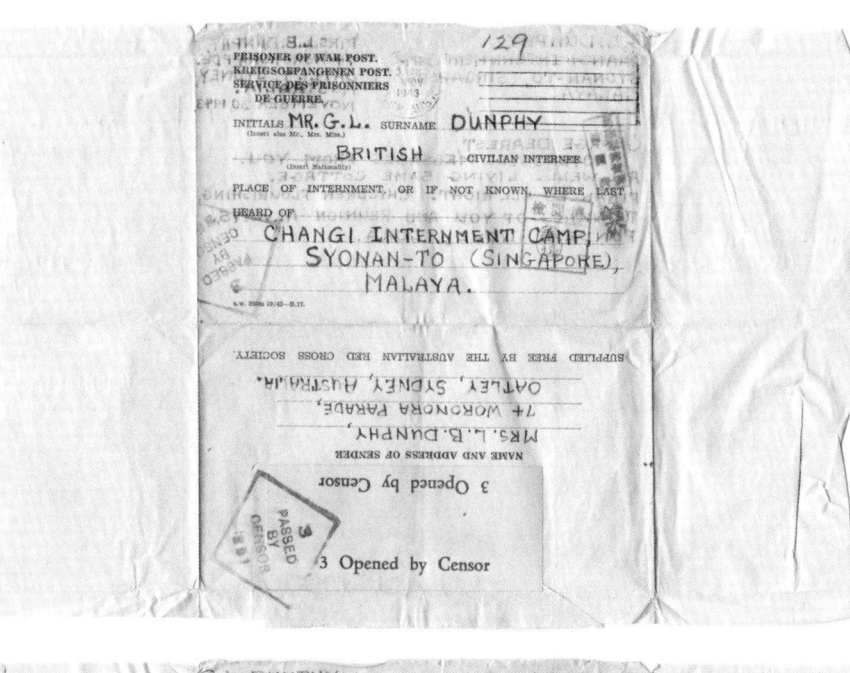

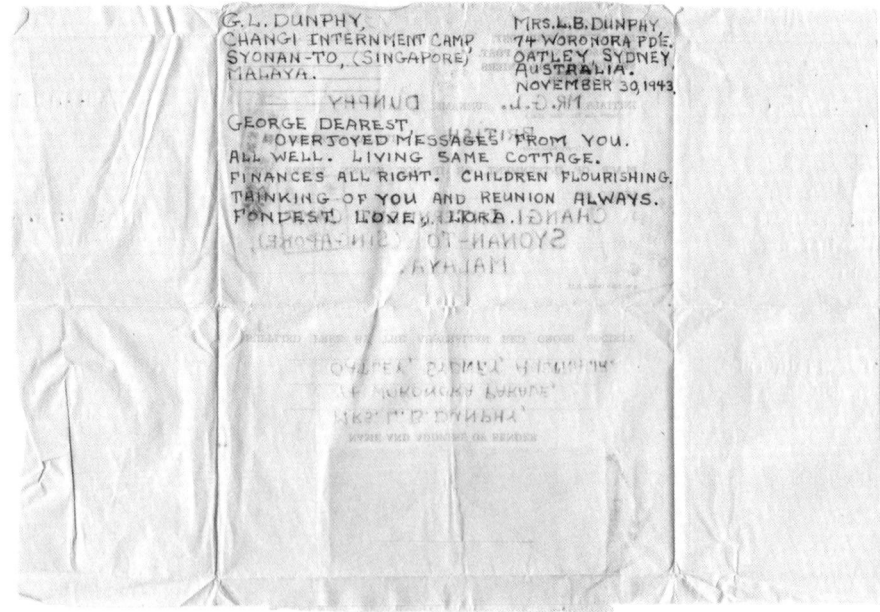

*Letter from Lora to the author, via
the Red Cross Prisoner of War Post*

BOOK II
SIME ROAD JOURNAL

November 1, 1944 Have decided to keep a diary, to give Lora some idea what our life was like in this camp. It will be a trivial, petty record, but it may be interesting to her.

November 6 The Japanese have granted permission to six of the European nursing sisters from the women's camp to work in the men's hospital. A very noteworthy and valuable concession.

We have now completed six months in the Sime Road camp. The results of hard work with the changkol are astonishing. The whole camp, which was one vast sheet of lalang when we arrived, now looks like one vast market garden, planted with sweet potatoes, tapioca, spinach, beans and minor crops such as chillies, tomatoes, mint, etc. We have now 50 acres either planted or being dug for planting, all of which we have opened up from thick lalang, except 16 acres of good valley gardens that we found when we came here. We have also 3500 papaya trees planted, and have been told by General Saito to bring it up to 10,000. The quantity of vegetables produced by the camp gardens last month was a record for the internment — 53,400 pounds. The quantity supplied by the Japanese was also a record — 49,400 pounds. So we got one-and-a-half times the standard ration of vegetables last month; but most of this was greens, and what we want now is more carbohydrates to fill our bellies.

November 8 Dr and Mrs N came back from town yesterday. They're both in comparatively good condition. There are now four left in town.

Nearly 6000 pounds of fish were supplied by the Japanese. This was an improvement on September and about 53.4% of the ration. The camp in addition bought 3000 pounds of dried fish. The October issue of sugar supplied by the Japanese was 84 ounces; the prescribed ration per inmate: salt 94 ounces, and tea 97 ounces.

Five thousand four hundred pounds of pork fat were received. This is being supplemented by our own supplies of coconut oil. The average daily shortage in the rice ration, owing to the difference between minimum and maximum weight of the rice bags, was 5.75%.

November 9 The last three European mental cases at Miyako were sent into the camp today. This is considered to be a pointer to something or other.

November 12 Another pointer! In fact an absolutely unquestionably indisputable pointer, a veritable pointer of pointers, in the opinion of the camp cranks and prognosticators. Last night the remaining five British Europeans who have been working in Singapore since the fall came into the camp. This is thought to presage a move of some sort. There are still optimists who prefer to believe in repatriation. Others talk of a move to another camp. Heaven forbid! There is a crop of stories at present about what so-and-so is supposed to have said, hinting at an impending move. In the meantime we are getting more and more impatient, and, since the spectacle last Sunday, every mutter of thunder causes us to prick up our ears.

Three hours later: I ought to erase the foregoing paragraph, the whole story now turns out to be untrue. The five in town have not come back and nobody knows how the story got around. But I shall leave it in this diary as a reminder of the extraordinary way in which rumours spread in this place. Here we are, only a few hundred yards from the camp headquarters office, and yet this completely false report remains current in our huts for several hours.

November 14 We have entered into one of those lean periods that happen nowadays owing to the fact that the actual weight of the rice sacks is less than the nominal weight. Today's ration consisted of less than a pound per head of cereals, rice, peanuts and green vegetables.

The menu is as follows:
Breakfast: coffee and peanut kunji.
Tiffin: rice and vegetable soup.
Tea: rice loaf, tea, fried spinach, pumpkin and potato stew.

This looks better than it really is; actually it is the worst menu we have had in some time in the all-important factor of bulk. All we get at tea, to sustain us from 6 p.m. to 8 a.m. the next morning, is a form of rice bread, a spoonful of spinach and a spoonful of "spread." The usual plate of kunji is missing.

November 15 My neighbour has just shown me a handful of dried chillies, which he has bought from a Jew at a price equivalent to $40 a kati (about 1⅓ pounds). Yet chillies are a local crop that can be grown in any backyard. The price of gula malaka has suddenly gone down to $18 a kati in Aldgate (the Jewish quarter of the camp).

I attended this morning the funeral of Miss Jackson, an old retired missionary of the Methodist Mission, who died in the women's camp yesterday. The end of her years in Malaya. A number of women and girls from the women's camp were permitted to come over from the women's camp to attend the service. They sat on one side of the church and the men on the other. This was the first time I had been in a mixed group of women and men since the captivity began nearly three years ago. The singing of the women affected me well-nigh to tears. During the service one of the Japanese officers in charge of the camp came in and paid his respects, bowing to the coffin.

I was struck by the following words in the burial service to our present situation: "Who shall separate us from the love of Christ? Shall tribulation or distress, or persecution, or famine, or nakedness, or peril or the sword? Nay, in all these things we are more than conquerors through Him that loved us." Fortunate indeed are those in this camp for whom these words are true. One felt a shock of surprise after the service, to see the coffin put into a lorry. But its ugliness was redeemed by a profusion of flowers. Only the officiating minister, himself an internee, was allowed to go in the lorry to Bidadari cemetery, so he had a lonely journey with the coffin. A sad end to Miss Jackson's 40 years in Malaya.

On the way back I came upon a veritable drift of yellow flowers in the grass under a small grove of rubber trees. I had never seen this plant before coming to the Sime Road camp. It is one of the most attractive wild flowers in Malaya, and the only one so far as I know that will grow in short turf, like daffodils and crocus at home. It has a tall, green stalk, about a foot high, and a flower made up of three large yellow petals which folds up into a tapering bulb, and in the morning it rather looks like a dim candle in the grass. I am told that it is a wild iris.

November 18 Today, by the order of Sergeant Major Tanaka, we are celebrating "Gardens Festival Day." All internees working in the gardens and all others doing heavy work are having a whole-day holiday; an extra issue of 250 kg of rice has been made for the gardeners; and, again by order, four pigs in the camp farm have been slaughtered for the evening meal.

More mail today. Ten thousand five hundred letters were released this afternoon and this is the largest amount of mail that we have yet had in a single batch. Moreover, it was released much more promptly than before. It only came into the camp yesterday afternoon, and here it is being distributed today. Such a thing has never happened before. Strange how some people, as soon as some little concession is made or favour shown, invariably read into it some development for our captors. The simple and natural explanation that they occasionally wish to do us a good turn seems not to occur to them. I got a letter from England written last December, nearly a year old, but some are as recent as May of this year, which is very good under present conditions.

November 19 Visited a friend in the hospital this afternoon. Saw one of the European nursing sisters on duty for the first time. How strange it seemed to see a woman in the professional nursing uniform moving about the ward. It seemed like a harbinger of our return to normal life, which we hope is near. The camp air-raid sirens sounded an alarm this morning, and we heard what we thought was a fire-fight in the direction of Johor. We only saw a few planes, flying at great height, probably Japanese. On my way back through the vegetable gardens I saw something I had never seen before: seven or eight doves together, feeding under the large leaves of the pumpkin vine. Usually one sees them only in ones and twos. I also saw in my afternoon walk a bush of the big purple Thunbergia in flower, the first I have seen in the camp, and a hedge of pink Lantana. It is remarkable what a variety of flowers are appearing in the camp now (Heaven only knows where they came from), and what attractive flowerbeds one sees outside some of the huts.

November 20 Sergeant Major Tanaka has warned us that it is becoming increasingly difficult for the Japanese to supply the camp with vegetables, because of the shortage in town, and that we shall have to rely more and more on the produce of own gardens. We are already self-supporting with green vegetables, but it is very doubtful we can keep up an output of carbohydrate vegetables (sweet potatoes and tapioca) sufficient to feed 3400 people for any length of time, assuming, that is to say, that the rice gives out and we have to feed ourselves entirely.

November 21 Another typhus victim has died; there are three more typhus cases in the hospital, making five in all. Also J.S.M. Rennie, one of the old-timers of Singapore, who came out in the first decade of this century.

This evening while we were having tea, there was a burst of anti-aircraft fire. We saw a single plane, very high, flying over the town. The Japanese were apparently caught napping, for although they had had fighters patrolling all day they had none up when this plane appeared. Moreover, the sirens were not sounded until the visitor had turned out to sea to go home. There were several unmistakable bomb explosions and the ack-ack was the heaviest we have yet seen over the town. For the first time there was also ack-ack fire almost overhead. We have no protection against shrapnel, only open slit trenches. Everybody is very excited. We have had nothing but reconnaissance raids so far, but every distant mutter of thunder causes us to prick up our ears.

November 22 Another hungry day. Our rations today consisted only of a rice and maize meal, less than a pound per man, and thin vegetable soup. For the evening meal we are to have only a mug of tea, a piece of rice bread and a spoonful of fried spinach. We are getting practically no animal protein now, the supply of dried fish being only sufficient to provide us a spoonful of fish paste once or twice a week. This is equivalent to only 5 g of animal protein per day, whereas, according to the scientists, the minimum consumption per day should be 35 g. We are thus alarmingly below the requirements of a properly balanced diet in respect of animal protein, and also fats. Yet one must admit that most of us are keeping fit and able to do a fairly hard day's work in the sun, although some people are shockingly thin. On the other hand, some men, especially in the younger categories, are keeping up their weight astonishingly well; but these are usually individuals whose work does not require them to sweat in the sun.

One of the Norwegians has brought a big bunch of Roupellia into the hut, picked from the garden of one of the Adam Park houses. It is the first I have seen since the days of freedom. One of the pleasures of life in this camp has been to see again the flowering shrubs and trees that were so familiar in one's former life in Singapore and almost forgotten within the grey walls of Changi Gaol. Seeing them again in and around the Sime Road camp has been like meeting old friends.

Who knows what is coming in this phase of internment. This afternoon we had pineapples for the huts — 16 men to a pineapple. The only fresh fruit I've had besides this, since coming to the Sime Road camp six months ago, is one piece of papaya, one or two rambutans and an unripe jambu; I also had some small tomatoes while in hospital.

November 23 "The Blue Angel" (Schweizer's lorry) came in yesterday afternoon with about 4000 pounds of maize and beans. This is only about six day's supply for the camp, but it is very welcome indeed. Moreover, the Japanese are now allowing the Neutral Agent to send in a lorry twice a month, instead of once as formerly, so we may expect more supplies shortly. There were also 300 pounds of coffee and some honey—the first we have had in some months—on yesterday's lorry, as well as cheroots, cigarettes and tobacco. Today the shop lorry was in, with more tobacco, so smokers are well-off at the moment. The honey was issued this afternoon; one tablespoonful.

Kedgeree with ikan bilis in it for tiffin today, as well as fried spinach. A very tasty dish. I got a second helping so I'm feeling really satisfied for once.

As a matter of record, to show what smokers are getting at the present stage of the internment, I may mention that this afternoon's issue consisted of 14 cheroots, 12 cigarettes and three-quarters of an ounce tobacco. Cheroots cost 25¢ each, cigarettes 10¢, and tobacco $1.50 an ounce. An issue like this comes along every week or 10 days. These are the very cheapest grades, manufactured normally for the coolie class, the cheroots being of the type which were selling three years ago at 1¢ each and the cigarettes at 10¢ per pack of 20.

Went to a concert by the Glee Singers last night. This took one back to those delightful evenings in the laundry in Changi Gaol. It was the first time we have heard this male voice choir since all recreational activities were stopped 15 months ago. Our hut quartermaster has just had a knotty problem to solve.

Our evening meal tonight has a new feature. We are to have boiled rice instead of kunji for the first time, to eat with our "vegetable hash." Shall the seconds be put on the roster for midday rice or evening kunji? Vote is solemnly taken and we decide to follow the former roster.

Four ounces of liquid gula malaka were issued today at $2. I mention this as another instance of the toothsome morsels that still come our way now and then. Overheard: "The only cheap thing in this camp is Labour at 40¢ a day," yes, 40¢ a day!

Another appointment with the dentist this morning. Rinsed my mouth out with a mug made out of a food tin and spat into a rice dish. Such is the equipment with which our dentists are working. Still, up to now they have had the essentials for relieving toothache, though not for permanent work. But while I was there a small boy came in with an aching tooth, and I heard one dentist say to the other, "Have we any anaesthetic?" The reply was, "Only a little." However they took the youngster up to the operating theatre of the hospital, and I think they gave him something or other. The dental anaesthetic now used in the clinic is made in the camp, certain drugs being made available for the purpose. Thank Heaven we have chemists among us. But medical supplies are running out, and that is one of the most urgent reasons we are praying for early release.

Also whilst at the dentist a young Japanese soldier came in, one of the camp guards; he leant his rifle against the wall and came in and waited to be treated. I was seated in the torture chair, grinned at him and he grinned at me. In that moment I saw him as he was: a simple peasant boy from the countryside of Japan, embarrassed by the situation in which he found himself. In that moment there it seemed absurd to regard him as an enemy; not a trace of racial hatred. The accursed, forced, artificial hatred that we are supposed to feel for our racial enemies disappeared and a simple human relationship took its place. But only for a moment. What a relief it will be when this is all over and we can meet these people without forcing ourselves to hate them. It is all very well to talk about hating a vague, vast, impersonal entity called "The Japanese," but when you meet an individual Japanese you find as often as not that he is a very likeable, friendly and decent sort of human being, as we have found in a number of contacts during this captivity. The saying that "war is made between governments, not between individuals" expresses a fact of human nature, although it would be most indignantly repudiated by many people in this camp.

The wages — or perhaps one should say pocket money — paid by the Japanese to internees at present are 40¢ a day for full-time workers (who put in three hours in the morning and three hours in the afternoon), so that most people have about $12 a month to spend, in addition to whatever money they may still possess after nearly three years of internment. Twelve dollars a month does not go far at present prices, and some people in the hut had to refuse their gula malaka today. But there is still a surprising amount of money in circulation in the camp. Many people have sold watches or other belongings, or have borrowed money, giving cheques to be presented after the war. The money comes chiefly from the Jews, who regard it a good investment to convert their large stocks of inflated wartime currency into securities which can be realised after the return to normal life.

I hear that the Jews had over 200 eggs on sale last night and were retailing them at $1.50 each; some days ago they were selling in the camp at $5 each. It is remarkable what the Jews manage to get in. Aldgate is a regular market for gula malaka, coffee, palm oil, cheroots and other black-market goods, and the prices prevailing there fluctuate from day to day and are well-known throughout the camp, just as if it were the produce market of peacetime in the environs of "Change Alley."

I shall have to stop. Three beds away a voice which is an extraordinary combination of the accents of Aberdeen and New York, is droning on and on, holding forth on world affairs, and it is impossible to concentrate.

Later: a further 3500 letters, mostly dating from the latter half of last year, were distributed today, leaving 9000 still in the hands of the Nipponese. Mail is now being received more frequently and in greater volume than ever before.

Two more members of the "Bodies Disposal Squad" came in this afternoon and have gone into the hospital. They are the last two out of five who were sentenced soon after the fall, of whom two died later in hospital in town, one came back recently, and these are the last. They have been in prison in town since May 1942, most of the time in the Outram Road Gaol.

Overheard an internee explaining that one of his daily jobs used to be to take the snails collected by the gardeners up to the farm, where they were cooked to feed the ducks, but now they were no longer required for the ducks, or there weren't any more ducks. The narrator wasn't sure what the true explanation was; in any case the snails are now used to feed the camp cats. This is done by a certain internee on his own initiative. Evidently the cats, like ourselves, have learned to eat strange foods.

Overheard: "Saturday tomorrow, there always used to be something festive about Saturday outside, but there's nothing festive about it here."

The camp shop is offering Chinese food bowls at $3.50 each; they cost 10¢ in normal times.

The G-string has come in again. This morning I saw a fellow with the smallest apologies of clothing I have ever seen.

November 24 Another typhus victim died today: D.J. Fraser, a planter from Selangor. This makes the sixth. A new malaria case in our hut today. This is the first we have had, apart from relapses, since the early days in this camp five or six months ago, when there were never fewer than four or five in the hut down with malaria at one time. We hoped we had got rid of the typhus when we cleared the lalang but not so. The rats are still here and come into the huts. Several of the victims have not been doing any outdoor work at all.

November 25 Sunday morning. I have just spent an industrious half-hour pouring oil onto the sections of my charpoy. This is the latest treatment for bugs.

Pigeon orchids are out today all over the camp. There is a glorious spray on an old rubber tree in the wooded ravine near our hut.

Outside fatigues report that shelter holes have been dug all along Bukit Timah Road. This looks as if more frequent air raids are expected.

November 26 After several peaceful days the sirens went again this morning; both the "Alert" and "Raiders Overhead" are being sounded. Japanese fighters buzzed about like angry wasps for two hours, but nothing happened.

Two more men died in the camp hospital today: Manning, a typhus victim, and Lee, of malaria. We seem to hear of another death almost every day now.

Gardens produced 46,000 pounds of green vegetables, or seven ounces per head per day, and also 8000 pounds of sweet potatoes.

Sergeant Major Tanaka has warned us again to take seriously the need to increase the production of food in our own gardens, "in view of the difficult conditions prevailing in Syonan and elsewhere." He has taken 100 men off other fatigues and ordered them to go into the gardens. Yet there are four fit men in our hut alone (three of them Dutchmen) who are refusing to do any work whatever, and no action is taken to compel them to work. It is only a very small minority, however, that is behaving like this.

I am rereading Middleton Murray's *Shakespeare*. I had this book for years in my former life, yet it seems as if I were coming to it for the first time, so much more receptive and responsive is one's mind in here, when one is free from the perpetual brain-fag and eye strain that made it so difficult to do any serious reading after office hours in ordinary life.

November 27 Another death in the camp hospital today.

November 28 Have bought a small supply of gula malaka in Aldgate at $15 a kati, a fantastic price by pre-war standards, when it was equivalent to just under $2, but cheap compared with the prices that were being paid in the black market a few weeks ago.

November 29 As an illustration of how hard these present conditions bear upon the older men in the camp, I may instance the case of my neighbour. He is 65. In order to avoid semi-starvation and qualify for "worker's rations" he has to turn out every day from nine in the morning to noon and from 2 p.m. to 5 p.m., to work outdoors in the heat, with an hour's break in the morning and afternoon, this last being a concession to men over 60. Within the past week he has had two bad falls on the concrete paths, caused by some failure of his sense of balance or coordination. Obviously at his age and on the present diet of rice and green vegetables, he ought to be resting in the afternoons at least. That he cannot do so without becoming a part-time worker, which means living on quarter of a pint of kunji in the morning, a pint of rice at midday and another pint of watery kunji and a piece of bread in the evening. And, with practically no other food except green vegetables (spinach, sweet potato leaves), those rations mean continuous hunger. The non-workers' rations are still worse: the same amount in the morning, three-quarters of a pint of rice at midday and three-quarters of a pint of watery kunji in the evening.

November 30 Once again we have to make another mental readjustment. After the air raid 25 days ago, a wave of optimism went through the camp. People assumed that the end really must be near at last. Hopes of being "out by Christmas" rose high. But since then we have not seen a single air raid, beyond one or two reconnaissance flights, and the disturbing conclusion is being borne upon us that the Allied forces may still be a very long distance away. The planes we have seen are said to be big bombers capable of flying 1000 miles each way with ease, and it may be some time yet before the attack on Sumatra and Malaya begins. We do not know where the British forces are or what is happening in Burma. In fact, we are completely in the dark as to the war situation in the Far East in general, and also in Europe. But one thing is certain, we are so eager for release, and time goes so slowly for us in here, that you always expect the course of events in the war to be faster than it is. It now seems wise to change one's focus again, to assume that we may still have another six months in this place, and to settle down again, after the recent excitement, back to Malay and Dutch studies and to making the most of each day as it comes, without worrying unduly about the future.

December 1 A procession of highly interesting noises this morning: big crumps in the distance, but no sirens or visible ack-ack.

A death in the camp hospital announced today: Moss, a middle-aged Eurasian. I happened to hear of his history. Lost his job and never worked again. Went out of his mind through worry in Changi and was placed in Miyako.

And now for a note that will be amusing to read in days to come, and when we may have forgotten how firmly we were in the grip of hunger in the Sime Road camp, and how trivial things assumed vital importance. We have just had a row in the hut over the question of "seconds." One school of thought maintains that the first helping of rice or soup should be larger, thus reducing the number of second helpings (which vary from one or two to 20 at each meal, and are given in strict rotation). In other words, the malcontents argue that they should get a little more rice or soup at each meal, and seconds less frequently. The quartermaster points out that if there are ten pints of kunji — equivalent to 20 "seconds" left over, it would be necessary to increase the first helping by only one-tenth of a pint if "seconds" are to be avoided, and it is beyond the skill of any food server to estimate such a small amount. That would result in unequal distribution, whereas at present everybody gets exactly the same amount, the top and sides of the tin used for ladling out of the food being carefully scraped so as to prevent any extra titbits falling on to the plate of the hungry internee.

December 3 Sunday morning. I'm so sick of life in this hut that I sometimes feel as if I shall go crazy if it lasts much longer. It is not the lack of the amenities of civilised life, for we are used to that by now, nor the cramped space in which we have to live, for I have neighbours who make that as easy as possible. No, it is the strain of having to live constantly within hearing of other people's voices, which becomes at times a form of refined mental torture. Quiet, pleasant conversation does not have this effect, but argumentative, angry, intolerant, uncharitable, grousing talk is so trying to listen to. At this moment an example: a heated argument about religion is going on between an excited Dutchman and a conventional Anglican, 15 feet away, and my hope of spending a quiet hour with my book has had to be abandoned. On my right are three Norwegian seamen who talk every night for about an hour or more after lights out. Heaven only knows what they find to talk about. Most of us find that our conversational resources have run dry after nearly three years of captivity. The chief topic of conversation in the camp at present is the technique of growing sweet potatoes, which is a chief activity. My Norwegian neighbours are markedly anti-British and never lose an opportunity of remarking that England will fight to the last American, the last Frenchman, etc. Their favourite theme is the coming decline of the British Empire and the world dominance of the United States. If there were any liquor in this camp we should see some lovely rows. As it is, one merely sits and suffers in silence. The secret of peace in this existence is to live next to people who talk little and read much. Unfortunately I live next to a group of seamen and others who are all of the type which habitually spend most of their leisure sitting about and talking. However harmless this habit may be outside, it is a damned nuisance in here. It is not the voices themselves as the feeling they give one of being constantly in contact with antipathetic personalities that is trying. Theoretically this should be a good training in tolerance. Actually, it makes one more and more intolerant of the unpleasant aspects of human nature. On the other hand, it makes one appreciative as never before of the pleasant qualities of courtesy, considerateness, kindness, patience, helpfulness and self-control as manifested by the majority in this crowded hut. And it makes one more determined than ever to try to practise these virtues oneself, so one is not likely to emerge from this experience a misanthrope. One's reactions to human nature will be much more decided and sincere than they used to be. One will respond more freely and openly to people and admirers, and avoid more deliberately and determinedly the types one has learnt in this forced community life to detest: the egotistical, the intellectually arrogant and conceited, the dogmatic and didactic, the sarcastic, the selfish, the uncharitable, the grown-up child that will have its own way or will go into the adult equivalent of tantrums. At the age of 42, and having just spent 10 weeks amid the sights and sounds of the camp hospital, one knows that life is too short and too precious to waste on such people. But the devil of it is that the qualities that evoke these responses in directly opposite directions are often found in the same personality! So after relieving my feelings by putting all this down, I arrive at the conclusion that tolerance of the bad, because of the good, is the answer after all. Moreover, while I have been writing laboriously on my charpoy, the religious argument has petered out, thank God! Yes, literally thanks to God, for this question will never be answered on the intellectual plane. So now I feel better and can address myself in a relaxed frame of mind to our Sunday tiffin of rice and vegetable soup.

Dr Lawson died today.

Later at tea-time: one-eighth of a papaya for tea. How delicious this fruit, the commonest and cheapest in Malayan tastes when we are getting practically no fresh fruit. In one's former life, one used to eat papaya as a duty rather than a pleasure, because it was supposed to be good for one, but familiarity bred indifference. Now it seems as full of flavour as the most luscious exotic fruit one has ever eaten.

Attended the Presbyterian communion service in the Church in the Glen. Wondered whether it had ever happened before in the history of the Christian Church that the bread used for the sacrament was made of rice. The preacher remarked that one of the things that had surprised him in this internment was his craving for a loaf of plain wheaten bread. I must say that while we have been on this rice diet I have had no such craving and indeed have forgotten all about real bread.

The preacher very truly remarked that one of the compensations in living the simple life, without the comforts of civilised life, is that we are bound to nature more than ever before.

December 4 Heard one internee giving another his recipe for home-made pipe tobacco: cheroots, butt ends, Sikh's beard and gula malaka.

Spent three hours cropping sweet potato leaves this morning. A scorching hot day. We sent 170 pounds of sweet potato leaves from our hut garden to the kitchen today. The objective now is to provide twelve ounces of vegetable per head per day from the gardens, presumably to meet the possible contingency of the Japanese supplies from town ceasing altogether.

December 5 Five hundred letters were released by the Japanese today. My neighbour got one from England dated April 1943, 20 months old!

Was given a pat of tinned butter — real butter, not margarine — to eat with my rice bread this afternoon. Was astonished that such things still existed in the camp. It must be nearly three years since I ate butter. It tasted delicious. Yet before the captivity we would have turned up our noses at tinned butter in Singapore. This took me back to the meals in the boarding house in Cavenagh Road 20 years ago. Since then we learnt to turn up our noses at tinned butter in Singapore, it having been replaced except for cooking purposes by the butter imported in bulk in Cold Storage, although I think the difference is really one of consistency rather than flavour. While eating my rice bread and butter with H and his companions in his hut, I thought of the preacher's remarks last Sunday evening that every meal should be a sacrament. Butter is a very precious commodity in this camp, and there was perhaps something of a sacrament of friendship in that occasion. It is curious how certain things stick in my mind. I have never forgotten an address on the sacramental view of everyday life that was heard from a fine young Anglo-Catholic priest in a village in Essex more than 20 years ago.... But in spite of this pleasant meeting at tea-time, I felt intensely depressed during the evening. That mood has been getting more frequent of late. The fact that the way in which the captivity drags on and on, with no evidence that the relieving forces are any nearer, with the certainty of another Christmas in internment, and the prospect of at least part of 1945 in this place, and not even a leaflet from the occasional raiding planes to tell us where our forces are or what is happening in the world outside, all this makes it difficult to keep up our spirits.

December 6 The first case of tropical typhus has occurred in the women's camp.

December 7 Yesterday afternoon, while tea was being served, the Japanese sent round an order to get into the slit trenches immediately, a surprise A.R.P. practice. In our hut we left our plates and mugs and obeyed the order promptly, but a hut near us took their time over it and were still filing leisurely out when an unsuspecting party of Japanese officials came round. The result was at dawn today they were ordered into their slit trenches as a punishment, and there they all were, their heads sticking up in rows along the hillside, when we woke up. And there they had to stay for an hour and a half without their breakfast. Truly a melancholy spectacle. And yet another reminder that it pays to obey Japanese orders quickly and lively.

In the women's camp a hut showed a light during the practice, and as punishment the Saturday night concert in the women's camp has been cancelled and also the usual meeting between women internees and their relatives in the men's camp next Sunday afternoon.

Our supplies of beans and peas have given out, so our breakfast porridge is plain rice and water. For tea we get no kunji but a piece of rice bread and half a pint of "hash" made by frying spinach and sweet potato leaves, and a small proportion of sweet potato tubers and other vegetables, with a little ikan bilis. Sounds dreadful but it is really surprisingly tasty. But it requires great effort of will to keep some rice over from tiffin to eat with the hash. If one doesn't, it makes for a wretchedly small meal to exist on until eight o'clock in the morning. This evening, for an example, all we are to get for tea is a piece of bread and a tablespoon of fried spinach.

Attended an open-air concert yesterday evening. Listened to one of the lesser-known Beethoven sonatas for the first time and found myself listening with real appreciation. It would have been quite beyond me three years ago. I have also heard the "New World" Symphony and Dvorak at the last two gramophone concerts and felt in myself the awakening of a new response to Dvorak. And on Saturday evening we are to have Schubert's Symphony in C minor. Certainly I am hearing more good music in this internment than perhaps ever shall hear again. But these notes do not convey the real mood in which one listens to the concerts. I find it impossible to listen with the complete detachment and wholehearted enjoyment that I hope to experience in the future, in peacetime. In here, no matter how keen my musical sensitivity, and it is still at an elementary stage, I am always conscious of depression over the apparently slow progress of the war, foreboding of starvation and worse dangers in this camp like running out of anaesthetic. Sadness over the unending separation from one's wife and children, irritation over the unpleasant human types one has to hear and see every day in the hut, and above all a feeling that there is something unreal in the peaceful atmosphere of these concerts, with such unimaginable horrors going on in the world outside.

December 8 Two years ago, at four o'clock in the morning, the first bombs dropped on Singapore and the Japanese landed at Kota Bahru. We have been hoping that our friends would realise that dramatic fitness of the day for a really convincing air raid, but alas! You would never know there was a war on, so quiet and peaceful are the sky and the Singapore countryside.

December 11 A further 2500 letters released today. I got one 20 months old, written in May, 1943, at which time, over a year after the fall of Singapore, my wife had had no news of me. There has been no air activity here for some days, and we are all very depressed. It looks as if release may still be a long way away after all.

December 12 Another 4000 letters today. This makes 60,000 since we came into this camp last May, or 300 a day.

A lorry came in yesterday, and another lorry today, but neither brought any of the badly needed pulses, so we are still living solely on rice, green vegetables, two ounces of sweet potato and tapioca from our garden today, and a very small amount of ikan bilis. Fortunately part of the rice is "cargo rice," so the beriberi menace is being staved off, but it will go hard with us if this type of rice gives out and no pulses come in. We are growing beans to provide vitamin B1 for the hospital to use, but there are not enough for all of us. However, nearly everybody showed a slight gain of weight in the monthly weighing last week, so our condition cannot be too bad. Moreover, a large proportion of internees, those doing digging and other heavy work, are getting 100 g of rice extra per day, and we are obviously benefiting.

To show the extraordinary way in which the Jews get stuff into the camp, I may mention that the quantity of gula malaka which they got in yesterday and which was on sale on the black market, was actually larger by one third than the amount which came in to the camp through official channels on the same day. As much as one dislikes the profiteering by the black-market operators and the ruthless spirit in which they exploit the needs of the internees, there is no denying that the Jews' business activities are of a real public benefit in this time of scarcity. They are distributing quantities of palm oil as well and coffee and a little of this oil makes all the difference in the kunji for a source of fat. The kunji at tea, by the way, has been absent from the menu for some days and it looks as if it will remain so. The value of the black-market retail business put through Aldgate last week is valued at $32,000.

I am reading Wells's *The Shape of Things to Come*. Intensely stimulating as always. Am also reading through a volume of Wesley's sermons actually!

December 13 The camp siren sounded the "Alert" this morning but nothing happened.

There is a general feeling of weariness, disillusionment and disappointment in the camp. The apparent quietness of this region so late in the war is hard to understand. We do not know where the British forces are or what they are doing, still less do we know of the Allied strategy in the Far East, but we had certainly expected an attack on Sumatra and Malaya before this, and judging by the rarity of raids on Singapore, that has not come yet.

A man in our hut went to the dentist with an abscessed tooth today and came back with the information that there were no more drugs available at the dentist's.

We have been told that in view of the extreme difficulty of the food position, the most that the authorities can do to supplement at Christmas will be to grant an extra 400 pounds of rice for the whole camp and 70 ducks from the farm, this apart from whatever the Neutral Agent may be able to send in.

A growing sense of the seriousness of the outlook, particularly with respect to food and drugs, is evident in the camp.

December 16 We were informed today that H.W. Long was executed on November 27, having been tried before a military tribunal and convicted of spying. A further grave warning has been issued against any contacts, no matter how slight or apparently innocuous, with members of the local population. Three internees are still in custody in town; we do not know what has happened to them.

December 18 We are to muster for roll-call morning and evening in future, and the roll-call will be taken by the Nipponese officials. Hitherto, with the exception of a few musters of the whole camp, we have had only roll-call taken by our own officials in the huts every day.

A concession has been made by the Nipponese in respect to the hours of work by the older men, who have been finding six hours a day in the sun very trying, particularly the 2 p.m.-to-5 p.m. spell, as that, according to sun time, is 12 p.m. till 3 p.m., the hottest part of the Malayan day, as we are working on Tokyo time. In future, men over 50 will turn out in the afternoon at 3 p.m. instead of 2 p.m., thus giving them a three-hour rest in the middle of the day and only two hours of work in the afternoon.

While lifting sweet potatoes in the hut garden this morning, sloshing about in the mud after a rainy night, it occurred to me that this is the first time in the lives of most internees that they have actually worked with their hands in the soil of Malaya. If they were planters in their former lives they merely supervised coolies; if they were suburbanites, they merely told the kabun what to do. Some planted their own flowerbeds, but very few did any actual digging. As for the vegetable-growing, I do not suppose there was a single man in the squad which I worked with this morning that had ever, in his peacetime life in Malaya, lifted any sort of food crop with his own hands out of Malayan soil. That is one of the most marked contrasts between European life out here and at home, the absence of contact with Mother Earth which even the city-dweller at home gets when he lifts a crop up of potatoes in his own garden.

Another 7500 letters and postcards, some of them as recent as July of last year, were released today. I received by very happy coincidence, a letter written on May 23, 1943, our wedding anniversary, when Lora had had no news of me and feared I might be dead; and the first letter dated the first week of October, written by Lora after she had had news of me, through a radio message and postcard. I have put down in this diary only matters suitable for general reading, but from now onwards I shall include private observations as well.

December 20 We hear mysterious thumps in the distance almost every day now. They may be only ack-ack practice or blasting. Our ears are now hypersensitive to thunder. In ordinary life my impression was that there was singularly little thunder in Singapore, but now I hear it every day.

I have sold my wristwatch for $175, to buy extra food (palm oil and gula malaka). I bought this watch for about $30 ten years ago on Battery Road, so I have received nearly six times the original price in the present inflated "banana money." The only foodstuffs I can buy in the black market are coffee of very poor quality (apparently only coffee grounds mixed with something else), gula malaka and palm oil.

Hobart came in today to invite me to attend a special communion for the Methodists in the camp to be held next Sunday morning; but I cannot bring myself to change my rule of never taking the sacrament.

Today has been one of those rare days when the clouds suddenly roll away and one feels a different being. I'd been feeling very dispirited for some time, feeling as if this captivity was going on forever and not able to fix my mind on reading or writing, but today, for no apparent reason, this has all gone. I have returned to my Dutch and Malay studies, read a chapter of *Shakespeare* by Murray, and am generally in a cheerful, serene and collected state of mind. Alas these blissful moods never last long.

December 22 Suzaki's and Schweizer's lorries came in this afternoon, bringing supplies for Christmas in cigarettes, a small amount of gula malaka, rock sugar and honey, and some red beans and maize, the last two items being the first supplies of pulses and cereals we have received in some time. We have had nothing to supplement the rice and flour with for about three weeks. One lorry sent in little besides cigarettes today, but the other has got together quite a varied collection of goods (including eight cases of clothing) and another lorry is expected tomorrow. They have obviously been scraping together everything they could for our Christmas, but we imagine that there is very little to be had in Singapore these days.

December 23 We have had several wet days in succession. Life here is very depressing in such weather. Rations have to be fetched in the rain along muddy paths from distant kitchens. All latrines are outdoors. One can only sit on one's bed in the hut, and there it is too dark to read with comfort, and we're dreadfully crowded. It is not so bad in the hut with a veranda but ours has none.

December 24 The lorries brought in 3000 pounds of dried fish today, a most welcome gift on Christmas Eve.

A fit of intense depression to start the day. Took a holiday from work in the garden and spent the morning doing domestic chores, airing my belongings after the rain, debugging the mattress, sweeping out my place and washing clothes. Special issues today were six ounces of gula batu (lump sugar), two spoonfuls of honey, and, from our hut garden, one spring onion and some mint and sweet basil. I also received five ounces of gula malaka, the fruit of an investment in the Adam Park fatigue. It is surprising what a difference these little bits and pieces make in helping to evoke a Christmas atmosphere. There is a very cheery spirit in the hut this afternoon. As with our two previous Christmases in internment, one thinks in advance that one will never be able to feel the Christmas spirit in such circumstances, but the power of old associations and tradition is such that when the time comes the apathy, the dreariness and the depression of the internment are dispelled like magic, as has happened this afternoon. And this time we really are sure — alas, as we were twelve months ago — that this really is the last Christmas we shall spend in imprisonment. This evening the usual church services are not to be held and we are having a united carol service in the orchard instead. A noteworthy concession is that the women are to be allowed to attend this service, although they will have to sit separately.

I have been very conscious of Lora and the children during the past week, and also my parents.

Christmas Day The carol service yesterday evening was a memorable experience. The grassy dell in the "orchard" provided a natural amphitheatre, bounded by heavy-foliaged fruit trees, opening out vistas of the suburbs of the city but shutting out from the view the ugly parts of the camp. The women sat slightly apart but close to the men, this being the first united service of the two camps that the Japanese have permitted. The choir of the men's camp sang a very good selection of carols, and the congregational singing of the Christmas hymns was deeply moving, the blend of men's and women's voices affecting us as if we were hearing it for the first time in our lives. Strange to say, the terrible hypocrisy of singing such hymns and listening to such carols in the sixth year of the Second World War did not seem to be hypocrisy at all. To the mind yes; to the soul no.

This morning I had an invitation to breakfast and four of us ate our kunji on the grass plot in front of a hut. A very pleasant change from the usual routine of eating more or less hurriedly in the gloomy, ill-lit hut before turning out to work at 7 a.m. (9 a.m. Tokyo time). Why did we never try having breakfast in the open air in our former lives?

The various area kitchens have given the camp a very pleasant surprise today. We had the most pessimistic expectations as to Christmas fare, but actually we've all had more than enough to eat, for once, and the food has been astonishingly good, considering the difficulties.

Today's menu for our area was:

Breakfast: tea, red bean and coconut kunji.

Lunch: ikan bilis, kedgeree, curry sauce, fried spinach and Christmas cake (made of rice flour, sweetened with gula malaka and flavoured with ginger and cinnamon).

Tea: sweet potato and onion hash, rice bread sweetened with honey, a spread for the bread and tea.

We have also had a little fresh fruit, a piece of papaya, a slice of pineapple, and bananas. All this has only been made possible by keeping back a small part of our rations for several days beforehand, but it has been a great treat to feed really well relatively speaking for one day.

There has been a very friendly atmosphere in the hut today. Christmas relieves the tension of this crowded and crude manner of existence in a wonderful way. This afternoon, after lunch, there was a meeting between the women and their relatives and friends on this side. This was the first time during the internment that the Japanese have allowed the women to meet friends, as distinct from relatives. Each woman was allowed to invite three men, so that some hundreds of internees from the men's camp were able to attend this party. It looked like a huge garden party, spread out under the trees and in the grassy glades of the orchard. I was a guest of Miss Rank and Miss Sadler. Lora would have been surprised at the number of our peacetime friends who were in our group: Hobart, Tyler, Gerald, Burr, Hinch, Gulland, Tipson and Cheeseman (during the day I also exchanged greetings with Le Doux, Bennett, Franklin, Charlie Jackson and others whom we knew in our former life).

The gathering in the orchard this afternoon was the happiest time I have had since internment began. It was as if the internment had been suspended for an hour and as if we had suddenly been transported back to normal life. The family gatherings, the sight of children with their parents, the women's dresses, the little touches of refinement that they brought to their hospitality, the return to the conventions and courtesies of normal life, the spirit of happiness that pervaded the whole gathering, these things made one feel civilised again, and they also made one realise with a sudden shock of enlightenment how ugly and crude and altogether extraordinary is our daily life in the men's camp. We have lived like this so long that we take it for granted, until we find ourselves in the presence of women again. I came away feeling that the party had helped me to face the remaining months of the internment, in so much as it had given me a foretaste of the life awaiting us after it is all over, and a renewed determination to get through the rest of it somehow, no matter how many hardships may be between us and freedom.

After the party I visited the hospital. Typhus, stomach ulcers, tropical ulcers, diabetes and other chronic cases. That ward is a truly tragic place at this stage of the internment. I came back to the hut and ate a huge tea, the best meal I have had in a very long time.

There is a camp concert this evening, but I have had all the gadding about I can stand for one day, so I am sitting peacefully on Mac's bed outside the hut writing up my diary.

We are now only one hour behind Sydney, being on Tokyo time, so that I and my family have been sitting down to meals almost at the same time. During lunch I had thoughts (I am almost inclined to believe) from the cottage in Bolingbroke Parade, which suddenly came into my mind with intense feeling. Lora and the children and Dad and Mother have been in my thoughts throughout the day.

It has been a good Christmas. We all feel it will be our last in captivity, and the surroundings here are so much pleasanter than they were at Changi, as is also the regime in general. The last Christmas in Changi Gaol was overclouded by the gloom, suspicion and ill-will following the Double Tenth. This time the tone of the camp has been very much better in every way. The change that has come over the place today, as compared with the usual atmosphere, is wonderful. We have all been cheered up and fortified to settle down to the routine of internment life and the waiting, alas it may be long, that we shall have to endure in 1945.

The Japanese have handed to us a Christmas message sent to prisoners of all nations by the International Red Cross, and one from the Prime Minister of Canada to Canadian prisoners; there are a few Canadians in the camp. Eight representative internees have been allowed to reply.

December 28 The camp gardens produced over 60,000 pounds of vegetables last month. Not bad for amateur European gardeners working in a tropical climate! This output was equivalent to ten ounces per day per head, for 3400 people. There was a big jump in the production of sweet potatoes and tapioca, from 6000 pounds to 17,000 pounds.

December 29 New Year messages from all the dominions, but not from Great Britain, were read out this afternoon. We should not forget that the Japanese took the trouble to receive and distribute such messages. I have received a second card from Miriam, written last April. Major, to my great surprise, is in an electrical job with free training.

New Year's Eve A dreadful day. Woke up in a state of nervous irritation. Unable to settle down to Dutch or Malay. The drone of Macrae's voice three beds away nearly drove me crazy. I felt an irrational and morbid detestation for the man. Eventually I gave up the effort to do anything useful and spent the whole day reading Bruce Lockhart's *Retreat From Glory*. By the evening I was in such a dull and depressed state that I was quite unable to go to the Sunday evening service. It was one of those black moods which used to come over me occasionally in peacetime. Evidently the internment has not cured the trouble. But what shall I do at such times when I am with my family again? Shall I again withdraw into myself and drug my mind with food and some worthless book? At any rate I failed completely today.

New Year's Day Thank God 1944 is behind us. I know what Lora is thinking this morning; I too believe that the end will come this year. But when? The Japanese (who have a festival of their own at this time) have granted a holiday today. Doesn't this sound as if we were back at school! And that is very much what it is like sometimes. However, I put in an hour's work this morning picking sweet potato leaf for our area kitchen.

January 2, 1945 Happening to notice this morning a pair of shoes belonging to a neighbour who still has some shoe polish and has been using some of it to spruce himself up for the recent festivities, it suddenly struck me what a pleasure it will be to wear a pair of well-polished shoes again. As for a hot bath… that is a luxury I have not known since the captivity began.

   Later: a wet evening. We are sitting in the hut listening to the rain come down. One of my neighbours has just passed the remark,

"Things have come to a pretty pass when the game of bridge has to be abandoned owing to the rain." That, I imagine, will be, for the reader in times to come, a startling and revealing insight on our accommodation here.

January 3 Attended a public sale of a deceased person's effects this evening. Over 50 people queued up to buy a collection of badly worn clothing, etc. I had an uncomfortable feeling of being in a pack of ghouls, myself as ghoulish as the rest. A bottle of palm oil and a small quantity of salt, gula malaka, sugar and cheroots provided the bait which drew several persons to queue up for two hours before the sale was due to open. I bought a fork, having been without one since 15.2.1942. Here is an instance of the extraordinary change of values in this camp. A friend of mine has bought a noiseless portable typewriter in very good condition for $50, which is only $10 more than the price paid for a pound and a half of sugar at this evening sale.

January 5 There is so much gloom and irritation (expressed or otherwise) in existence chronicled in this journal that I must not fail to record one of the best moments. This morning I positively enjoyed cropping sweet potato leaf. I was blissfully free from evil and malicious thoughts and able to surrender myself wholly to the beauty of the peaceful sunny morning.

Three hundred of our heavy changkollers (the 100g-extra-rice-a-day brigade) were taken out of camp this morning to open up a new area. We hope it is not to be the Dunearn Road fatigue all over again. There we worked for months, digging over a large area about two miles from the camp, and now it is being cultivated by Chinese and we are getting no benefit from it at all.

The camp has again run out of supplementary cereals, so that we are back to plain rice-and-water kunji for breakfast and rice bread for tea. To make matters worse, the black market has been without supplies for some days, though judging by past experience it will probably be in full swing again soon.

We now turn out to roll-call at 7.45 a.m. every morning Tokyo time, which means that for the first time in my life I see the sunrise every day. The evening roll-call has been dropped.

A neighbour has just read out from a book by Siegfried Sassoon a parody which expresses perfectly the internees' anticipations of life after release: "God's in his Heaven and sausages for breakfast."

Enjoyed Dvorak's Cello Concerto and Handel's "Water Music" at the gramophone concert this evening.

A pleasant surprise at tiffin today. For some unknown reason the rice issue was two pints instead of the usual one-and-a-half. It was in the form of a salt-fish kedgeree, and I got a second, so that for once I feel really satisfied. What a relief it will be after this is all over not to have to think about food, to take each meal as it comes and never give a thought to the next!

January 7 Looking at the new Dunearn Road fatigue going out this morning, it struck me what an effective scene this would make for a coloured film of our internment: the long, straggling column of several hundred white men carrying changkols, their half-naked bodies showing up reddish-brown on the grassy hillside.

One of my neighbours went into town yesterday on the sludge fatigue. This is the most unpleasant job in the camp. It involves going to the city's sewage treatment works, standing knee-deep in the treatment beds and shovelling the semi-liquid sludge into trolleys, then loading the lorry, and coming back with shirt and shorts and one's whole body caked with a substance that was originally human excrement. But this is the only fertiliser we have to keep up the output of home-grown food, except the urine which is used daily. The sludge fatigue is sought-after, in spite of its unpleasantness, because it is often rewarded with a haul of cheroots, gula malaka, etc., but yesterday they were unlucky.

Heard "Scheherazade" by Rimsky-Korsakov, in full for the first time, at the gramophone concert this evening, and at the same time watched yellow-breasted sunbirds (or flowerpeckers) hopping about in a bush of white mimosa only three feet away. This is the first time I have seen this relative of the common pink-flowered sensitive plant.

The sprays of white fluff projecting from the feathery foliage are very pleasing. Le Doux was with me.

Spent the morning washing my clothes and smearing my abominable charpoy with oil to keep down the bugs. Fried rice and crackling at tiffin. As usual I made a deal with McLeod: half my tea-time bread for his crackling.

A letter from Lora arrived today. It was written in March 1944, so I am now only nine months behind with family news. Surprised and very pleased to learn that they are now living with uncle Henry. I feel immensely gratified, but alas, I feel that uncle Henry's house is no longer the peaceful and quiet place it used to be. Perhaps it was too quiet without aunt Elsie. The children are all attending Balgowlah school, even Ronnie, who was only two-and-a-half when I last saw him. It helps greatly to get these letters, even though they are only 25 words. I wondered as I ate my tiffin what would they be having for Sunday dinner in that kitchen in 124 Wanganella Street that I remember so well. I ate only rice and red beans (the ingredients of this morning's kunji and last night's bread) and was quite satisfied. How long will this capacity to enjoy the very plainest of food last when we go back to normal life?

I am keeping this diary with a view to giving Lora some idea of what this life is like, or I should say, was like, for it will be all over when Lora reads these jottings, if she ever does. Sometimes, in the view of the absence of any sign that relief is getting nearer, we cannot help wondering whether we shall ever get out of here alive. If we only knew that relief would come in three months or six months, or some definite period, it would not be so bad; it is this uncertainty as to how much longer that is so trying.

January 8 There was a short but very loud burst of ack-ack in the north while we were having tiffin, and some people saw a single plane and heard sirens in town. This is the first sign of air activity we have seen for about seven weeks.

Weighed this afternoon. Nearly everyone in the hut has put on from one to four pounds in the last four weeks, so we can't say we're being starved. I am up four pounds. One of my neighbours, who works five hours daily in the garden, is also up four. But black-market purchases of palm oil and gula malaka have a good deal to do with it.

January 9 Seven new internees have arrived. They are Dutchmen and have been working on a suction dredge in the Palembang River for over two years. At first they were allowed ashore once a week. But during the last 14 months they never left the dredge. What a life! Before coming to this camp they spent three days in Changi Gaol with the POWs and they say the food there was excellent, including meat and fish. It appears that the POWs are faring better than we are, as we are getting no meat and only a very small amount of dried fish. Today, for example the menu was purely vegetarian, the only ingredients being rice, vegetables mostly green, and a little coconut oil.

I returned the book of Wesley's sermons to the religious library today having actually read half of them. I was curious to find out the sort of preaching that converted my Methodist forebears in Wylam and Lincolnshire. I am now starting on Bishop McConnell's book on Wesley, having already been through it once in Changi. I also returned today Niebuhr's *An Interpretation of Christian Ethics*, but I was out of my depth there, or unable to give my mind to it amid the distractions, irritations and gloomy thoughts that harass me at the present time.

My unconscious mind is still exploring the past. This morning, while studying Dutch, I suddenly remembered a particular hedge at Cottingham as I saw it one winter's day when I was ten years old. Why it should have come to mind at that moment, I cannot imagine. This sort of thing is constantly happening. Alas, so many of these early memories are not happy ones: Hull, Kingswood, Colchester....[†] I can only do my best to see that the corresponding years are different for my own children. But I do not and cannot blame my parents. They did their best according to their own lights and in a very difficult situation. I feel no condemnation (except for myself in later years) when I

† [The author's father was a Wesleyan Methodist minister, hence they moved around the "circuits" quite frequently. — ED.]

reflect on our family life, but only a deep sadness. I now begin to see how much unhappiness my mother and father have suffered, and how lacking in understanding and affection I myself have been and now it is too late.

January 10 Ack-ack again this morning, over the town this time, and fighters flying very high. The usual pessimists are to be heard arguing that it was only a practice.

My neighbour has gone into hospital. It is remarkable what a difference to one's comfort three feet of extra space makes when under present conditions.

It is Wednesday afternoon, one of our two weekly half-holidays, so everyone has been sleeping or reading in the hut. It has rained most of the afternoon and I have passed the time in reading *No Return From Bali*, a highly coloured novel, in bad light. It was a relief during tea to go outside and look at our flowerbeds and walk with bare feet on the rain-wet grass.

January 11 An exciting day. This morning we heard the siren sounding the "Alert." Soon afterwards came the "Wailing Willie" signal. One of my neighbours was most supercilious in ridiculing suggestions that we were in for a real raid. But he looked foolish a few minutes later when the crump-crump of bombs and the sharp crack of ack-ack was heard towards the north. These noises swelled in volume and seemed to spread all over the island lasting half an hour or more. It was the biggest raid we have had so far. For the first time I saw the Allied bombers, big silver planes flying very high. Also for the first time, I got into our slit trench and put something over my head as protection against shrapnel. A number of fighters were up and we heard a great deal of machine-gun fire in the clouds. Whatever else it may have achieved, this raid has had a great effect on the spirits of the internees, for we have all been getting very depressed by the apparently endless waiting for something to happen in this part of the world. We can only guess as to where the bombers came from. Most of us have resigned ourselves to being here at least another six months, and probably longer, but this is pure speculation. We are completely cut off from the outside world. We were given today a grim reminder of the price that will be paid for our freedom, for we saw one of these big bombers hit by the ack-ack and burst into flames in mid-air. The horror behind that sight has been haunting my mind today. And we also saw a Japanese fighter go down in flames. When will this insensate savagery end?

In the evening I listened to Schubert's "Unfinished Symphony" in the Church in the Glen and watched the clouds drifting across the quiet sky. What a contrast!

January 12 The siren sounded the "Raiders Overhead" again this afternoon but nothing happened.

January 13 The rice issue today is the lowest it has ever been. The amount of rice and rice flour for the 900 men in our area of the camp is 730 pounds. General Saito has done his best to combat the practice of sending us bags of rice containing less than their nominal weights, the effect of which is to reduce our rice ration by 10% to 20%, but he has not succeeded.

I came across an extraordinarily prescient comment on the Japanese by Sir Stamford Raffles in Emerson's *Malaysia* today. In a lecture delivered in Java 130 years ago, Raffles spoke of "the stationary nature of Chinese society," whereas in comparison, "the slightest impulse seems sufficient to give a determination to the Japanese character which would progressively improve until it has attained the same height of civilisation with the European." That was in 1815, and now in 1945 I see bomber and fighter aeroplanes built in Japan and manned by Japanese airmen flying over the former European stronghold of Singapore, Raffles's own creation.

January 14, Sunday There was more ack-ack this morning, directed at a single plane which was presumably on reconnaissance. For the first time shrapnel fell within the camp and one man had a very narrow escape. This danger is taken too lightly, but in truth there is practically nothing we can do, as there are no materials to construct covered shelters and the attap roofs of the huts give no protection. We are advised to contrive head-cover with mattresses or something of the sort and are warned that the hospital is so desperately short of drugs that it cannot cope with the large influx of air-raid casualties. But so far scarcely anybody has taken this precaution during raids, probably owing to a belief that this is of very little use.

I have devoted the last three days to a concentrated attack on Emerson's *Malaysia*. Although the deep cleavage between past and future affected by the Japanese occupation relegates this work to the sphere of history, it is intensely interesting to read at this time — what we hope to be the final phase of the war in the Far East — as showing the extreme diversity and complexity of the problems that will have to be faced in Malaya after the war.

One of my neighbours is having a miserable day with a swollen face caused by an abscessed tooth, and the camp dentist has no more anaesthetic for extractions. This is one of the situations you don't think of when you enter upon internment.

January 16 My neighbour's gumboil burst just as he was about to enter the dental clinic. A direct intervention by Providence.

The camp has bought a goat and three kids to provide milk for hospital patients. The price was $3000 (know I have not had an extra nought by mistake — $3000!).

The rice issue today has set a new low record.

We are faced with a serious menace to health. No more "cargo rice" is available and other foodstuffs on which we have relied in the past to give us the B vitamins, particularly beans and groundnuts, are either extremely scarce or unobtainable, so that serious epidemics of beri-beri and pellagra must be expected if the position does not improve. The probability is that it will actually get worse as the war becomes intensified in this region. We believe that the Nipponese officials in charge of the camp are genuinely doing their best but that conditions outside are extremely difficult. If one allows oneself to think about it, the remainder of the internment looks like being a dangerous period, particularly if one is in a weakened condition already. But one lives for the day and tries not to think about the seemingly interminable period that lies between us and the joy of freedom.

I ate raw sweet potato roots and raw spinach today. Hobart told me that in their hut they are eating raw sweet potato leaves every day. I go to bed very hungry every night now and as a result dream most vividly, usually unpleasant dreams, but on the other hand hunger so far has not prevented me from sleeping fairly well.

January 19 Lorinne is eight years old today. I only know the date because Lora mentioned it in a letter written on January 19 last year. I still know only the months in which Georgie's and Ronnie's birthdays fall, not the dates. Lorinne has been in my thoughts today and I got out the picture of her hugging the big doll given to her by aunt Elsie which I like so much.

It has been a bad day, culminating in a fit of nerves at tea-time in which I was absolutely miserable. I keep wondering what I shall be like when these fits come on me when I am with the family again. At least I have more self-control than I used to have. It may be that the cause of these moods is partly physical. Good food, interesting work and a variety of other interests should help, whereas the monotonous, squalid, irritating existence in this hut is enough to cause depression.

Schweizer's lorry brought in about 2000 pounds of papayas and the same quantity of bananas today. I record this as a reminder of the way in which he is constantly trying to help the camp. But these supplies don't go far when distributed among 3500 people.

Some people in the camp are still feeding comparatively well. The members of the charcoal fatigue, which works outside the camp, are able to buy all the cheroots, gula malaka and coffee they want. They keep themselves in funds by retailing part of their purchases at a high profit. A Norwegian seaman who lives near me today bought four fresh eggs from the black market at $5 each. He is a member of the poker school which meets beside my bed to my annoyance and in which the players readily lose amounts ranging from $10 to $70 in one evening. And this after nearly three years imprisonment! Where the money comes from is a mystery, particularly in the case of the merchant seaman.

January 20 Heard a work by Tchaikovsky and Beethoven's First Symphony at the gramophone concert yesterday evening. My enjoyment of classical music is unmistakably improving.

We have been granted a half-holiday today to celebrate some anniversary or other. How like being back at school it is!

January 22 An alarm today, but nothing happened.

Some cases of a more severe malaria than that met with hitherto have occurred in the camp, and persons possessing mosquito nets are warned to get inside them by 10 p.m. Unfortunately many internees, including myself, do not own a mosquito net. Not a pleasant situation to be in, to be living in a malarial area with no mosquito net, practically no drugs, and a diet which makes recovery from sickness difficult. But so far I have been lucky with regard to malaria, although plagued by mosquitoes in bed at night.

I have just finished the second reading of Aldous Huxley's *Ends and Means*, which I read for the first time in 1938. Certainly one of the outstanding books I've read during the internment. A book of this quality, which makes one think and lifts one out of this squalid and petty life in the hut, is a great boon.

January 23 I actually saw a red rose in bloom this morning. I did not think there was such a thing in the camp. In the same hut garden there were also the finest specimens of the pagoda flower, a native of Malaya, that I have ever seen. I was also able to observe closely for the first time the colouring of one of those brown lizards, which I happened to see in a sunny patch in a flowerbed. Its back was a beautiful dull brown with black markings, like a piece of old damascene work. (I mention these trifles to show how different our environment is in this camp from what it was in that abominable Gaol. Here one can have rare moods of real happiness, such as were felt when strolling back from the library this morning.)

January 25 Last night, a fine, moonlit night, we had our first night alarm, but nothing happened. The sudden wailing of the sirens out of the darkness brought back memories of Singapore three years ago.

January 26 The siren sounded again last night, but I slept through it. A member of the poker school which meets near my bed announced today that he was eating six eggs a day. This represents an expenditure of $900 a month. So there are still some people in the camp managing to live very well at a time when the diet is as bad as it has ever been. This particular individual is a mystery. He is an English Jew who was in Gaol for fraud before the fall of Singapore and was therefore, presumably, without funds. Now he appears to have an inexhaustible supply of money.

A single plane flew over this morning and was fired on. We are at last beginning to feel that something is happening in this region.

Book reading: *Crome Yellow*, Aldous Huxley.

January 30 The blue flag (preliminary air-raid warning) was hoisted in the camp this morning, and we think two of our planes flew over, but nothing more happened.

January 31 Dreary weather. We have had a succession of wet evenings and this afternoon we are sitting in the hut listening to the patter of the rain on the attap roof.

Ten more huts are to be built for 400 new internees, said to be coming in the near future. Who are they?

The Aldgate black market has little to sell these days. I must admit that, doing only one-and-a-half hours' work, I am not hungry on the present rations, although they include practically no animal protein. Yet I am expending nearly as much energy as I did in normal life when I spent the day in the office and took no exercise beyond a leisurely stroll in the evening. I know now that I need a very much smaller quantity of food than I used to think was necessary in a sedentary life.

Some excitement has been caused by an order from the Japanese to supply lists of (a) all internees over 65, (b) all under 65 who are "permanently sick," (c) families. It would indeed be surprising if repatriation for these categories came at this late date, long after we had abandoned all hope of it.

I am afraid the really significant moods, those which will show in days to come how one really felt during this internment, are rarely entered in this journal, partly because I am often too bored and apathetic and too sick of it all to make the necessary effort. Yesterday afternoon, for example, between 4 p.m. and 5 p.m., the hut suddenly became absolutely unbearable. Yet, being only 2 p.m. by the sun, it was too hot to sit outside. Later I fled to my favourite corner in the Church in the Glen, by the white mimosa bush, looking across to the grassy slope on the other side of the ravine, and, as always, felt an immediate and blissful relaxation of tension, so that within a minute or two, after having been totally unable to settle down to reading or study in the hut, I was happily engaged in reading aloud from the Jawi version of Luke's Gospel. Soon I was driven back to the hut again by rain, but the few minutes outdoors in a quiet place had made all the difference.

February 1 Today we had the biggest raid so far. Over 90 bombers came over. It was an incredibly lovely sight. One hates to use that word of bombers, and yet those formations sailing serenely through the blue gulfs between the masses of white cloud and gleaming bright silver in the sunlight were lovely. I have never seen anything more exciting and stirring in my life. Fortunately there was no bombing anywhere near the city. The general comment is, "I wish we knew where they came from!"

February 2 The siren sounded again this morning as a single plane flew over, presumably on reconnaissance.

Greatly enjoyed a symphony by Bizet at the gramophone concert yesterday evening. I find myself looking forward to these concerts these days. We usually have them on Mondays, Thursdays and Saturdays. I should certainly not have been able to listen to so much classical music a few years ago, but I imagine it will be a regularly recurring need in the future.

February 3 A reconnaissance plane was over again this morning.

Book reading: *Wesley*, by Bishop McConnell. I've been trying to understand Methodist beliefs, traditions and history since these things are part of my personal heritage and I have hitherto known very little about them.

February 6 Bad news today. By order of the Nipponese High Command, the rice ration is to be cut by 20%.

Continued proximity to the Glasgow-Bronx hybrid, Macrae, otherwise known as "The Black Market King," is driving me nearly crazy. I sometimes wonder if I shall ever be perfectly sane again after the strain of this life in the hut. Nearly three years with no privacy whatever!

Book reading: *Guns and Butter*, by Bruce Lockhart.

A miserable wet Singapore evening and I'm trying to study Jawi.

February 8 Schweizer sent in today 4000 pounds of maize, 1300 pounds of red beans, 1800 pounds of dried fish, 900 pounds of noodles, eight bags of coffee and ten tins of honey, besides smokes. Blessings on him! A most timely contribution.

Can't I write about anything in this existence except food!

February 9 The monthly weighing today showed nearly everyone down several pounds.

An official notice states that books are being returned to the library with batches of leaves torn out, presumably for toilet paper, and this at a time when our scanty stock of books is already decreasing from three years' wear and tear.

A friend of mine has sold his watch in Aldgate. It cost him $50 a few years ago. The price he got for it here was $1000, less 10% to the broker.

An unforgettable moment of insight and illumination came at about 7.30 p.m. this evening, as I was sitting on the concrete steps overlooking Hut 129-A. I felt like Christian when he reached the top of the hill. Everybody else was discussing the new rice rations.

February 10 The new scale of rice rations came into force today. The non-worker gets six ounces of boiled rice at midday, the main meal of the day. Part-time workers get a little more, full-time workers twice as much. There are small extra allowances for woodcutters, charcoal-burners, heavy changkollers, construction workers and a proportion of the gardeners. The hours of work for those not drawing these allowances are reduced: they are now 9 a.m. to 11 a.m. and 3 p.m. to 5 p.m. The heavy workers will still turn out six hours a day. The Nipponese have warned us that further gradual deterioration in the food position must be expected. Evidently we are now entering upon the most dangerous phase in the internment.

A reconnaissance plane flew over today, the first for five days.

The weather continues to be miserably wet in the afternoons and evenings.

My neighbour Macrae has come back from hospital, so I shall no longer enjoy the comfort and convenience of being able to use his extra floor space.

The black market is again getting in large quantities of gula malaka ($25 a kati), and palm oil is also coming in.

February 11, Sunday There was a muster of the whole camp, grouped according to nationalities, this morning. Twenty-five nationalities (including the dominions) were represented. During the roll-call the sirens sounded, a single plane flew over, and we heard cannon fire in the clouds.

With their shirts on, hiding their thinness, the majority of internees looked quite healthy. I am sure that a non-medical man, seeing them for the first time, would not have noticed any signs of ill-health or malnutrition. And yet there is no doubt that by orthodox medical standards we are seriously underfed in respect of calories, protein and vitamin B1.

The camp presented a striking picture after the roll-call, with long lines of internees streaming down and up the valley slopes on their way back to their huts.

Four p.m.: How many times in this internment have I wished I could sketch! I've just seen, silhouetted on the bank above our hut, the gaunt form of my neighbour X, a senior officer of the M.C.S., industriously searching in the sweet potato beds for the dead leaves to put in his pipe.

Book reading: *In the Steps of St Francis*, by Ernest Raymond. Very fine.

February 12 More bad news! The Nipponese have informed us that there will be a further cut in the rice ration next month and yet another cut in the following month. They have also stated that within "a few months" they may not be able to give us any rice at all and that we shall have to live solely on the produce of the camp gardens. There is to be a further comb-out of fatigues so as to put every available man into the garden. The fat ration has been cut by 35%, sugar and salt by 25%. The petrol allowance for the camp lorries has been reduced from 600 gallons to a nominal 20 gallons a month.

February 16 The fourth year of the captivity begins today; we are all utterly tired of it. The community in our hut continues to be admirably patient and cheerful on the whole, but it is very trying not knowing how much longer it will last. For myself, I must confess I feel apathetic, listless and disheartened, but I try outwardly to be as cheerful as possible.

February 22 Wet morning. We are sitting in the hut; I do not remember such a wet February in Singapore. Feeling utterly fed up. Very little air activity since my last entry in the diary — only an occasional reconnaissance. We simply do not know what is happening. It is extraordinary how completely cut off we are from the world outside our boundary fence, even from the city five miles away. My black moods continue. I cannot purge my system of the hatred, disgust and humiliation engendered by life in that cell at Changi. Indeed, the feeling aroused by continual contacts with aspects of human nature that I dislike have become such an obsession that I find constructive, impersonal thinking most difficult. However, yesterday evening I was lifted completely above the plane of prison camp life by a fine concert by the camp choir. Beethoven's "Creation Hymn," the "Eriskay Love Lilt," "The Road to the Isles," Mendelssohn's "On the Lagoons" and three haunting Russian songs moved me deeply. On the way to the concert I overheard someone asking one of the "Asia Boys," a very crude specimen, whether he was going to the concert. His reply was, "Why the hell should I go to hear them? Howlers! I had to put up with their howling for two years in Changi and I don't want no more of it." But there were other "Asia Boys" at the concert, obviously enjoying it. It is impossible to generalise about them. There are some very decent fellows among them.

A reminder to the future: I have just heard Doc Byron, our quartermaster, utter his usual midday call, "Come and collect your saline, please." This saline drink is issued to those whose work makes them sweat freely.

Tiffin today: rice with potato and papaya soup, precious little of either.

Outside a Straits robin is singing sweetly after the rain. I am about to read another chapter of Lin Yu Tang's *My Country and My People*. Life is not so bad after all.

February 25 Sunday afternoon. A raid yesterday by about 100 planes, evidently carrying incendiary bombs. Five huge fires and several smaller ones could be seen along the southern skyline, where the city lies (hidden from us by low hills), and a pall of thick black smoke stretched for miles, reminding us of the last days of the siege three years ago. This morning a reconnaissance plane came over. One fire is still sending up a thick pillar of smoke. The raiders again were four-engined planes, so they may have come from 1000 miles away, and we still have no evidence that the relieving forces are any nearer than that. What would we not give to listen to BBC bulletin! This feeling of being cut off from the outside world, and not being able to do more than make blind guesses as to how much longer we shall be here, is one of the hardest things to bear in this internment.

The food is getting worse, as we are now solely dependent on the camp gardens for vegetables. The outlook is considered by the Nipponese to be so serious that even boys of ten years and upwards have been ordered to work in the gardens in the mornings. We are digging up an area on the golf course outside the camp and planting it with tapioca, which takes eight or nine months to mature. Pray Heaven we are not here to eat it!

Hinch is in hospital, having had a serious abdominal operation. Gerald Summers is also there with nutritional diarrhoea, which you cannot get rid of on this coarse diet. My neighbour McLeod is in hospital again with stomach ulcers. He cannot digest rice at all, so I give him my bread and eat his rice. I keep well but am very easily tired. I'm rather worried as to whether I am physically capable of taking on the strenuous work that awaits me immediately after release.

I am continually haunted by the thought that I shall have to stay in Singapore while the children are growing up and never see them again except during the hoped-for leave after internment and thereafter every three years or so. Moreover, Lora may not be able to come here again until they are older. I see ahead an endless succession of Sunday afternoons as dreary and melancholy as this one. All my interests lie in Malaya, but I have this longing to be with my family. Shall I ever be able to do good work again, with this inner conflict going on? And what further sadness will this problem mean for Lora? I long to spend the next five years in Sydney but do not see any chances of this being possible. I shall have to talk it over with Lora when I go to Sydney on leave. But when?

Book reading: *My Country and My People*, Lin Yu Tang.

February 28 This evening we actually had a little fresh fish.

March 1 Another reconnaissance plane over this morning. They are coming almost every day now and are sometimes met with no opposition whatever, but they are still very large, long-range machines and there is still no evidence that the war has come any nearer to Singapore, on land, at any rate. This waiting seems interminable.

There is now very little to be had in the black market. Some coffee is being sold at $35 a kati. No palm oil has come in for some time. I am living solely on the camp rations, except for palm oil.

March 2 After writing the lament above, two tins of palm oil came to the hut from a black-market operator yesterday evening. What a queer spectacle, 80 men eagerly queuing up for half a pint of this yellow, unpleasant-smelling, messy liquid which would have revolted us in our former lives! But it is precious at the present time, when our diet is very deficient in fats. Moreover, all we get for breakfast is a watery rice porridge, a very poor meal on which to start a morning's work in the gardens, and a teaspoonful of palm oil added to it makes a great difference.

I saw a completely new bird yesterday evening in the white mimosa bush. About the size of a wren, whitish-grey breast, brown back and very handsome bronze-red patches on the back.

I am reading *The Martyrdom of Man* with great appreciation but there are so many interruptions and distractions in this life that I get through very little reading. Only two evenings a week are free, as I go to church on Sundays, gramophone concerts on Mondays, Thursdays and Saturdays, and have a regular engagement on Fridays.

Later: A raid by 55 planes this morning. We watched them flying in groups of different sizes on a course to the north of us. A great deal of ack-ack was sent up.

March 3 Three significant items of news:

A. An order has been issued that all jewellery in the camp must be declared.

B. No more petrol is to be supplied to the camp lorries, so a special "hauling gang" is to be formed. Carts have always been hauled by human draught animals during the internment, so this new order presumably means that the lorries will have to be hauled as well. This was what the POWs were doing with their firewood lorries at Changi when we were there, but they had a much bigger supply of strong young men than we have, and we were getting much more and better food in those days. We are wondering whether this means that Suzaki's lorry and Schweizer's lorry, which bring in smokes, foodstuffs (to supplement the Japanese rations) and other necessities, will have to be hauled from town, a distance of six miles.

C. The flowers which have given us so much pleasure in this camp are to disappear. All flowerbeds and grass plots in front of the huts, where we sit in the evenings, are to be planted with vegetables forthwith, by Nipponese order. There is no doubt they are taking the food position very seriously indeed. There is a three-month supply of rice in the camp, but a large influx of new internees is expected shortly.

One forty-five p.m. after lunch. F.K. Wilson, propped up on his camp-bed six feet away, has been reading aloud extracts from a book on psychology for the last half-hour, while I have been trying to study Dutch. Shall I ever sit in a quiet, empty room again!

March 4 Today is the 1111th day of internment.

March 6 When breaking up a piece of new ground outside the fence yesterday, the graves of eight soldiers were found, marked only by the mounds and the steel helmets of the dead men. There are two other small cemeteries inside the camp where men who fell in the fighting over this area are buried.

March 7 The Nipponese have enquired whether any internees wish to sell jewellery at the market price.

A notice read out today reminds us that we are reduced to living like savages. Some internees, it appears, are using leaves and grass at the flush latrines, and this practice must stop, though it baffles the imagination to see how the camp police can enforce this rule during the hours of darkness. One of my secret fears is that I shall run out of toilet paper and have to acquire the bottle-of-water technique.

Monthly weighing today: I'm down two pounds. I now weigh 138.

March 8 Schweizer delivered today 2000 pounds of dried fish and 300 gallons of palm oil.

March 9 Food report for February: 14,800 pounds of fish (10,500 pounds from the Japanese), 72,000 pounds vegetable from the camp gardens, 9200 pounds of papayas from camp gardens. The Japanese supply of vegetables, which had been sent in three times a week, ceased, as also did the six pints of buffalo milk a day which they had been supplying for the children. The petrol supply was cut by two-thirds.

Book reading: *The Martyrdom of Man*, by Winwood Reade.

The rice rations have been cut again. Four-hour workers, of which I am one, a cut from 17½ ounces (nominal) per day to 10½ ounces. Part-time workers 8½ ounces, nonworkers and women 7 ounces.

Three cows are to be bought by the camp at $16,000 each. The Nipponese Red Cross promised to refund the money a month hence. Some postcards posted in Sumatra last September (six months to travel 500 miles) were delivered to the camp today.

My neighbour McLeod has gone into hospital. He is going downhill, being unable to get a proper diet for his stomach ulcers.

March 10 Saturday evening. Raining. I have made another mental readjustment. I have decided not to allow myself any more cheerful assumption that this is almost certainly the last year. I am not going to be unsettled anymore by foolish hopes, speculations and rumours. I've made up my mind that the remainder of the internment is going to be an increasingly hungry and miserable time. I am going to carry on with Malay and Dutch as far as possible. I'm going to try to suppress impatience and restlessness and settle down to the routine with all the resignation I can muster. The one consolation in our present situation is that if we have to endure semi-starvation some time it may be necessary to give us home leave immediately after release. One thing is certain, if the food position in Singapore is as serious as it is in this camp, thousands of people will die of famine if the recapture of Malaya is delayed much longer. Why is it so long in coming, we cannot imagine.

A notice read out while I was writing the words above stated that Sergeant Major Tanaka has told the Men's Representative that further cuts in the rice ration must be expected and that by August the rice stocks may be entirely finished, so we are warned to plant all the food crops we can. Schweizer today sent in maize, barley and red beans, and, as usual, a small quantity of honey. His help is invaluable.

March 11 Sunday 1 p.m. Rain all morning. Tiffin: vegetable soup and half a pint of rice (a cupful). Smokers much cheered by an issue of four ounces of shag from Schweizer. Have swapped mine for the next issue of sugar. I'm reading Kirkby Page's *Jesus or Christianity*. Am making a practice now at mealtimes of imagining myself at table with Lora and the children, as I hope to be again some day.

March 12 Minor raid today with incendiaries. About 16 planes. But these raids by long-range bombers no longer cheer me up. The only thing that interests me now is when are we going to get out?

The weather continues wretchedly wet and chilly. So far the hut has taken the new rice ration with admirable cheerfulness. I am trying to keep up my Dutch and Malay. But life really is dismal and bound to get worse.

March 13 The camp medical authorities advise us that on our present diet we should not waste energy by walking for the sake of exercise or by visiting in distant parts of the camp but should rest as much as possible, preferably lying down.

March 15 Three p.m. in the hut. Raining again. An extraordinarily long spell of rainy weather. We've actually had rain every day for 37 days.

March 17 Sergeant Major Tanaka has given yet another proof of his genuine keenness to keep up the food supply as far as possible. He has arranged for a supply of tapioca to be supplied by the Nipponese, so that heavy workers will receive seven ounces per day and others one-and-a-half ounces. The "heavy changkoller" gang is now planting a new area of 23 acres with tapioca outside the boundary fence, and this will be invaluable if we are still here in six months' time.

Book reading: *Secret China*, by Kisch.
Saturday evening again; how the weeks fly by!

March 18 Sunday afternoon. Raining. Eaten nothing today except a small amount of rice, maize and palm oil. Oh for a Sunday tea with my family! Trying to read Jawi (St Luke's Gospel) with the poker school on one side and a discussion on the technique of growing sweet potatoes going on the other side. What a life!

March 22 We have learned to recognise the deep drone of our four-engined bombers. Reconnaissance planes flying over yesterday and today were spotted at once by the sound. It seems a long time since the last raid, and for some days past we have not heard troops singing on the march on the roads around the camp, so everything is very quiet. We carry on with the daily routine in the gardens, enjoying every mouthful of our plain and scanty food, do a little reading or play bridge after tea, and wait for the end. My own guess is another six months. I indulge in a lot of daydreaming about the future, particularly my return to Sydney, but have a real fear that these years of inactivity will make it very hard to start again professionally. I have intensely realistic dreams, unusually horrid ones, presumably as a result of going to bed on an empty stomach.

Book reading: *Poets and Prophets*, Andre Maurois, and *Twice Born Men*, Harold Begbie.

Since January our chaps have dug and planted 20 acres at Watten Estate, on the golf course and outside the fence adjacent to the camp. Good going for white labour!

March 23 There has been a sudden influx of palm oil and everybody has laid in a stock. I actually now have six pints in hand, having received a loan with which to pay for it at $8 per half-pint. But it is worth it, for it adds largely to the calories in our diet and in fact makes all the difference between hunger and a tolerably satisfying meal. Here I am writing about food again! I am in danger of letting it become an obsession.

March 25, Sunday About 700 new internees arrived today, mostly Jews and Eurasians from Singapore. About two-thirds are women and children. After the comfort of their own houses they now find themselves in attap huts which are, without exaggeration, no better than the poorest sort of cattle shed, with an area of floor space per man two feet eight inches wide. These huts have been built entirely by internees in recent weeks. This influx probably means shorter rations all round, but it has at least broken the monotony and given us something fresh to talk about. The camp is buzzing with excitement and there is intense curiosity as to the conditions of life outside. It is pathetic to see the children, neatly dressed, who have suddenly been brought into captivity. I thank God again that our own trio are far away from all this. As I write these words a new internee has come into the hut to look up friends. Here's an elderly Eurasian, dressed in a white suit, with topee and shoes, and it is extraordinary to see this typical figure of peacetime Singapore greeting half-naked internees, sitting on camp-beds or stools in the crowded hut. The men whom he is greeting are his former European superiors in the Singapore Municipality, and it must be a shock to him to see how we are living. Actually it is not half as bad as it looks, once you get used to it!

March 28 More internees arrived today. They are Singapore Eurasians who went to "New Syonan," the land settlement at Bahau. They seem glad to be here.

March 30, Good Friday An air-raid last night. Huge fire in the south. More internees from Penang arrived today. The camp population is now well over 4000. The Nipponese supply of vegetables from town has been resumed. I hear that the children in the women's camp, whose rice ration is just over six ounces a day, are dreadfully hungry, and the mothers, who themselves receive only seven ounces, are going short for the sake of the children. I myself am not feeling hungry on a diet of 10½ ounces of rice or other cereal, a pint of vegetable soup, an ounce of dried fish and two teaspoons of palm oil a day. Yet I am doing four hours light work a day in the garden.

Book reading: *Arctic Adventure*, by Freuchen.

Today and Easter Sunday are holidays. I have a feeling that there is a picnic today at Manly. I am now at the lowest level of depression I have ever known in my life. The usual afternoon rain is blowing up. A most extraordinary spell of rainy weather. Nearly 60 days on which some rain has fallen every day, and lately every afternoon has been wet.

I am getting clear sensations of giddiness when lying down. Probably deficiency in my diet.

All the talk is about the Red Cross parcels which have arrived in camp. The war has been completely forgotten.

April 1, Easter Sunday A united service for the men's and women's camps is to be held in the orchard this evening, by permission of the Nipponese. I am in no mood for it and shall not go. This afternoon, sitting in the hut, memories of the children at Mount Rosie (only three miles away) have been coming back with overwhelming sadness.

The new internees have been eagerly questioned about life outside. From what they say, the inflation of the currency has gone so far that fantastic, incredible prices rule for all kinds of goods, including local produce. One hears of rickshaw coolies pulling out rolls of $10 notes, and so forth. To buy a day's supply of vegetables, one takes $30 or $40 to the market. A bedsheet costs $150, a bicycle $2000, a refrigerator $20,000, and so on. Nobody can live on his salary, and people are apparently existing by selling their personal belongings one after another. How long can this go on? One cannot see how the labouring class manages to live at all, but an elderly Jew said to me: "There are no coolies any more, only towkays." There seems to be very little business, the only imports coming from Java, but a lot of buying and selling of houses and land is still going on. With regard to events in the outside world, the new internees seem apathetic and indifferent. The war has gone on so long that they have largely lost interest in it and have no hope of an early release. No doubt they have been too preoccupied with the problems of everyday personal and family life under present conditions to pay much attention to what is going on in the wider world. At any rate, they can tell us very little about the progress of the war, but from what they do say I begin to feel horrible fear that we may spend another Christmas in this camp after all. If we do not die of famine before we are out of this we shall be lucky. One is conscious too of the unending strain and anxiety that this must mean for Lora and perhaps for my Father and Mother too. I begin to realise more and more, as I grow older, that my parents care for me more than I knew, and that I have been cold and unresponsive towards them.

April 3 I was invited to a coffee party outside the area hospital last night. Now that I drink coffee only rarely, the stuff acts on me like a potent drug. I was in a queer state of mental exhilaration, excitableness and abnormal activities for hours last night. The explanation may be that when I drank the coffee at 8 p.m. I had eaten nothing since the midday meal, and I ate nothing afterwards. I am doubtful whether any good results accrue from mental stimulation induced in this way.

I have just read Cheeseman's paper on books about Malaya. What painful memories it conjures up! How many times I have cursed myself for not sending my Malayan library for storage in Sydney. But I could not look to the end of the war in those days, although I was prompted to pack up the books and send them away many times. Of course, I never really thought that Singapore would fall.†

Book reading: *History of the English People*, by Halévy. What a pity there is nothing like this on a social history of Malaya. One feels that one's thought on reading should be directed towards the country one is living in. Yet how rarely it is, among British people in Malaya. It seems as if most people can only take a keen interest in social problems if studied in their own native environment. Thus British people in Malaya would read Halévy's work with interest while a similar work about Malaya would leave them cold.

† [The author's collection was donated by his children to the Murdoch University library in Western Australia. His rarer books were stamped with a black Japanese seal — translation "Singapore Library" — his newer books with a red seal. This helped him identify his books and claim them after the war — they were in the Raffles Library. — Ed.]

April 4 Some of us have become positively childish about food. There is now an agitation in the hut to start three separate rosters for second helpings of the midday soup. The suggested categories are (1) vegetable soup, (2) soup with fish in it, (3) soup with rice in it. All this fuss about half a pint of watery soup which comes around once in two or three weeks.

April 5 Lora's birthday; I've been conscious of her since waking up. Thoughts of her keep on breaking into the daily routine. I shall celebrate by thinking about her during my solitary meditation after dark tonight. Perhaps some of her thoughts today are getting through to me and mine to her. If only we could be sure that the family will be reunited, or even that we shall be able to communicate, this time next year!

April 8 Three pounds down at the monthly weighing, now 135 pounds, as compared with my pre-war weight of 160. In spite of the continuing loss of weight, and the general thinness, most people confess that they feel remarkably well. The rice ration has been cut again, this time 6%.

April 9 Great excitement this afternoon. The Nipponese authorities have agreed to release the Red Cross parcels on a basis of one per man for old internees and one between five for the new internees. Thus ends a controversy which has shaken the camp to its depths. The first proposal, unless there was a misunderstanding, was that the parcels should be released in instalments on the basis of one per 22 men, or something equally futile. The matter has been harshly discussed throughout the camp. So distorted has our sense of proportion become in this queer, isolated community of ours that for several days the single small Red Cross parcel waiting for each internee has suddenly become the most important thing in life, literally the most important, more important than the war or the daily rations or any of the usual matters to occupy our minds. The internees, particularly the more simple-minded, are behaving just like kids a day or two before Christmas. It has all seemed rather childish and undignified, but a doctor friend of mine tells me that many signs of infantilism are to be seen in the camp. No doubt this is inevitable, in the fourth year of captivity. Personally, I have avoided discussion as to the confounded parcels, but privately I find myself thinking a great deal about food, the food that I intend to eat after release. But, curiously enough, I have no craving for expensive, rich foods. My thoughts run on the very plainest fare, rice, soya bean, groundnuts, palm oil, green vegetables, sweet potatoes, fish, eggs and cheese. These are the foodstuffs (together with milk) that I hope to live on in the future. I wonder what I shall think of this prediction when I reread it after I have settled down again to peacetime life, if that time ever comes. At present we are in a state of depression. No air raids, not even reconnaissance flights, no evidence of an early attack on Malaya, and the account of the situation in the Far East given to us by the new internees is far from encouraging from our point of view. We have at least another six months ahead of us, as far as I can see, and perhaps more. Meantime, we are not starving. Suzaki's lorry brought in 2300 pounds of ragi (millet) yesterday, and very large areas around the camp are being planted with tapioca.

April 15, Sunday The Nipponese have given us a whole holiday today; why? we don't know. Debugged my charpoy and mattress. Patched mattress, which is fast perishing. Reconnaissance plane over this morning. After a period of quietness, visits by single planes have become frequent again. The Red Cross parcels have not yet been given out. There is a general irritation and disappointment over the matter, and people are now inclined to write off the parcels altogether.

April 17 I'm feeling more than ever before the dreary monotony, the deprivation of freedom, the inability to get away from people (which is very much worse since the new internees came in), and the utter uncertainty as to how long this will go on. How I loathe this life!

April 23, 1945 A gala day. The Red Cross parcels have been distributed at last. We got a parcel each, containing about eight pounds of tinned foods. This is the second time during the last three years and two months that we have received Red Cross comforts. The first time was in Changi in 1943, when we got one parcel between seven men. American cigarettes were selling today at $5 each. I have actually eaten chocolate again. It was mouldy and full of weevils, but I ate it just the same. The British parcels are dated May 1942, so are nearly three years old.

April 24 Radio message from Lora! Very surprised and delighted, it has probably gone from Sydney to Tokyo and thence to Singapore. I spend a lot of time nowadays thinking about that reunion which I suppose will come some day, although sometimes I almost despair of this internment ever ending.

April 25 I finished *The Excursion*, and I'm now reading *The Prelude*. The line, "that still spirit shed from evening air," is peculiarly expressive of my own state of mind when I get right away from the hut and go to some quiet spot with a book during the two hours of daylight left after tea.

April 26 An elderly Eurasian and two Jews (one speaking only Malay and Arabic) have joined our garden squad. The easy, unselfconscious and friendly manner with which they have been received is in very striking contrast with what would have been our demeanour had we found ourselves working side by side with such people four years ago.

April 28 Overheard: "This new toilet paper (from the Red Cross) is no good for cigarettes. The Bible paper is much better." Being a non-smoker, I have only just found out that for a long time there has been a brisk trade in Bible, prayer book and hymn-book pages, at 15¢ a sheet, for cigarette-making.
    A typical menu at the present time:
Breakfast: rice millet kunji.
Lunch: vegetable stew.
Tea: rice bread, sweet potato spread, tea.

May 1, May Day Labor Day in Sydney. The beginning of summer in Europe. How we long to know what are the feelings of people at home on this day! Is it to be a summer of peace and happiness? Or is this bestial savagery to continue? It is very hard to have to live in ignorance and mystification, not knowing what the true situation is in Europe or Burma or anywhere else. Singapore seems to have been forgotten. We have not even seen a reconnaissance plane over for some days. Personally, I'm resigned to being here until the end of the year. I dare not look farther ahead than that.

Payday today. I drew $11.80 per month.

A characteristic sound of life in this hut is the meticulous scraping of plates and bowls at meal times. People are so hungry that they do not waste a single grain of rice. I am still reading Wordsworth. What an enviable boyhood is revealed in *The Prelude*!

I visited old Mr Robson and others in hospital this afternoon. As always, I found it a great ordeal. The walk up the valley and over the bridge at three o'clock in the afternoon (1 p.m. by the sun) was exhausting. The extent of the new tapioca areas planted by internees outside the boundary fence is now really impressive. Trying my best to preserve a calm state of mind. Cannot endure life when this tension is troubling me.

May 2 This afternoon I saw a merchant seaman, one of the crudest of them, returning to his hut after collecting his rations elsewhere. He was dissatisfied with his helping of vegetable hash, and as he stood on the concrete path, angrily holding out his plate, gesticulating and chattering, he looked exactly like an ape. Just one of the coarse, ugly, animal sights that we see around us every day in this camp. As for the bore-holes (excrementalists)....

May 4 The gardens are now producing ten ounces of vegetables (seven of leaf and three of root) per head per day. Considering that the camp population is now at 4000, this is a really big achievement. It has certainly saved us from beriberi and scurvy. I sold five cigarettes (Red Cross) for $5 each. This together with my month's wages, enabled me to buy a kati of gula malaka for $35. Black-market goods are now very scarce. No palm oil has come in for some time.

Seven thousand letters have arrived.

I've come to the conclusion that the only thing that really matters in this camp is to preserve one's tranquillity, peace of mind, and detachment from petty details and irritations. But how hard that is! Silence is a constant refuge when the hut becomes too trying.

I came across a wonderful line while reading *The Prelude* at breakfast this morning: "Clothed in the sunshine of the withering fern." What a perfect description of bracken in the autumn!

May 5 Another fine thing from *The Prelude*: "the still overflow of present happiness." Were it not for memory, these words would sound utterly meaningless in an internment camp.

May 6 Sunday evening. Started the seventh book of *The Prelude* while sitting in the cemetery.

May 7 Down three pounds at the monthly weighing. Now 132.

Book reading: *Forbidden Journey*, Ella Maillart.

May 9 Current rumours are that our rations are to be increased and that we shall be out of the camp by the end of the month.

An exhibit showing the dry weight of the internees' daily rations at the present time is doing the rounds of the huts. Quantities of rice, rice flour and maize are staggeringly small.

Suzaki's lorry came in today, after three weeks' interval, with cheroots and palm oil. The tobacco famine has been so bad lately that people have been paying $2.50 for a small cheroot.

Archdeacon Graham White died today, four months after the death of his wife.

May 12 Sent a wireless message to Lora. Hobart also did so. Was struck this morning before breakfast by the fact that we appreciate the beauty of the early morning sky so much more in this life than outside.

The first thing in the morning one goes outside the hut to wash and clean one's teeth, half an hour after dawn, and the whole dome of the sky is visible in this treeless spot from east to west and in the south, so that one sees some magnificent skies. Unfortunately one is very rarely in a mood to enjoy them, but I used to miss them altogether in normal life, when I rarely went outside the house before I left for the office.

May 13, 1945, a typical Sunday in the Sime Road camp Gong went at 7.30 a.m. Tokyo time (5.30 a.m. former time). Went outside to wash and clean teeth. A lovely cloud picture in the sky. Made my bed (such as it is). Breakfast: a pint of rice-maize kunji, with a spoonful of palm oil, and tea without milk or sugar.

Cropped sweet potato leaf, while others manured beds with urine. At 10.20 a.m. the usual half-hour break and a mug of tea. Afterwards debugged my charpoy and mattress and swept out my place. I should have carried on in the garden until noon, but I must get my domestic chores done some time. I then had a shower (Sunday afternoon being a half-holiday).

Lunch: plate of rice and vegetable stew, with a flavouring of dried fish. In the afternoon slept and read, feeling utterly sick of internment life, my fellow internees, myself, the hut, and everything connected with this miserable, and at times well-nigh unbearable existence.

Tea at 5.30 p.m.: a piece of rice maize bread, half a pint of rice and vegetable hash with a little dried fish in it, and tea. Our last meal until 8.15 a.m. the following morning.

Went along the valley to the cemetery, where I read Wordsworth's *Tintern Abbey*, and, as usual, lost that nervous tension as soon as I found myself in a quiet and solitary place with a view of the countryside. Heard the hymns sung at the communion service in the Church in the Glen. Came back at sunset, calmed and tranquil in mind, and ate the food I had saved for supper (having gone without tea). After lights-out I had a talk with friends under the stars, but felt unsociable and felt afterwards that my friends could not have enjoyed my company. Went to bed about 11; an undeniably wretched day on the whole.

May 15 The cereal issue today is a new low record. In our area it is 411 pounds for 700 men. So much for the rumour the rations were to be increased.

May 16 The continuous silence in the skies over Singapore has become almost uncanny. For over a month the place has been left alone entirely by Allied aircraft, not even a reconnaissance plane having been seen! We are all speculating as to the meaning of this.

The night before last, two Eurasian youths escaped from the camp. Their absence was discovered the following morning and reported to the Nipponese. Last night they came back and were taken up to the Green House. To our amazement, they were let off with a caution. If this had happened a year ago, a very severe beating would have been the least they could have expected. This was the first escape during the internment since the "Barrel" Roberts case in early 1942 so far as we know.

Today I ate a duck's egg which had cost me $9 in banana money and for which I shall have to pay in good Straits currency after the war. I was almost ashamed to do it, but the almost complete absence of protein is beginning to tell. I cannot now walk 300 yards without fatigue, and I could not run if my life depended on it.

On every hand nowadays one hears incessant talk about palm oil, gula malaka and eggs. Nothing seems to matter except getting a little extra food. The black market has been reformed and regularised, so that everybody now gets an equal opportunity to buy at relatively moderate prices.

Loathing of this life in the hut has grown on me so much recently, together with lethargy caused by shortages of food, I'm finding it increasingly hard to keep on with Malay and Dutch studies. The temptation to escape from all this by lapsing into reverie is growing, and I'm doing practically no reading.

May 18 The black-market price of palm oil has risen to $30 a pint. I have invested $90 in a reserve supply.

People are talking excitedly about something that is to happen, or some good news that we are about to be told, on May 21. Of course, nothing will happen on that date, but some people will never learn. It is amazing how rumours like this gain currency time after time. I've just heard an announcement in the afternoon bulletin that a Jewish internee has been fined $20, deprived of privileges and sentenced to three days' police custody for eating a sweet potato! Stealing from the gardens is becoming increasingly serious. The same bulletin this afternoon stated that thefts of Red Cross foodstuffs and other articles are on the increase throughout the camp. Not only do we have to endure captivity and live like coolies but we have to mix with real slum types on top of it all.

May 23, Wednesday Celebrating my wedding anniversary. A beautiful, serene, still morning. I hope my thoughts are reaching Balgowlah. Somehow, I feel that they are, and vice versa. On coming in from cropping at the 10.30 a.m. tea interval I found a charming note and gift of gula malaka from Gordon. Hobart, who has a special personal interest in this anniversary, since he married us, also gave me congratulations. Tonight Syd and I are celebrating with a moonlight supper at which I propose to open a tin of apple pudding. I resolved not to start on my Red Cross parcel until today, and by a great effort of will I have kept that vow, so now I have a few treats in store. How I long to be in Uncle Henry's house today!

May 27, Sunday My 43rd birthday. My thoughts have been at 124 Wanganella Street. Celebrated with a special tiffin of three courses, as follows: vegetable soup; salad of raw Ceylon spinach, onion and mint, with dressing of palm oil, curry powder and gula malaka; a Red Cross tin of creamed rice (to think that in my youth I hated rice pudding!).

Visited old Mr Robson at the hospital this afternoon. One of the hospital doctors has told H that on the present rations we are undergoing, literally, slow starvation is imminent. I'm feeling the scantiness of the food more than ever before. In particular the midday meal of the four-hour worker — a pint of vegetable soup with scarcely any rice in it — is most inadequate. Without a private stock of palm oil we would be starving in the lay as well as in the medical sense.

I'm finding it increasingly difficult to keep on with my Dutch and Malay or to carry on any mental effort. This life becomes more and more unbearable. But I'm beginning to think that we may be here next Christmas after all. Losing weight at the rate of three pounds a month, and now down to 132 pounds; how long can it go on?

May 29 It is two months since the last air raid. People are getting very depressed. They're beginning to fear that we shall be kept here until Japan is defeated at home, which may mean another year.

I am reading the political and economic chapters of *Towards the Christian Revolution* with much profit. A most stimulating book. At last I begin to get some understanding of the ideas of Marxism.

Still quite unable to control foul thoughts about people I dislike. Have come to the conclusion that we have all sunk into a state of childishness about food. It is disgusting to hear middle-aged men (including myself) solemnly discussing "seconds" which amount to a couple of spoonfuls of kunji or soup. One of the greatest pleasures of freedom is going to be escape from this everlasting and ubiquitous talk about food, about the menu for today or tomorrow, about the prospects for "seconds," about whether it was the half-pint or the ⅝-pint measure used to serve the rice and potato hash, and a dozen other trivialities of the same sort.

May 30 The very day after writing the remarks above, we heard the sirens again. But the air-raid did not materialise; believed to be a practice.

The two Eurasian youths who broke out of the camp were released yesterday. They got a beating, three days without food and a fortnight's imprisonment with rations. The general opinion is they got off lightly.

May 31 I got a close-up view of a pair of water hens while sitting on a tree stump beside the anti-malarial drain in the western valley yesterday evening. Afterwards I sat by the two wells farther up the valley and for the first time discovered that there are fish in them. The presence of these fish is a pretty problem for the field naturalist. The wells were dug about a year ago. They are far from any stream or pond. The small concrete drain nearby is dry nearly every day. Yet there are now fish a foot long in the wells. Unless they travelled overland, or lay dormant in the mud of the old streambed in the ravine, they must have swum up the small drain from the main drain half a mile away during heavy rain, climbed the grassy side of the drain and flopped another six feet across the grass to the wells.

I bought a duck's egg at $9 and a kati of gula malaka at $34. The black market is bringing in Australian tinned butter, cheese, sausages, jam and other luxuries, and these things are fetching fantastic prices. A tinned cake sold for $600.

Sirens again this morning, in a burst of ack-ack. Perhaps we are not forgotten after all. About 8000 letters have been delivered. We have been notified that Schweizer is to get no more funds from Geneva and we shall receive no more supplies from him.

June 1 Celebrated Syd's wedding anniversary last night by sharing a tin of American pork. Had coffee with milk and sugar in it the first time in about three years. Absolute nectar! A very pleasant chat and meal, following the Thursday evening gramophone concert. I was invited to dinner at Syd's house on the same anniversary next year. I wonder....

June 5 Utterly sick of the daily routine of coolie work in the hut garden. I feel very tempted to tear up this diary. Such an ugly, degrading, petty, animal existence does not deserve to be recorded. But some people succeed in rising above it occasionally, particularly those in my circle who attend the 7.30 a.m. (really 5.30 a.m.) communion service in the Church in the Glen on Sunday mornings. At this open-air rite at dawn in a sequestered corner of the camp, they must be conscious of the beauty of nature in a way that is impossible in the ordinary routine of life around these ugly huts and vegetable gardens.

June 6 Mysterious tunnelling operations have been started in the camp. We are officially informed that the tunnels are for our use, but we do not know whether they are intended to be shelters or underground stores.

I never want to hear the words palm oil and gula malaka again as long as I live, once I get out of this place. What bliss it will be to live again among normal people who are not forever talking about food!

June 7 Yesterday, in a conference with General Saito and Lieutenant Suzuki, the Men's Representative appealed for more food, pointing to the general and continuing loss of weight and the prevalence of sickness in the camp, and declaring that the camp medical authorities took a serious view of the situation. General Saito was sympathetic but said nothing could be done, as there was a very serious food shortage throughout Malaya as a result of disrupted communications and the sinking of ships, even small ones, between Malaya and adjacent countries. The general also said that the Nipponese themselves were suffering and they could not give us what they did not have. This looks as if our people are getting nearer at last, but everything around here remains very peaceful. Down another three pounds at the monthly weighing, now 129 pounds. Just heard one elderly man in the hut say he is within a few pounds off 100 pounds lost during the internment. Another has lost 60 pounds. Another has lost weight during the last three months at the rate of half a stone a month. Generally, the younger men are standing the semi-starvation better than the elderly. Some of the latter show really serious losses. If we have to endure this another six months many of us will be living skeletons when released, indeed some are already. My ribs already have a gruesome likeness to that state, judging by the feel of them when I lie down at night.

We have had no protein food whatever during the last three days; still, in spite of it all there is good programme at the gramophone concert this evening, and I shall enjoy my vegetarian supper afterwards. I finished reading *Romeo and Juliet* yesterday evening. I have never read it with such keen appreciation and close attention before.

June 9 I bought half a kati of gula malaka for $17 and half a pint of palm oil (camp issue) for $2.

Most people in the camp are now spending at the rate of $20 a month, and many, much more, on gula, palm oil, coffee and tobacco in the black market. This money is mostly borrowed. Nearly all of us are going to come out of this internment with a load of debt. Our hut garden is now planted with the third successive crop of sweet potatoes.

The Sikhs have been armed with poles to which a nasty-looking spike is attached, instead of the plain lathis previously carried. It is thought that reconnaissance planes have been over several times during the last few days. But if so, it has been nothing more than a swift dash across the island at a great height. This is Saturday evening. Shall I ever enjoy a real Saturday evening with Lora again?

Today's menu:

Breakfast: a pint of rice kunji.

Lunch: vegetable and rice stew, one pint.

Tea: rice bread, vegetable and rice hash, ⅜ of a pint, and a spoonful of fried spinach.

I am now going to the Church in the Glen, taking with me Nora Waln's *The House of Exile*, and Shakespeare's tragedies.

Stop press! Great excitement. The news has just gone round that the remainder of the Red Cross parcels are to be released tomorrow, one parcel to two persons.

June 11 I saw Willmot this morning. I was shocked by his shrunken, emaciated condition. He is only a shadow of his former self.

June 12 In Nora Waln's *The House of Exile* there is a delicious description of a meal in a Chinese house. The first course comprised three dishes, one being breast of chicken, another red cabbage and green pepper, and the third tenderloin of chicken with chestnuts. The second course was fish soup. The third was steamed rice, plain steamed rice. This seems curious, read in this camp. We should consider a bowl of rice very much of an anti-climax after the savoury dishes that preceded it, but evidently the Chinese (at any rate in north China) consider that rice has a delicate flavour and should be eaten by itself. Or perhaps this course is served only as the Malays serve a banana at the end of a meal, the purpose they describe as "chuchi mulut" (clean mouth).

After tea this afternoon, M, who had opened a Red Cross tin, very thoroughly licked his plate.

A queer spectacle: old Abdullah, a Basra Jew, late owner of a piece-goods shop in Selegie Road, squatting on the sill of Dawson's doorway and haggling over a tin of bacon, which his religion forbids him to eat. He got $160 for it. I heard later that the same sort of tin was fetching as high as $280.

Another case of tropical typhus has occurred in this hut. This makes five cases out of 80-odd men in the hut.

I have at last identified the tailor bird.

June 13 A wet morning. J, who has just come up from the Eurasian hut, complains he hears nothing all day in that hut but bargaining and arguing over food. It is the same everywhere. On Sunday morning, when the parcels were distributed, I heard a man in the garden say, "I hate to go back to the hut! I shall hear nothing but parcels, parcels, parcels." In our own hut we have just taken most elaborate precautions to ensure equitable distribution of a small surplus of Red Cross food amounting to about one-and-a-half tins per man. I suppose I shall recall these days when I gaze once again on the well-stocked shelves of M.S. Ally — if I ever do.

I have been promoted from the grade of four-hour gardener to that of six-hour gardener. This means that I not only work longer hours but am expected to wield a changkol and do heavy work generally. As compensation I get a supplementary ration of about two-and-a-half ounces of rice and a little tapioca.

I finished Nora Waln's book *The House of Exile*. Outside, in former life, I tried to read this book and could not settle down to it. In here, I enjoyed every page.

June 15 Suzaki's lorry brought in over 2000 pounds of ragi. I got half a kati of gula malaka through the "grey market." Had supper with J and shared a tin of bully beef.

June 19 I bought four ounces of salt from the grey market at $10.60. I am back on four-hour rations. I finished *Towards a Christian Revolution*, having read it with keen interest. We are all sceptical, cynical, apathetic, and pessimistic about prospects of early release, and utterly bored.

June 20 I bought a duck's egg at $11.50. The black market operators are already going around the huts offering $20 for this afternoon's issue of grey-market eggs.

Human nature stark naked — this is what we see in this hut life. A man is known as he really is, not as he appears in the superficial and occasional contacts of ordinary life. In particular, the selfishness and meanness which sometimes lie beneath a genial or affable manner are quickly revealed.

June 21 Three-quarters of a pint of palm oil from the grey market today. I am eating raw Ceylon spinach every day, to fill out the rations. With curry powder and palm oil, it makes a tolerable salad.

June 25 The camp is passing through a tobacco famine. Cheroots are selling at $3 each. As much as $12 has been paid for a single American cigarette. I saw J out this morning gathering sweet potato leaves. He must've been desperate to do this, as hitherto he has always scorned tobacco substitutes. Thank Heaven I am a non-smoker.

The midday meal today consisted of a watery vegetable soup with a flavouring of blachan (dried prawn). Being a rainy, chilly, blustery day, I felt confoundedly hungry.

June 26 Three-quarters of a pint of palm oil through the grey market.

June 27 While standing in the coffee queue at the kitchen yesterday evening, I heard a man, not an educated man, judging by his voice, say that he had learnt Latin during the internment and was at present translating Virgil and finding it most interesting. Yet another indication, of the many afforded by this internment, of what adult education might be in a social order which gave security and leisure to the common man.

July 1 Sunday morning. A dreadful day yesterday. Fighting irritation all the morning. Leisure time between two and four wasted. Utterly unable to shake off depression or settle down to language study. But in the evening I heard Beethoven's Violin Concerto, exquisitely played by Heifetz, and this had a magical effect. This morning I feel distinctly cheered by the thought that we have entered on the second half of 1945, although there are at present no indications whatever of early release.

July 3 The camp now has 73 acres under tapioca and sweet potatoes. All internees of 15 to 48 years of age with male relatives in Syonan are required to give their names. Does this mean parole?

July 4 The physique and health of the heavy changkollers, on 300 g of rice plus an extra allowance of 110 g of rice and two tablespoonfuls of tapioca, is remarkable. Note that 300 g is only three-and-a-half ounces. True, they take it easily, but even so they expend as much energy as they would as office workers in normal life. One concludes, therefore, that the amount of food necessary to maintain health in a sedentary mode of life is enormously less than is generally supposed.

July 6 All men between the ages of 15 and 55 paraded today for a medical examination. Special attention was paid to the legs and feet. It looks as if we have a long walk coming. There are other indications that a move to another camp is imminent.

July 7 Monthly weighing. Up two pounds, now 132.

July 9 Two internees have escaped during the last few days, a Eurasian and a Jew. As a result the inmates of the huts to which they belong have been put on half-rations; the Jews in our part of the camp are to be transferred to two huts in the central area, and the Eurasians are all to be cleared out of their hut and distributed among the huts in the central and southern areas. Such is the inconvenience which these two persons have caused their fellows.

The Eurasian hut has afforded a marked contrast with the two Jewish huts near here. The Eurasians have been quiet and orderly, whereas the Jews have been conspicuously noisy, quarrelsome and generally unpleasant as neighbours. Heard a chorus of jolly, spontaneous laughter in the Eurasian hut the other day. This is a very rare thing in this camp. The effect of this long captivity has been to make men taciturn, repressed and frequently morose, but the Eurasians, having only been a few months in internment, still behave like normal people. They are helped to do so by the presence of a number of boys in their hut, some of them having their sons or nephews with them, so that something of a family atmosphere exists there.

July 11 F.K. told me this morning that he had just read two odes of Horace with genuine enjoyment. Although a good classical scholar, he lost interest in the classics after leaving the university and therefore read only for amusement, continuing to do so throughout his peacetime life in Malaya. During the internment his reading tastes have changed. He has, for example, read most of Dickens and a good deal of Scott. His new appreciation of Scott struck me particularly, as I have always found Scott's novels very tedious myself.

Colonel Cecil Rae died today. Also another diabetes patient.

July 12 Six ounces of gula malaka at $19.

July 13 Fifteen cheroots from Suzaki at $1 each. Issues of smokes are few and far between nowadays. Tobacco seedlings have been distributed throughout the camp today at the rate of two per man. This must be the first instance in Malaya of Europeans trying to grow their own tobacco.

July 14, Saturday I visited Le Doux today. He is looking old, weak and shaky. I fear for him if the internment goes on much longer. The drugs needed for the treatment of his ailments are not in the camp.

It is thought that there have been reconnaissance flights over the island this week, but we're not sure. We wait patiently, utterly weary of it all. I cannot believe that I shall ever live a normal life again, or sit down to supper with my wife and children again.

July 15 I talked with O.J. today. With his teaching Latin and Greek, in addition to doing ordinary fatigues, I have never heard him talk better. His mind is clear and vigorous. Yet he has not had home leave for 15 years. This is another case of internment having done a man a great deal of good. In his former life, O.J. was perpetually sodden with alcohol and harassed by indebtedness. In internment the essentials of existence are provided, and everybody is teetotal perforce. Consequently one sees O.J. in here at his best, as he might be in normal life but for his weaknesses.

July 16 A camp issue of one pint of palm oil at $10. Usual ten-day ration of sugar (4.8 ounces).

Suzaki-san's lorry today brought in 1900 pounds of ragi (six-days' supply), 500 katis of gula malaka, cheroots and cigarettes (nine cheroots and five cigarettes per man).

I am at present well-supplied with palm oil, gula malaka and coffee. Moreover, I still have in hand, of the Red Cross goods, two tins of bacon, one of galantine (pressed meat in aspic), two of margarine and one of golden syrup. I'm trying to keep a famine reserve, for I think we may have days with no food whatsoever before the end.

I go off worker's rations tomorrow, having been ordered to rest a swollen foot. The difference is half a pint of kunji for breakfast instead of a pint. The other meals are the same. No more gramophone concerts, because of the evening roll-call; I miss them very much.

July 18 An issue of hen's eggs at $17 each. Refused mine. Sweets are being sold at a dollar each. A "brown market" has been started in the camp to import cheroots and gula malaka, in addition to the existing grey and black markets.

I read Edith Sitwell's book on Bath. Am now reading *The Far East Comes Nearer*, by H. Hessell Tiltman, and *Moral Man and Immoral Society*.

July 19 Six thousand letters have arrived. Nipponese rations received today: 500 pounds of blachan, 500 pounds of ikan bilis.

My breakfast as a non-worker: half a pint of kunji.

July 20 The Indian POWs in the wired-off huts have been replaced by Europeans, whose nationality we do not know.

July 21 I attended the funeral of J.H.M. Robson.

July 23 Eight ounces of gula malaka $20. Borrowed $500 and repaid $100 to Hobart.

Noticed for the first time this afternoon how thin Hobart has become. I was shocked by his worn, skeleton-like appearance. Hinch is still an invalid, cannot get his operation wound healed. Gerald Summers is in hospital with an ulcer and looking pitifully thin. Tapioca leaves, dehydrated, are to be used as food in the future.

July 24 A room, a desk, chair; silence, solitude and privacy… that is my idea of bliss at the moment.

July 25 A list of all owners of watches in the camp has been asked for. Those are willing to dispose of their watches are to be offered butter, cheese, coffee and sugar for them.

A reconnaissance plane was over today.

July 26 A letter from Lora dated September, 1944, with a snapshot of the children. A very delightful surprise. It comes at a time when one has almost given up hope of ever getting out of this place.

July 29, Sunday The trouble is that we only see the ugly side of life in here.

August 2 I finish my fortnight spell of non-worker's rations. Became a heavy changkoller, working outside, with supplementary rations of 150 g of rice (three-quarters of a pint of boiled rice) and three ounces of tapioca. The basic rations are 300 g of rice nominally — actually about 260.

August 3 I spent my first morning outside the camp, digging on the racecourse. A heavenly feeling when I breasted the ridge and saw the landscape of greensward, forests and lake. It rained after tiffin. Mustered in the mud at three o'clock. Weeded in the tapioca in a drizzle for half an hour, drank a mug of tea, and came home.

Three ounces of sugar from Suzaki was $9. Passed over an egg at $18. Money getting very hard to raise.

I'm feeling more and more restless. Dutch and Malay have almost come to a standstill.

Five p.m. in the hut. I have just received a card from my sister Miriam. It's dated December 1944 and delighted to hear of a daughter for my brother Major and Sylvia.

August 4 An air raid at last, the first since March, but only a small one.

August 5, Sunday Monthly weighing: 131 pounds, down one.

A whole holiday today. I took my Ceylon spinach and chillies to Le Doux. Took out charpoy and mattress and debugged. Swept out my place. Collected one pint of palm oil ($6.50) from a special Tanaka issue to heavy workers. Collected the fatigue rice and tapioca. Took the rice down to Hobart for Miss Rank's birthday party, with a present of ten toffees ($1 each) from myself. Cut more spinach and prepared salad with onion tops. Put Gordon's 30 cheroots in another container. Collected crackling on fatigue rice, the first crackling I have had for some months. Finally bathed and had tiffin after a very busy morning entirely taken up with petty duties and tasks. In spite of all this rushing about, entirely satisfied with a pint of vegetable stew (containing rice flour and palm oil) and a small amount of kunji for tiffin. Now raining hard, so relatives' meeting in the orchard looks like being a washout. I will now settle down to Galsworthy's novel, *To Let*.

August 6 There are now no fewer than eight tunnels under construction in the camp.

Hobart has learned, in a letter from Celeste, that the radio message he sent to Lora in December, 1943, was received.

The pith of the papaya tree is to be used in our food. It has no food value but will provide bulk.

August 9 I visited McLeod in the area hospital this afternoon. What a place on a wet afternoon! Kajang walls, attap roof, mud floors, semi-darkness, no lights, too dark to read… the hut crowded with beds, tropical ulcer cases with legs propped up….

Syd confessed last night that his ideal after so long in internment is to live alone in a lighthouse with a library.

In this existence one enjoys what one can. The 20-minute interval while changkolling on the golf course this afternoon was very pleasant, sitting alone in the turf in the sunshine. Enjoyed the landscape of ploughed earth and jungle.

August 11 I saw the Malayan buttonquail for the first time, on the edge of the belukar in the ravine below the cemetery. I was walking in bare feet along a grassy path, so got within a few feet of it. F.K. tells me the meaning of Padang Pyioyu.†

More symptoms of internment childishness. A leading Johor planter scampering like a schoolboy to get away from his job after the afternoon's work and get a shower before the rush begins. Middle-aged men actually running to get into the queue for tea at the mid-morning

---

† [*Padang* is literally "field" in Malay, while *pyioyu* is likely *puyuh*, "quail." What was meant by the phrase, however, is not revealed. — Ed.]

break on the golf course, so as to get their tea two minutes before the other people.

I am more and more impressed by the resemblance between this camp and boarding school. Really cannot see much difference between these men and the boys I was at school with. Have we not developed and changed at all in the intervening years? Or have we relapsed into boyishness, shedding the conventions and inhibitions acquired in adult life under the stress of captivity?

August 12 Sunday afternoon. Another of the Jews ran away in the night, leaving his wife and child behind him in internment. The most perfect cad I have ever heard of.

Seven persons have died in the camp in the last two days, including G.C. Meredith, who had a fine record in the last war, joined up again in this one while on leave and went through the Dunkirk show, and then came back to Singapore after the Japanese attack on the Malaya, arriving here on February 6, nine days before the end.

August 13 A good supply of mixed drugs was received last month from the Nipponese High Command.

The morning and evening roll-call yesterday and again today were taken by Sikh guards. This has never happened before. At our hut we did not bow, as we do for the Nipponese officers, but stood at attention.

A siren was heard at midday today and the blue flag (preliminary warning) went up at the Green House, so the peace rumours which have so excited the camp during the last two days proved once again to be baseless.

Today, Monday, the heavy changkollers and wood haulers were not allowed outside the camp.

August 14 No more funerals in town are to be allowed. Internees who die in the camp will have to be buried inside the camp. (All the crosses over the military graves were removed, and a central memorial erected, several weeks ago.)

Don't forget the snails! On Thursday of last week we were told that "all snails found inside and outside the camp were camp property." Collecting depots for snails were established. Well-known M.C.S. member in charge of the snail farm. They say the giant snails look and taste like gristle when cooked, and if cooked with palm oil and curry powder they taste of palm oil and curry powder. Our hut had a very narrow escape, the first delivery of cooked snails having been on Friday.

August 18 The day of the Great Disappointment. At one o'clock today the camp was firmly convinced that peace had been signed and that we would be released next week. This belief had been inspired by a succession of events, stories and rumours.

Peace rumours were rife last weekend. Then on Thursday a POW officer was said to have shouted over the fence that the war was over and that the relieving troops would arrive on the 25th. Yesterday afternoon a couple of lorries loaded with Asiatics passed the camp and their occupants were said to have shouted the same news. Today we heard that work on the tunnels had been stopped, that the tunnellers had been told to occupy themselves in tidying up the camp and gardens "during the next five days," that there would be no more outside fatigues, that the sawmill had stopped work, and that the remaining 300-odd Red Cross parcels have been released. As a result excitement rose to fever heat and even the most sceptical began to be really shaken. But alas! While we were eating our midday meal the deep drone of one of our planes was heard and the thudding of ack-ack all over the island. So the war was not over. What a deflation!

Hut 66 after tiffin resembled nothing so much as a pricked balloon. And now it looks very much as if we are due for a move to another camp in the next few days. This is the worst shock the camp has yet had.

I worked in the garden in the afternoon, bedding up and planting sweet potato cuttings, never felt less like work in my life. Nobody in the squad spoke an unnecessary word. However, when we finished work and came back to the hut about 4.45 p.m. we found a fresh crop of stories which suggested that the war was really over after all.

This was Saturday evening. Tokinaga had been seen weeping and reading a newspaper. Otski's path-raking squad, waiting outside the North gate, sent a Malay guard up to the Green House for orders. He came back with the order "Return to camp," etc., etc. But my mind was not made up until ---- came just before tea and told me that he had seen a newspaper of the 16th, which said that the position of the Japanese had become untenable and that the Emperor was about to issue rescripts to the fighting forces.

By this evening, Saturday, everybody was practically convinced. It was on this evening, too, that we first heard the amazing story of a meeting between British commanders and the Japanese commander-in-chief Malaya, at Penang. We were almost wild with excitement this evening.

Just before lights out on Saturday night came the final conclusive proof. An increase of rations. The whole camp was raised from 300 to 500 g of rice. This finally removed all lingering doubt. Later we heard that the keys of the foodstore had been handed over to Jarrett. So by lights-out on Saturday night, the 18th, we were finally convinced.

I did not sleep at all on Saturday night. Atmosphere in the hut was like ten Christmases rolled into one. All night long sleepless figures were wandering about or sitting on the veranda.

Two women internees were buried today. So near the end.

August 19, Sunday First indication at the dawn roll-call. Two Sikhs came round and dismissed us without counting. Afterwards we learned that one of the Sikhs had told the Area Commandant during the rounds of huts that all the stories we were hearing were true. A quiet morning. Cropped sweet potato leaf in the hut garden.

No fresh news on Sunday. Stuffed myself at tiffin and tea. For first time since Christmas had as much as I wanted to eat. In fact, ate too much.

The grave-digging fatigue was working again this morning.

During the afternoon it was pouring with rain; suddenly there was a burst of cheering from the Dutch POWs. Dekling went up and was told they had just been informed that the war was over and had been for the past three days.

We were all waiting for a statement today, but the Green House remained silent. Exciting rumours went around that the reoccupation of Singapore would begin tomorrow and that British officers would arrive at the camp in the morning.

In the evening, two more significant developments. The last four internees in the hands of the military police were returned to camp, to the joy of everybody. Moreover, the last four Europeans working in town were sent into camp, having been outside ever since the internment began. They say the reoccupation begins tomorrow and lasts until the 24th.

A long talk and usual Sunday evening meeting with Hobart.

Sunday evening roll-call taken by one of the Nipponese camp officials. We duly kyotski'd and kiri'd — we hope, for the last time.

August 20, 1945, Monday I worked in the garden until 11 a.m., cropping leaf and sweet potatoes. Morning roll-call washed out with rain. Twelve forty-five p.m., still not a word from the Nipponese. No sign of our people. Menu today:

Breakfast: rice kunji with palm oil in it.

Tiffin: rice and vegetable stew.

Tea: bun and vegetable hash.

Four p.m. An official statement at last. General Saito saw Collinge, the Men's Representative, today. He told him that, "It is possible you will all, in a short time, be going back to your normal times." But, he added, negotiations are still going on, a decision has not yet been reached, matters are in a critical stage, and the Japanese are still in charge of the camp.

August 21, Tuesday It's Tuesday morning. We are now doing no work except cropping sweet potato leaves and tubers.

More new arrivals in the camp last night: seven Dutchmen who have been working on Pulau Damar Laut, and local-born "enemy aliens." It was from them that we heard the first time the news of the recent atomic bomb blast and the signing of peace.

August 22, Wednesday A quiet day. Dug sweet potatoes until 10.15 a.m. We're still waiting for our troops. Still no official information as to when the changeover takes place.

Volunteers for grave-digging were called for this morning.

August 23, Thursday Six hundred Red Cross parcels have come in, and a lorry load of supplies from Schweizer, who has lost no time in getting in touch with us.

I felt worried and nervous all day, trying desperately to write a leader — the first leader — terribly afraid I will never be able to do it.

I'm trying to detach myself from all of this, so as to realise fully the incredible fact that I shall soon hear from Lora and that our separation is nearly over.

August 24, Friday This evening's bulletin:

General Saito told Collinge today that "the war is over and we shall all go back to our normal lives in the very near future." Pressed, he said he thought the British will take charge in the beginning of next month and Lord Louis Mountbatten and General Terauchi had to settle certain points. The Japanese will supply us with news of any important world events, also the local English papers.

All lighting and smoking restrictions are cancelled.

All livestock in the camp farm are to be slaughtered.

The Nipponese will try to send in fish and eggs for the women's camp and boots and shoes for all who need them.

RAF planes will begin to fly over Singapore at 5 a.m. tomorrow dropping food parcels. The Japanese camp commander, Lieutenant Suzuki, has strictly forbidden us to cheer. The Japanese officials here are very nervous lest we provoke an incident with their military.

August 25, Saturday Eleven a.m. in the hut. It's raining and I'm drinking sweetened coffee!

No RAF planes yet.

The menu for tea today: rice flour and palm oil loaf, savoury rice, fried ikan bilis, meat and vegetable pie, devilled sauce.

August 26, Sunday Fresh fish for tea; visited Bennett.

August 27, Monday Seven ounces of Australian butter. Five ounces of sugar. A tin of Kraft cheese.

August 28, Tuesday All too bewildering. I'm desperately trying to write the leader. I'm very worried.

August 29, Wednesday One tin of pineapple each.

August 31, Friday First British uniforms seen in the camp about 4 p.m. Two officers of the Parachute Regiment. Intense excitement.
I listened to the BBC for the first time since this all began.

September 1, Saturday Gerald Summers died.

September 2, Sunday I finished the leader.
The signing of the surrender in Tokyo heard in camp. Dozens of internees went into town. Hundreds of people came out from town and into the camp. Restrictions are rapidly breaking down. The Japanese flag is still flying over the Cathay.
Two-and-a-half pounds of butter received.

September 3, Monday The Union Jack was hoisted in the camp. I shaved off my beard and moustache.

FIRST LETTER HOME ON RELEASE FROM INTERNMENT

Sime Road Camp,
Singapore
September 2, 1945

My Dearest Lora,

I could hardly believe that I am able to write to you freely at last. On August 27th I wrote an airmail postcard to you in a hurry, because there seemed to be a chance of getting it sent off in a day or so, but afterwards I wished I hadn't posted it, because we have been sitting in this camp ever since — and I have had quite enough of trying to tell you all I want to within a postcard, and I'm sure you don't want any more 25-word cards from me either. However, that last card may arrive before this letter, and it will at least tell you that I am reasonably well. I expect you have been perturbed by the wireless news about bad health conditions among the prisoners of war here.

My dear, there is so much to tell you that I just don't know where to begin, and I think I shall have to leave most of it until I can tell you the whole story myself when I arrive in Sydney. I am very lucky to have come through safely. I had a miraculous escape from drowning on a ship on which David Waite and a number of my late colleagues lost their lives. Then I spent three months under an assumed name living as a private soldier in an A.I.F. camp. Then I spent six weeks in hospital with dysentery. Then I was sent to this civilian internment camp in Changi Jail. Halfway through the imprisonment there the Japanese Gestapo found out who I was, in the course of an enquiry in which 15 out of 45 internees died in the hands of the Japanese military police, but I was miraculously left alone. And while in this camp I had a close call with tropical typhus and pneumonia. However, it's all over now. I don't think there are any permanent ill-effects, and a month or two of good feeding is all I need until I can get a good long holiday with you and the children and forget all about this experience.

I know what you too must have gone through until you heard that I was still alive, for I heard through letters reaching other people here that the story of the sinking of the steamboat *Giang Bee* and of my having left on her had reached you. It was an immense relief when I learnt, some time in 1944, the messages from me had got through and that that worry at least was off your mind.

I am looking forward very eagerly to my first letter from you and perhaps from the children too. (It has only just occurred to me that they are at an age now when that is possible!) We are still in this camp waiting for the British forces. The Japanese troops are still in Singapore, but today for the first time people from the city flocked out to the camp in hundreds and all restrictions are rapidly breaking down. The British reoccupation is expected in two or three days, and immediately after that I hope to go into town with two or three other newspapermen in the camp and restart *The Straits Times*. I don't really feel like tackling that job straight away, but there are several reasons why I think it must be done. Seabridge will probably return very soon and relieve me of the responsibility. I expect I shall have to stay a few more weeks, but after that there is every prospect of my leaving for Sydney. The fact is that none of us are really fit for normal work, and the general intention appears to be to get everybody away as soon as possible. Burns, managing director of *The Straits Times*, is a neighbour of mine in the camp and knows conditions here, so it shouldn't be long before I get away. It just doesn't seem possible that our reunion is really near, but I think we can be sure of that now.

Letters have been a wonderful help and consolation. If it hadn't been for them I'm afraid I would almost have given up hope at times. The last letter was dated September 1944, but I have also received a radio message from you which I think was sent in February of this year. I am very anxious to hear that all is well with you and the children. I shall write to Uncle Henry at the earliest opportunity after release. I shall also write as soon as possible to Dad and Mother. I received three cards from Miriam, the latest dated December of last year. There are innumerable questions I want to ask about the relations in Sydney and your family and everybody at home, but we can't do it all at once!

The photograph of the children which you sent was a great help. I think about them a great deal and try to imagine how they have changed since I last saw them.

This is Sunday evening, and I expect you are thinking about me in Uncle Henry's house at Balgowlah as I'm thinking of you. (I am writing this in the camp cemetery! It is the only place where I can get away from the wild excitement and continual distractions of life in this camp in these last days.) I don't think I have yet to fully realise that it is all over and that I'm going back to normal life and that I shall soon be in touch with you again as in normal times. Perhaps the full consciousness of all this will not come until I get out of this camp. (Mount Rosie is only three miles away — we are near the golf course and the racecourse — but we have been kept strictly within the boundary fence.) In the meantime I'm writing this so as to have a letter ready to send off to you as soon as the mails are recommenced after our release. I have already sent greetings to all the relatives in my postcard and will be writing to them after I have settled down in town.

All my love and dearest thoughts to you and Georgie, Lorrine and Ronnie. I am longing to see you all again.

George

*The author, with Lora
and (from left) George B.,
Ronald and Lorinne, in
Sydney, November 14, 1945*